FREIGHTMASTER
The National Railfreight Timetable

Spring 2016 edition

CONTENTS

PART ONE : **Freight 'Hotspots'**   4

Key to tables   5
SOUTH WEST ENGLAND/SOUTH WALES ......   6 - 18
SOUTH EAST ENGLAND ....   19 - 51
CENTRAL ENGLAND ....   52 - 81
NORTH WEST ENGLAND/NORTH WALES ......   82 - 96
SCOTLAND ....   97 - 104
NORTH EAST ENGLAND ....   105 - 125
Freightmaster Online   126
Glossary   127
Guest Timetable   128

PART TWO : **On Location**   *i* - xv

PART THREE: **Freight Flows**   129 - 144

INDEX TO HOTSPOTS   145

Published by : **Freightmaster Publishing**
158 Overbrook, SWINDON, SN3 6AY

Printed by : Stephens & George, Merthyr Tydfil, CF48 3TD

Research & Design : Mark Rawlinson
(e-mail) : mark@freightmaster.net

Managing Editor : Martin Buck
(e-mail) : martin.buck@btconnect.com
(tel) : 01793 - 644957

Our Websites...

Book Titles : www.freightmasterpublishing.co.uk

Freightmaster 'OnLine' : www.freightmaster.net/offers

EDITORIAL

WELCOME to Issue No.81; it's Spring, the clocks have gone forward and we can, hopefully, put behind us landslips, line closures and diversions.

Speaking of diversions, the closure of the WCML at Lamington, whilst inconvenient and disruptive to West Coast train services, did present enthusiasts with the opportunity to photograph a variety of freight traffic on the ex-Glasgow & South Western route via Dumfries. Many took up the challenge and I have seen some stunning photographs, many of which will appear in the 2017 edition of *Loco Review*!

NEWSWORTHY freight developments continue for Colas, who have now moved into the construction sector hauling cement trains on behalf of Tarmac out of the Oxwellmains plant near Dunbar. The services, which are all 60-hauled, are as follows:

- 6A65 Oxwellmains to Aberdeen   6B36 return
- 6H51 Oxwellmains to Inverness   6B31 return
- 6D62 Oxwellmains to Viewpark   6B34 return
- 6E92 Oxwellmains to Seaham   6S26 return
- 6M01 Oxwellmains to Carlisle Brunthill   6S01 return

In high summer, a colourful Colas 'tug' working cement over the Highland Line should be a sight to behold - the pages of Loco Review eagerly awaits!

ON LOCATION in this edition features:

DONCASTER   and   *HATFIELD & STAINFORTH*

I am pleased to welcome a new 'Guest photographer' - *Alan Padley* - who has kindly made a selection of his superb images available for this feature. Alan hails from Doncaster and is well placed to illustrate freight traffic in this busy part of South Yorkshire. Many enthusiasts flock to Doncaster station, one of the most visited freight 'hotspots' on the network; GBRf has a significant presence hauling coal, gypsum, intermodal and industrial sand trains, which attract a good selection of the many different liveried Class 66/7 locos.

There are plenty of good vantage points within a seven mile radius of the station, including Hexthorpe, Arksey, Kirk Sandall, Hatfield & Stainforth, Bessacarr and Rossington, for example. This is one 'location' certainly worth a visit.

Martin Buck

April 2016

PART ONE: freight hotspots

The timetables in this part of the book have been carefully chosen to give maximum coverage of the network, so as well as busy locations such as Doncaster and Stafford, there are also a number of more 'scenic' locations such as the Settle and Carlisle line.

The locations are grouped into geographical areas. At the start of each area there is a map showing all freight terminals/yards within that area, plus the location of the 'hotspots'.

A full index of locations covered can be found at the back of the book.

TRAIN PERFORMANCE

The tables list the trains that were running at the of going to press, including many additional services not shown in working timetables, plus most MGR coal workings, although services to East Midlands/Aire Valley power stations cannot be included due to their unpredictable nature.

Important Note - Please Read!!

Please note that the tables in this book provide a guide to the usual timings of trains which should pass a given location on a 'perfect day'.

Despite our best efforts to make the tables as accurate as possible, the actual running of freight services can vary significantly from day to day, and individual trains can:

1. run late (just like passenger trains!)

2. run early, due to an over-generous schedule, or a booked stop being missed out

3. run on the 'wrong' day(s), if required by the customer.

4. be cancelled altogether.

So please, do not expect every train to run exactly as shown in the tables - freight trains are simply not that reliable/predictable!

Finally, due to the nature of railfreight traffic, many trains will be retimed/rerouted/finish altogether during the currency of this publication.

Full details of all such changes are regularly added to **Freightmaster Online** - see the advert at the back of this book for further details.

Key to tables

The following conventions are used throughout this book:

Times: Split into columns for North/South; East/West, etc., with the following codes:
18:20 = passing time (train not booked to stop)
18c20 = stops for crew change(arrival time given unless otherwise noted)
18L20 = stops for loco change(arrival time given unless otherwise noted)
18R20 = stops to run round
18T20 = stops for traffic(arrival time given) - mail trains only.
18D20 = stops to set down wagons; **18U20** = stops to pick up wagons

Please note that brackets around originating times are used where a train runs consistently very early, which would otherwise make the originating time look incorrect.

Headcodes:
These are used by Network Rail and the FOCs to keep track of trains. The full 'Train i.d.' used by the 'TOPS' computer actually consists of ten characters, but in everyday use, a shortened form, consisting of four characters is used:

The first character is a number which denotes the train type:
0= light engine
2= stopping passenger train
4= 75 m.p.h. freight(e.g. Freightliners)
6= 60 m.p.h. freight
8= 35 m.p.h. freight

1= Mail/TPO(& express passenger)
3= 90 m.p.h. freight(rarely used)
5= empty mail vans/empty stock
7= 45 m.p.h. freight
9= Eurostar passenger services

The second character is a letter which represents the destination Network Rail 'zone':
E = Eastern
L = Anglia
M = London Midland

O = Southern
S = Scottish
V = Western

Other letters are used where the train remains within a former region for its whole journey.
One-off or short term special workings use a 'Z' code (**G** in the North East & South Wales), which is used where the train does not have a regular, fixed path with Network Rail.

The last two numbers identify the particular train, e.g. 1V64, 6S75, 4M30.

'Days Run'
For ease of use, each table is split into three sections: *Mondays-Fridays, Saturdays* and *Sundays*. In the Mondays to Fridays section, this column indicates the days each train is booked to run. (e.g. **TO**= **T**uesday **O**nly; **MX**=**M**ondays **ex**cepted(i.e. runs Tuesdays to Fridays). Trains which run as required are denoted by the suffix **-Q** e.g. **WFO-Q** indicates a train which runs on Wednesday and/or Friday (or neither!). Similarly, **W/FO** denotes a train which runs on Wednesdays or Fridays (but not both). Finally, **(Q)** on its own means the train can run on any or all days (or not at all!). If this column is blank, the train normally runs every day .

'Type of Train'
Trainload freight services: the type of wagons conveyed, e.g. bogie hoppers, 4-wheel tanks, etc.
Wagonload/mixed services: the train title - e.g. *Enterprise/Freightliner, etc.*

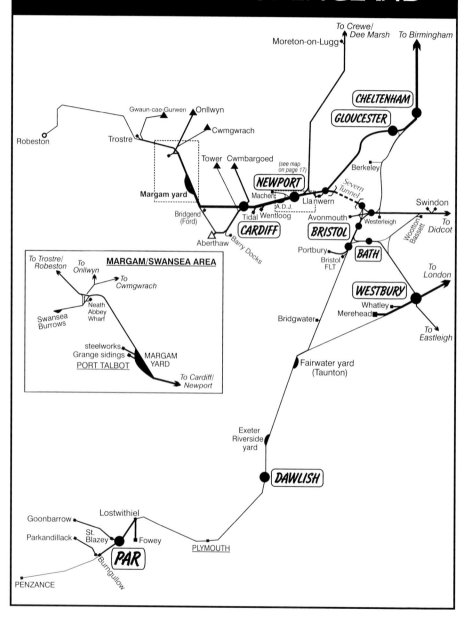

6

[24 hour]

Mondays-Fridays:

West	East	H'code	Runs	Train	Traction	Type of train
06:00	–	6G05	ThFO	05:08 Fowey-Goonbarrow	EWS 66	empty china clay hoppers
06:00	–	6C99	WO	21:47(Tue) Newport ADJ-St.Blazey	EWS 66	empty china clay
06T37	–	1C99	MX	23:45 Paddington-Penzance	fGW 57	"Night Riviera" sleeper
07T38	–	1C99	MO	23:50(Sun) Paddington-Penzance	fGW 57	"Night Riviera" sleeper
07:40	–	6P07	MTWO	06:55 Fowey-Parkandillack	EWS 66	empty china clay hoppers
07R40	–	6B00	ThO	07:15 St.Blazey-Parkandillack	EWS 66	empty china clay hoppers
–	08:00	6G06	ThFO	07:37 Goonbarrow-Fowey	EWS 66	loaded china clay hoppers
–	13R15	6C53	WO	12:29 Parkandillack-St.Blazey	EWS 66	loaded china clay
14:30	–	6G07	ThFO	13:20 Fowey-Goonbarrow	EWS 66	empty china clay hoppers
–	15:15	6P24	MTWO	14:25 Parkandillack-Fowey	EWS 66	loaded china clay hoppers
–	15:15	6C53	ThO	15:06 St.Blazey-Exeter Riverside	EWS 66	loaded china clay
–	16:40	6G08	ThFO	16:29 Goonbarrow-Fowey	EWS 66	loaded china clay hoppers
–	20:40	6C55	ThO	22:25 St.Blazey-Exeter Riverside	EWS 66	loaded china clay
22:45	–	6P25	FO	22:08 Fowey-St.Blazey	EWS 66	empty china clay hoppers
–	22T55	1A40		21:45 Penzance-Paddington	fGW 57	"Night Riviera" sleeper

Saturdays:

06T40	–	1C99		23:45(Fri) Paddington-Penzance	fGW 57	"Night Riviera" sleeper

Sundays: NO BOOKED TRAINS

[06:00-21:00]

Mondays-Fridays:

North	South	H'code	Runs	Train	Traction	Type of train
17:05	–	6C53	ThO	15:06 St.Blazey-Exeter Riverside	EWS 66	loaded china clay

Saturdays& Sundays: NO BOOKED TRAINS

BRISTOL NORTH
(Pilning, Filton __and__ Bristol Parkway)

[06:00-21:00]

Mondays-Fridays:

Pilning	Filton	Parkway	code	Runs	Train	Traction	Type of train
07:45	–	07:55	6B49	MO 07:08	Llanwern-Swindon steel term.	EWS 66	loaded steel
08:05	–	08:15	6B49	FO 06:46	Llanwern-Swindon steel term.	EWS 66	loaded steel
08:20	08:35	–	6V51	TThO 03:03	Warrington Arpley-Portbury	EWS 66	wagonload
08:45	09:00	–	6V54	WO-Q 05:35	Chirk-Exeter Riverside	Colas 70	empty timber carriers
10:00	–	–	6B68	MO-Q 09:25	Avonmouth-Aberthaw p.s.	EWS 66	loaded EWS coal hoppers
10:40	–	10:50	4070	09:58	Wentloog(Cardiff)-Southampton	F.Liner 70	Freightliner
–	11:10	11:15	4M18	MWFOQ 09:47	Fairwater yard-Washwood Heath	F.Liner 66	Departmental
–	11:45	11:40	6V80	MFX-Q 22:56	Gasgoigne Wood-Portbury	GBRf 66	gypsum(in box wagons)
12:35	–	12:25	6Z47	ThO-Q 08:49	Wembley-Cardiff Docks	EWS 66	empty bogie hoppers
–	13:10	13:15	6M63	WO-Q 11:58	Bridgwater-Crewe	2 DRS 37s	flasks
–	13:55	–	6A83	MO-Q 13:30	Avonmouth-Theale	EWS 66	loaded bogie hoppers
–	13:55	–	6A83	WFO-Q 13:30	Avonmouth-West Drayton	class 59	loaded bogie hoppers
14:25	–	14L15	6B35	MWFOQ 10:46	Hayes-Moreton on Lugg	EWS 66	empty bogie hoppers
14:10	–	14:15	4057	MO 13:29	Wentloog(Cardiff)-Southampton	F.Liner 66	Freightliner
15:15	–	15:05	6B50	MO 14:00	Swindon steel term.-Llanwern	EWS 66	steel empties
15:25	–	15:10	6V47	ThO-Q 10:26	Tilbury-Margam	EWS 66	empty cargowagons
16:25	–	16L15	6B33	MX-Q 13:00	Theale-Robeston	EWS 60	empty bogie tanks
16:35	–	16:25	6B50	FO 15:00	Swindon steel term.-Llanwern	EWS 66	steel empties
–	–	17c55	6V35	MWFOQ 14:53	Bescot-Avonmouth	EWS 66	loaded cement tanks
–	–	18:15	6V79	FO-Q 11:56	Angerstein-Avonmouth	GBRf 66	empty bogie hoppers
–	18:15	18:20	6E81	MFX-Q 17:00	Portbury-West Burton	GBRf 66	empty box wagons
18:20	–	18:30	6017	FO-Q 16:32	Barry Docks-Dollands Moor	EWS 66	Intermodal/covhops
18:35	18:25	–	6M51	ThO-Q 16:08	Exeter Riverside-Chirk	Colas 70	loaded timber carriers
18:30	18:20	–	6X52	TThO 17:33	Portbury-Mossend	EWS 66	loaded car carriers
20:15	–	20:25	6A29	18:58	Newport ADJ-Didcot yard	EWS 66	wagonload

Saturdays:

Pilning	Filton	Parkway	code	Runs	Train	Traction	Type of train
07:50	–	07:45	4V50	05:08	Millbrook-Wentloog(Cardiff)	F.Liner 66	Freightliner
11:45	–	11:55	4059	(Q) 11:06	Wentloog(Cardiff)-Southampton	F.Liner 66	Freightliner
12:50	12:55	–	0012		11:06 Margam-Westbury yard	EWS 66s	light engine 'convoy'
13:45	–	13:35	4V52	(Q) 10:00	Millbrook-Wentloog(Cardiff)	F.Liner 70	Freightliner
14:45	–	14:35	6B33		11:25 Theale-Margam	EWS 60	empty bogie tanks

Sundays: NO BOOKED TRAINS

8

BRISTOL SOUTH
(Bristol Temple Meads and Bath)

[06:00-21:00]

Mondays-Fridays:

Temple Meads	Bath	H'code	Runs	Train	Traction	Type of train
06c50	06:25	4V36	MX	23:34 Felixstowe-Bristol FLT	F.Liner 66	Freightliner
08c55	-	6V51	TTh0	03:03 Warrington Arpley-Portbury	EWS 66	wagonload
09:05	09:25	4L31		09:03 Bristol FLT-Felixstowe	F.Liner 66	Freightliner
09c15	-	6V54	WO-Q	05:35 Chirk-Exeter Riverside	Colas 70	empty timber carriers
11:00	-	4M18	MWFOQ	09:47 Fairwater Yard-Washwood Heath	F.Liner 66	Departmental
11:05	11:20	4L32		11:00 Bristol FLT-Tilbury/Gateway	F.Liner 66	Freightliner
11:00	-	6V80	MFX-Q	03:56 West Burton p.s.-Portbury	GBRf 66	gypsum(in box wagons)
12:30	-	6M63	WO-Q	11:58 Bridgwater-Crewe	2 DRS 37s	flasks
-	14:25	6A83	MO-Q	13:30 Avonmouth-Theale	EWS 66	loaded bogie hoppers
-	14:25	6A83	WFO-Q	13:30 Avonmouth-West Drayton	class 59	loaded bogie hoppers
16:30	16:50	4025	Th0-Q	16:25 Bristol FLT-Millbrook	F.Liner 66	Freightliner
17c50	-	6M51	Th0-Q	16:08 Exeter Riverside-Chirk	Colas 70	loaded timber carriers
17:50	-	6E81	MFX-Q	17:00 Portbury-West Burton	GBRf 66	empty box wagons
18:10	-	6X52	TTh0	17:33 Portbury-Mossend	EWS 66	loaded car carriers

Saturdays:

06c50	06:20	4V36		23:14(Fri) Felixstowe-Bristol FLT	F.Liner 66	Freightliner
-	13:20	0012		11:06 Margam-Westbury yard	EWS 66s	light engine 'convoy'

Sundays: NO BOOKED TRAINS

CARDIFF(station)

[06:00-21:00]

Mondays-Fridays:

West	East	H'code	Runs		Train	Traction	Type of train
-	07:05	4C93		05:35	Margam-Cwmbargoed	EWS 66	empty EWS coal hoppers
07:10	-	6B66	MX-Q	05:45	Avonmouth-Aberthaw p.s.	EWS 66	loaded EWS coal hoppers
07:35	-	6V49	TThO	19:34	Tees yard-Margam	EWS 66	empty steel
-	08:10	6B31	MX	06:30	Bridgend-Newport ADJ	EWS 66	Ford vans
08:15	-	6B06	FX	07:55	Newport ADJ-Barry Docks	EWS 66	wagonload
08:15	-	6V10	FO-Q	02:04	Dollands Moor-Barry	EWS 66	wagonload
-	08:20	6H35	(Q)	07:28	Margam-Birdport(Uskmouth)	EWS 66	loaded steel
08:55	-	6B42	ThO-Q	08:48	Cardiff Pengam-Neath	GBRf 66	empty bogie hoppers
08:55	-	6V54	WFO-Q	05:35	Chirk-Baglan Bay	Colas 70	empty timber carriers
-	09:35	6B13		05:00	Robeston-Westerleigh	EWS 60	loaded bogie tanks
09:35	-	6B58	FX-Q	08:50	Llanwern-Margam	EWS 66	empty steel
09:55	-	1V91		05:33	Holyhead-Cardiff	DB 67	Passenger
-	10:35	6H25	(Q)	09:22	Margam-Llanwern	EWS 66	loaded steel
11:00	-	6B68	MO-Q	09:25	Avonmouth-Aberthaw p.s.	EWS 66	loaded EWS coal hoppers
-	11:05	4V01	MFO-Q	00:22	Earles sidings-Cwmbargoed	EWS 66	empty EWS coal hoppers
-	11:05	4C94	MFX-Q	10:25	Aberthaw p.s.-Cwmbargoed	EWS 66	empty EWS coal hoppers
-	11:35	6M86	WO-Q	10:29	Margam-Dee Marsh	EWS 66	loaded steel(coil)
11:35	-	6B09	TX-Q	09:30	Newport Docks-Margam	EWS 66	empty steel
13:25	-	6B41	MTO-Q	11:10	Westerleigh-Robeston	EWS 60	empty bogie tanks
-	14:40	6H27	TWO-Q	13:53	Margam-Llanwern	EWS 66	loaded steel
15:05	-	6V05	(Q)	09:16	Round Oak-Margam	EWS 66	empty steel(covered)
15:20	-	6C93		14:00	Cwmbargoed-Aberthaw p.s.	EWS 66	loaded EWS coal hoppers
-	15:25	6B39	FX	14:32	Barry Docks-Newport ADJ	EWS 66	wagonload
-	15:40	6B75	ThO-Q	13:37	Neath-Cardiff Pengam	GBRf 66	loaded bogie hoppers
16:00	-	6H26	FX-Q	15:23	Llanwern-Margam	EWS 66	empty steel
16:20	-	6V75	(Q)	09:30	Dee Marsh-Margam	EWS 66	empty steel
16:30	-	6V47	ThO	10:26	Tilbury-Margam	EWS 66	empty cargowagons
16:35	-	6H36	(Q)	14:44	Birdport(Uskmouth)-Margam	EWS 66	empty steel
-	17:05	4Z45	FX-Q	15:28	Aberthaw p.s.-East Usk yard	EWS 66	empty EWS coal hoppers
-	17:15	6E30	FX-Q	16:21	Margam-Hartlepool	EWS 66	loaded steel(coil)
-	17:16	1W96			Cardiff-Holyhead	DB 67	Passenger
-	17:20	6017	FO-Q	16:32	Barry Docks-Dollands Moor	EWS 66	wagonload
-	17:20	6Z44	TO-Q	16:22	Aberthaw-Lindsey	EWS 66	fuel oil tanks
17:20	-	6B33	MX-Q	13:00	Theale-Robeston	EWS 60	empty bogie tanks
18:00	-	6V92	(Q)	10:22	Corby-Margam	EWS 66	empty steel
-	18:40	6M51	TThO	17:19	Baglan Bay-Chirk	Colas 70	loaded timber carriers
19:40	-	6F08	(Q)	17:30	Newport Docks-Margam	EWS 66	empty steel
19:45	-	6M77	MFO-Q	17:47	Cwmbargoed-Earles sidings	EWS 66	loaded EWS coal hoppers
19:45	-	6C94	MFX-Q	17:47	Cwmbargoed-Port Talbot	EWS 66	loaded EWS coal hoppers
-	19:45	6E09	TO-Q	13:54	Onllwyn-Immingham	EWS 66	loaded EWS coal hoppers
-	19:55	6E47	TThO	19:09	Margam-Middlesborough Goods	EWS 66	loaded steel
20:30	-	6B47		18:14	Westerleigh-Robeston	EWS 60	empty bogie tanks

Saturdays:

West	East	H'code	Runs	Train	Traction	Type of train
-	06:25	6B65	(Q)	05:31 Margam-Llanwern	EWS 66	loaded steel
07:35	-	6V49		19:34(Fri) Tees yard-Margam	EWS 66	empty steel
-	08:05	6B31		06:30 Bridgend-Newport ADJ	EWS 66	Ford vans
-	09:25	6B13		05:00 Robeston-Westerleigh	EWS 60	loaded MURCO bogie tanks
09:35	-	6B58	(Q)	08:50 Llanwern-Margam	EWS 66	empty steel
-	11:05	6H25		10:02 Margam-Llanwern	EWS 66	loaded steel
-	11:55	0012		11:06 Margam-Westbury yard	EWS 66s	light engine 'convoy'
14:05	-	6H26		13:30 Llanwern-Margam	EWS 66	empty steel
-	15:25	6H27		14:20 Margam-Llanwern	EWS 66	loaded steel
16:05	-	6F06	(Q)	14:17 Newport Docks-Margam	EWS 66	empty steel
16:15	-	6B33		11:25 Theale-Margam	EWS 60	empty bogie tanks
-	19:40	6H29		18:50 Margam-Llanwern	EWS 66	loaded steel

Sundays:

West	East	H'code	Runs	Train	Traction	Type of train
-	11:10	6H25		10:11 Margam-Llanwern	EWS 60	loaded steel
-	14:30	6E47		13:45 Margam-Middlesbrough	EWS 66	loaded steel
-	14:55	6H27		14:09 Margam-Llanwern	EWS 66	loaded steel
-	15:45	6E30	(Q)	14:54 Margam-Hartlepool	EWS 66	loaded steel(coil)
-	19:55	6M75		19:15 Margam-Hardendale	EWS 66	empty lime containers
20:25	-	6H28		19:45 Llanwern-Margam	EWS 66	empty steel

NEWPORT *(station)*

[24-hour]

Mondays-Fridays:

West	East	H'code	Runs	Train	Traction	Type of train
-	06:00	6M81	WX-Q 04:46	Margam-Round Oak	EWS 66	loaded steel
06:30	-	4V51	02:27	Southampton-Wentloog(Cardiff)	F.Liner 70	Freightliner
06:40	-	6V51	TTh0 03:05	Warrington Arpley-Portbury	EWS 66	wagonload
06:45	-	6B66	MX-Q 05:45	Avonmouth-Aberthaw p.s.	EWS 66	loaded EWS coal hoppers
07:05	-	6V49	TTh0 19:34	Tees yard-Margam	EWS 66	empty steel
-	07:05	6M96	F0-Q 05:51	Margam-Corby	EWS 66	loaded steel(coil)
07:25	-	6V10	F0-Q 02:04	Dollands Moor-Barry	EWS 66	wagonload
-	07:45	6V51	TTh0 03:03	Warrington Arpley-Portbury	EWS 66	wagonload
08:15	-	6F05	MF0-Q 07:55	Llanwern-Newport Docks	EWS 66	loaded steel
08:30	-	6V54	WF0-Q 05:35	Chirk-Baglan Bay	Colas 70	empty timber carriers
-	08:40	6H35	(Q) 07:28	Margam-Birdport(Uskmouth)	EWS 66	loaded steel
09:10	-	6B58	FX-Q 08:50	Llanwern-Margam	EWS 66	empty steel
09T40	-	1V91	05:33	Holyhead-Cardiff	DB 67	Passenger
-	10:00	6B13	05:00	Robeston-Westerleigh	EWS 60	loaded MURCO bogie tanks
-	10:10	4070	09:58	Wentloog(Cardiff)-Southampton	F.Liner 70	Freightliner
-	10:25	6Z34	T0-Q 09:46	Cardiff Tidal-Chaddesden(Derby)	DCR 56	empty box wagons
10:35	-	6B68	M0-Q 09:25	Avonmouth-Aberthaw p.s.	EWS 66	loaded EWS coal hoppers
-	11:00	6H25	(Q) 09:22	Margam-Llanwern	EWS 66	loaded steel
11:45	-	4V38	08:20	Daventry-Wentloog	DRS 66	'Tesco Express'
-	11:55	6M86	W0-Q 10:29	Margam-Dee Marsh	EWS 66	loaded steel(coil)
12:15	-	6F07	MX-Q 11:55	Llanwern-Newport Docks	EWS 66	loaded steel
13:10	-	6B41	MT0-Q 11:10	Westerleigh-Robeston	EWS 60	empty bogie tanks
13:15	-	6Z47	Th0-Q 08:49	Wembley-Cardiff Docks	EWS 66	empty bogie hoppers
-	13:40	4057	M0 13:29	Wentloog(Cardiff)-Southampton	F.Liner 66	Freightliner
-	14:30	6F06	MF0-Q 14:00	Newport Docks-Llanwern	EWS 66	empty steel
14:40	-	6V05	(Q) 09:16	Round Oak-Margam	EWS 66	empty steel(covered)
-	15:05	6H27	TW0-Q 13:53	Margam-Llanwern	EWS 66	loaded steel
15:35	-	6H26	FX-Q 15:23	Llanwern-Margam	EWS 66	empty steel
15:45	-	6V75	(Q) 09:30	Dee Marsh-Margam	EWS 66	empty steel
15:55	-	6V47	Th0 10:26	Tilbury-Margam	EWS 66	empty cargowagons
16:15	-	6H36	(Q) 14:44	Birdport(Uskmouth)-Margam	EWS 66	empty steel
16:55	-	6B33	MX-Q 13:00	Theale-Robeston	EWS 60	empty bogie tanks
-	17:25	4Z45	FX-Q 15:28	Aberthaw p.s.-East Usk yard	EWS 66	empty EWS coal hoppers
17:25	-	6V92	10:22	Corby-Margam	EWS 66	empty steel
-	17T31	1W96	17:16	Cardiff-Holyhead	DB 67	Passenger
-	17:40	6E30	FX-Q 16:21	Margam-Hartlepool	EWS 66	loaded steel(coil)
-	17:50	6017	F0-Q 16:32	Barry Docks-Dollands Moor	EWS 66	wagonload
-	17:50	6Z44	T0-Q 16:22	Aberthaw-Lindsey	EWS 66	fuel oil tanks

West	East	H'code	Runs	Train	Traction	Type of train
19:05	-	6X52	TTh0	17:33 Portbury-Mossend	EWS 66	wagonload
-	19:05	6A29		18:58 Newport ADJ-Didcot yard	EWS 66	wagonload
-	19:10	4M36		18:58 Wentloog-Daventry	DRS 66	'Tesco Express'
-	19:20	6M51	TTh0	17:19 Baglan Bay-Chirk	Colas 70	loaded timber carriers
19:35	-	6V06	TO-Q	15:10 Handsworth-Cardiff Tidal	EWS 66	loaded scrap
-	19:55	6X52	TTh0	17:33 Portbury-Mossend	EWS 66	wagonload
20:10	-	6B47		18:14 Westerleigh-Robeston	EWS 60	empty bogie tanks
-	20:20	6E09	TO-Q	13:54 Onllwyn-Immingham	EWS 66	loaded EWS coal hoppers
-	20:20	6E35	W/Th0	17:58 Cardiff Docks-Port Clarence	GBRf 66	empty bogie tanks
20:25	-	6V69	TO	16:58 Bescot-Newport ADJ	EWS 66	empty china clay
-	20:25	6E47	TTh0	19:09 Margam-Middlesborough Goods	EWS 66	loaded steel
-	20:55	6S16	Th0-Q	20:28 Cardiff Tidal-Mossend	EWS 66	loaded steel
21:25	-	6V07	WX-Q	14:27 Round Oak-Margam	EWS 66	empty steel(covered)
-	21c35	6L42	WO-Q	11:32 Trostre-Tilbury	EWS 66	Tinplate(in covered wagons)
-	21:35	6M75	TTh0	20:28 Margam-Carlisle yard	EWS 66	wagonload
-	21:50	6C99	TO	21:47 Newport ADJ-St.Blazey	EWS 66	empty china clay
-	21:55	6B21	MF0-Q	21:51 Newport ADJ-Llanwern	EWS 66	loaded steel
22:00	-	6V55	MWF0	15:30 Bedworth-Robeston	EWS 66	empty bogie tanks
22:15	-	6V73	F0	19:10 Swindon Cocklebury-Cardiff Tidal	EWS 66	loaded scrap
-	22:50	6L63	TF0-Q	21:25 Margam-Tilbury	EWS 66	loaded steel
23:35	-	6V04	WO-Q	19:59 Kingsbury-Cardiff Tidal	EWS 66	scrap(in bogie boxes)
-	23:55	6E80	TTh0	23:20 Cardiff Tidal-Rotherham	EWS 66	empty box wagons
23:55	-	6V81	MWF0	18:32 Rotherham-Cardiff Tidal	EWS 66	scrap(in bogie box wagons)
-	00:05	6M94	SX	22:44 Margam-Corby	EWS 66	loaded steel(coil)
-	00:10	6E49	TO-Q	23:30(Mon) Cardiff Tidal-Rotherham	EWS 66	slag(in box wagons)
-	00:25	6O03	WF0-Q	22:32 Cardiff Docks-Crawley	EWS 66	loaded bogie hoppers
00:25	-	6V97	TTh0	14:46 Beeston-Newport Docks	EWS 66	scrap(in bogie boxes)
-	01:30	6M11	SX	00:18 Margam-Round Oak	EWS 66	loaded steel
01:45	-	6V71	TThSO	18:26 Hardendale-Margam	EWS 66	containerised lime
-	01:45	6M76		00:38 Margam-Dee Marsh	EWS 66	loaded steel
-	01:50	6M77	TSO-Q	17:47 Cwmbargoed-Earles sidings	EWS 66	loaded EWS coal hoppers
-	02:05	6A28	TO	01:50 Cardiff Pengam-Colnbrook	GBRf 66	loaded bogie hoppers
-	02:35	6B17	(Q)	21:20 Robeston-Westerleigh	EWS 66	loaded MURCO bogie tanks
-	02:45	6H21		01:32 Margam-Llanwern	EWS 66	loaded steel
02:45	-	6B14		00:48 Didcot yard-Newport ADJ	EWS 66	wagonload
03:10	-	6V02		18:37 Tees yard-Margam	EWS 66	empty steel+lime
-	03:10	6M03	WF0	21:00 Robeston-Bedworth	EWS 66/60	loaded bogie tanks
-	03:25	6D98	SO	02:50 Cardiff Tidal-Handsworth	EWS 66	empty box wagons
-	03:30	6A11	TThF0	22:49 Robeston-Theale	EWS 60	loaded MURCO bogie tanks
04:25	-	6V00	WO-Q	19:30 Port Clarence-Cardiff Docks	GBRf 66	loaded bogie tanks
05:10	-	6V16	TO-Q	17:02(Mon) Mossend-Cardiff Tidal	EWS 66	empty steel

Saturdays:

West	East	H'code	Runs	Train	Traction	Type of train
-	06:50	6B65	(Q)	05:31 Margam-Llanwern	EWS 66	loaded steel
07:05	-	6V49		19:34(Fri) Tees yard-Margam	EWS 66	empty steel
08:10	-	6F05	(Q)	07:55 Llanwern-Newport Docks	EWS 66	loaded steel
08:15	-	4V50		05:08 Millbrook-Wentloog(Cardiff)	F.Liner 66	Freightliner
09:10	-	6B58	(Q)	08:50 Llanwern-Margam	EWS 66	empty steel
-	10:00	6B13		05:00 Robeston-Westerleigh	EWS 60	loaded MURCO bogie tanks
-	11:20	4059	(Q)	11:06 Wentloog(Cardiff)-Southampton	F.Liner 66	Freightliner
-	11:25	6H25		10:02 Margam-Llanwern	EWS 66	loaded steel
-	12:35	0012		11:06 Margam-Westbury yard	EWS 66s	light engine 'convoy'
13:45	-	6H26		13:30 Llanwern-Margam	EWS 66	empty steel
14:25	-	4V52	(Q)	10:00 Millbrook-Wentloog(Cardiff)	F.Liner 70	Freightliner
-	15:50	6H27		14:20 Margam-Llanwern	EWS 66	loaded steel
15:55	-	6B33		11:25 Theale-Margam	EWS 60	empty bogie tanks
19:45	-	6V06	(Q)	15:10 Handsworth-Cardiff Tidal	EWS 66	loaded scrap
-	20:00	6H29		18:50 Margam-Llanwern	EWS 66	loaded steel
20:25	-	6B47	(Q)	18:18 Westerleigh-Margam	EWS 60	empty MURCO bogie tanks

Sundays[to midnight]:

West	East	H'code	Runs	Train	Traction	Type of train
-	11:30	6H25		10:11 Margam-Llanwern	EWS 60	loaded steel
12:30	-	4V38		09:06 Daventry-Wentloog	DRS 66	'Tesco Express'
-	14:50	6E47		13:45 Margam-Middlesbrough	EWS 66	loaded steel
-	15:20	6H27		14:09 Margam-Llanwern	EWS 66	loaded steel
-	16:45	6E30	(Q)	14:54 Margam-Hartlepool	EWS 66	loaded steel(coil)
-	17:15	4M36		17:00 Wentloog-Daventry	DRS 66	'Tesco Express'
19:55	-	6H28		19:45 Llanwern-Margam	EWS 60	empty steel
-	20:25	6M75		19:15 Margam-Hardendale	EWS 66	empty lime containers
-	22:15	6L42	(Q)	13:48 Trostre-Tilbury	EWS 66	Tinplate(in covered wagons)
-	23:05	6M94		21:53 Margam-Corby	EWS 66	loaded steel(coil)

CHELTENHAM and GLOUCESTER

[06:00-21:00]

Mondays-Fridays:

Cheltenham	Gloucester	code	Runs	Train	Traction	Type of train
06:00	–	6M60	FO	03:05 Exeter Riverside-Bescot	EWS 66	loaded china clay
07:50	–	6V73	TO-Q	04:33 Crewe-Berkeley	2 DRS 37s	flasks
08:50	–	6V80	MFX-Q	22:56 Gasgoigne Wood-Portbury	GBRf 66	gypsum(in box wagons)
08:50	08:35	6M81	WX-Q	04:46 Margam-Round Oak	EWS 66	loaded steel
09:30	09:15	6M96	FO-Q	05:51 Margam-Corby	EWS 66	loaded steel(coil)
10:40	10:55	4V38		08:20 Daventry-Wentloog	DRS 66	'Tesco Express'
–	11:15	6B13		05:00 Robeston-Westerleigh	EWS 60	loaded MURCO bogie tanks
10:50	11:35	6V05	(Q)	09:16 Round Oak-Margam	EWS 66	empty steel(covered)
12:05	–	6B41	MTO-Q	11:10 Westerleigh-Robeston	EWS 60	empty bogie tanks
12:15	12:00	6Z34	TO-Q	09:46 Cardiff Tidal-Chaddesden	DCR 56	empty box wagons
13:25	–	6M56	TO-Q	13:41 Berkeley-Crewe	2 DRS 37s	flasks
14:20	–	6M63	WO	11:58 Bridgwater-Crewe	2 DRS 37s	flasks
14:50	15:05	6V92		10:22 Corby-Margam	EWS 66	empty steel
15:50	16:05	6V07	WX-Q	14:27 Round Oak-Margam	EWS 66	empty steel(covered)
17:00	–	6V35	MWFO	14:53 Bescot-Avonmouth	EWS 66	loaded cement tanks
18:15	18:25	6V06	TO-Q	15:10 Handsworth-Cardiff Tidal	EWS 66	loaded scrap
19:15	19:05	6Z44	TO-Q	16:22 Aberthaw-Lindsey	EWS 66	fuel oil tanks
–	19:05	6B47		18:14 Westerleigh-Robeston	EWS 60	empty MURCO bogie tanks
19:15	19:30	6V69	TO	16:58 Bescot-Newport ADJ	EWS 66	empty china clay
19:20	–	6E81	MFX-Q	17:00 Portbury-West Burton	GBRf 66	empty box wagons
19:45	19:55	6V65	ThO-Q	16:55 Saltley-Cardiff Tidal	EWS 66	scrap(in bogie boxes)
19:45	19:55	6V55	MWO-Q	16:08 Bedworth-Robeston	EWS 66	empty bogie tanks
20:10	–	4V18	MWFOQ	18:36 Washwood Heath-Fairwater	F.Liner 66	Departmental
20:30	20:15	6E30	FX	16:21 Margam-Hartlepool	EWS 66	loaded steel(coil)
20:35	20:25	4M36		18:58 Wentloog-Daventry	DRS 66	'Tesco Express'
20:40	20:50	6V55	FO	15:30 Bedworth-Robeston	EWS 66	empty bogie tanks

Saturdays:

Cheltenham	Gloucester	code	Runs	Train	Traction	Type of train
06:55	–	6E89		05:00 Portbury-Doncaster Hexthorpe	GBRf 66	empty box wagons
–	11:10	6B13	(Q)	05:00 Robeston-Westerleigh	EWS 60	loaded MURCO bogie tanks
18:05	–	6V06	(Q)	15:10 Handsworth-Cardiff Tidal	EWS 66	loaded scrap
–	19:25	6B47	(Q)	18:18 Westerleigh-Margam	EWS 60	empty MURCO bogie tanks

Sundays:

Cheltenham	Gloucester	code	Runs	Train	Traction	Type of train
11:25	11:40	4V38	(Q)	09:06 Daventry-Wentloog	DRS 66	'Tesco Express'
17:20	17:05	6E47		13:45 Margam-Middlesbrough	EWS 66	loaded steel
18:15	18:05	4M36		17:00 Wentloog-Daventry	DRS 66	'Tesco Express'
20:15	20:05	6E30	(Q)	14:54 Margam-Hartlepool	EWS 66	loaded steel(coil)

Other Locations:

- **ASHCHURCH** is 10 minutes running time north of Cheltenham;
- **LYDNEY** is 20 minutes running time south of Gloucester

15

SEVERN TUNNEL JUNCTION
(also Bishton, Undy, Magor, Chepstow, etc)

[06:00-21:00]

Mondays-Fridays:

West	East	H'code	Runs	Train	Traction	Type of train
06:10	–	4V51		02:27 Southampton-Wentloog(Cardiff)	F.Liner 70	Freightliner
06:55	–	6V10	FO-Q	02:04 Dollands Moor-Barry Docks	EWS 66	Intermodal/covhops
–	07:00	6B49	FO	06:46 Llanwern-Swindon steel term.	EWS 66	loaded steel
–	07:30	6B49	MO	07:08 Llanwern-Swindon steel term.	EWS 66	loaded steel
–	C07:45	6M81	WX-Q	04:46 Margam-Round Oak	EWS 66	loaded steel
–	08:05	6V51	TTh0	03:03 Warrington Arpley-Portbury	EWS 66	wagonload
–	C08:30	6M96	FO-Q	05:51 Margam-Corby	EWS 66	loaded steel(coil)
–	08:35	6V54	WO-Q	05:35 Chirk-Exeter Riverside	Colas 70	empty timber carriers
10:10	–	6B68	MO-Q	09:25 Avonmouth-Aberthaw p.s.	EWS 66	loaded EWS coal hoppers
–	C10:30	6B13		05:00 Robeston-Westerleigh	EWS 60	loaded bogie tanks
–	10:35	4070		09:58 Wentloog(Cardiff)-Southampton	F.Liner 70	Freightliner
–	C10:45	6Z34	TO-Q	09:46 Cardiff Tidal-Chaddesden(Derby)	DCR 56	empty box wagons
11:30C	–	4V38		08:20 Daventry-Wentloog	DRS 66	'Tesco Express'
12:30C	–	6V05	(Q)	09:16 Round Oak-Margam	EWS 66	empty steel(covered)
12:40	–	6Z47	ThO-Q	08:49 Wembley-Cardiff Docks	EWS 66	empty bogie hoppers
12:55C	–	6B41	MTO-Q	11:10 Westerleigh-Robeston	EWS 60	empty bogie tanks
–	14:00	4057	MO	13:29 Wentloog(Cardiff)-Southampton	F.Liner 70	Freightliner
14:30	–	6B35	MWFOQ	10:46 Hayes-Moreton on Lugg	EWS 66	empty bogie hoppers
15:35	–	6B50	MO	14:00 Swindon steel term.-Llanwern	EWS 66	steel empties
15:45C	–	6V92		10:22 Corby-Margam	EWS 66	empty steel
15:50	–	6V47	ThO-Q	10:26 Tilbury-Margam	EWS 66	empty cargowagons
16:30C	–	6V07	WX-Q	14:27 Round Oak-Margam	EWS 66	empty steel(covered)
16:40	–	6B33	MX-Q	13:00 Theale-Robeston	EWS 60	empty bogie tanks
17:05	–	6B50	FO	15:00 Swindon steel term.-Llanwern	EWS 66	steel empties
–	18:05	6O17	FO-Q	16:32 Barry Docks-Dollands Moor	EWS 66	Intermodal/covhops
–	C18:20	6Z44	TO-Q	16:22 Aberthaw-Lindsey	EWS 66	fuel oil tanks
18:40	–	6X52	TTh0	17:33 Portbury-Mossend	EWS 66	wagonload
18:45	–	6M51	ThO-Q	16:08 Exeter Riverside-Chirk	Colas 70	loaded timber carriers
19:20C	–	6V06	TO-Q	15:10 Handsworth-Cardiff Tidal	EWS 66	loaded scrap
–	19:30	6A29		18:58 Newport ADJ-Didcot yard	EWS 66	wagonload
–	C19:35	6E30	FX-Q	16:21 Margam-Hartlepool	EWS 66	loaded steel(coil)
–	C19:40	4M36		18:58 Wentloog-Daventry	DRS 66	'Tesco Express'
19:50C	–	6B47		18:14 Westerleigh-Robeston	EWS 60	empty bogie tanks

'Route Knowledge':   (blank) = to/from the Severn Tunnel;   C = to/from Chepstow

Saturdays:

West	East	H'code	Runs	Train	Traction	Type of train
08:00	–	4V50		05:08 Millbrook-Wentloog(Cardiff)	F.Liner 66	Freightliner
–	C10:30	6B13		05:00 Robeston-Westerleigh	EWS 60	loaded MURCO bogie tanks
–	11:35	4059	(Q)	11:06 Wentloog(Cardiff)-Southampton	F.Liner 66	Freightliner
–	12:35	0012		11:06 Margam-Westbury yard	EWS 66s	light engine 'convoy'
13:55	–	4V52	(Q)	10:00 Millbrook-Wentloog(Cardiff)	F.Liner 70	Freightliner
15:25	–	6B33		11:25 Theale-Margam	EWS 60	empty bogie tanks
19:15C	–	6V06	(Q)	15:10 Handsworth-Cardiff Tidal	EWS 66	loaded scrap
20:05C	–	6B47		18:18 Westerleigh-Margam	EWS 60	empty MURCO bogie tanks

Sundays:

West	East	H'code	Runs	Train	Traction	Type of train
12:15C	–	4V38	(Q)	09:06 Daventry-Wentloog	DRS 66	'Tesco Express'
–	C16:25	6E47		13:45 Margam-Middlesbrough	EWS 66	loaded steel
–	C17:30	4M36		17:00 Wentloog-Daventry	DRS 66	'Tesco Express'
–	C19:05	6E30	(Q)	14:54 Margam-Hartlepool	EWS 66	loaded steel(coil)

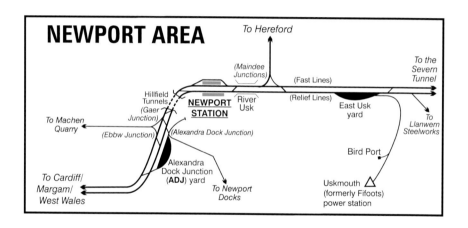

WESTBURY
(station and Fairwood Junction)

[06:00-21:00]

Mondays-Fridays:

Westbury station	Fairwood Junction	code	Runs	Train	Traction	Type of train
07:55	–	6M50	FX	07:55 Westbury VQ-Bescot VQ	Colas 70	Departmental
08c10	08:05	7A09		07:12 Merehead-Acton yard	MendipRail 59	loaded YEOMAN 'jumbo'
08c15	08:20	6C81	ThO	03:48 Colnbrook-Whatley	EWS 59	empty bogie hoppers
09R05	09:00	6M20	TO-Q	08:30 Whatley-St.Pancras	EWS 66	stone(in bogie hoppers)
09c10	09:25	7C29	MX	06:22 Acton yard-Merehead	MendipRail 59	empty bogie box wagons
09R35	09:30	6C72	(Q)	08:20 Fairwater yard-Westbury VQ	F.Liner 66	Departmental
10c10	10:30	6V33	WO-Q	07:15 Wembley-Whatley	EWS 66	empty bogie hoppers
10c10	10:30	6Z28	FO-Q	05:52 Hither Green-Whatley	MendipRail 59	empty bogie hoppers
11:05		7C31	WFO	08:40 Theale-Merehead	MendipRail 59	empty bogie hoppers
11c15	11:05	6M20	TWX-Q	10:37 Whatley-St.Pancras	EWS 66	stone(in bogie hoppers)
11:15		6M20	TO-Q	08:30 Whatley-St.Pancras	EWS 66	stone(in bogie hoppers)
11c15	11:05	6A26	WO-Q	10:37 Whatley-Hayes	EWS 66	stone(in bogie hoppers)
11:55		6M40		11:56 Westbury VQ-Stud Farm	GBRf 66	empty ballast boxes
–	11:55	7C31	WFO	08:40 Theale-Merehead	MendipRail 59	empty bogie hoppers
12c10	12:05	7B12	(Q)	11:35 Merehead-Wootton Bassett	MendipRail 59	loaded Yeoman hoppers
–	12:20	6C73	MX	12:12 Westbury VQ-Fairwater yard	F.Liner 66	Departmental
12c20	12:30	6V42	MX-Q	08:13 Wellingborough-Whatley	GBRf 66	empty bogie boxes
12c40	12:35	6A77	TThO	11:42 Merehead-Theale	MendipRail 59	loaded bogie hoppers
12c40	12:45	7C31	MO	09:55 Theale-Merehead	MendipRail 59	empty bogie hoppers
–	13:25	6Z84	MO-Q	13:17 Westbury VQ-Fairwater yard	F.Liner 66	Departmental
14c05	13:55	6L21		13:30 Whatley-Dagenham	MendipRail 59	loaded bogie hoppers
15c05	15:20	7C77		12:40 Acton yard-Merehead	MendipRail 59	empty 'jumbo' train
15:30	–	6C48	(Q)	13:30 Appleford-Westbury yard	MendipRail 59	empty box wagonss
–	15:40	6C78	FO-Q	15:27 Westbury VQ-Fairwater yard	F.Liner 66	Departmental
15c50	15:55	6V18		11:20 Allington-Whatley	class 59	empty bogie hoppers
–	16:20	7V07	ThO-Q	12:41 Chichester-Merehead	MendipRail 59	empty box wagons
17c05	17:00	7A15		16:16 Merehead-Acton yard	MendipRail 59	loaded bogie boxes
17c15	17:10	6M41	MX-Q	16:39 Whatley-Wellingborough	GBRf 66	empty bogie boxes
17:15	17:45	6C76	(Q)	14:40 Acton yard-Whatley	MendipRail 59	empty bogie hoppers
17c50	17:45	6A97	WFO	17:05 Merehead-Colnbrook	EWS 59	loaded bogie hoppers
–	18:25	6V12	ThX	15:38 Woking-Merehead	MendipRail 59	empty box wagons
–	18:35	7C64		15:24 Acton yard-Merehead	MendipRail 59	empty bogie hoppers
18c45	19:10	7C66	(Q)	17:47 Wootton Bassett-Merehead	MendipRail 59	empty bogie hoppers

Saturdays:

07c10	07:15	6C81		03:48 Colnbrook-Whatley	EWS 59	empty bogie hoppers
–	08:15	7C29		06:32 Acton yard-Merehead	MendipRail 59	empty bogie box wagons
13:45	–	0012		11:06 Margam-Westbury yard	EWS 66s	light engine 'convoy'
17:45	–	6V51	(Q)	14:35 St.Pancras-Westbury	EWS 59/66	empty bogie hoppers

Sundays: NO BOOKED TRAINS

18

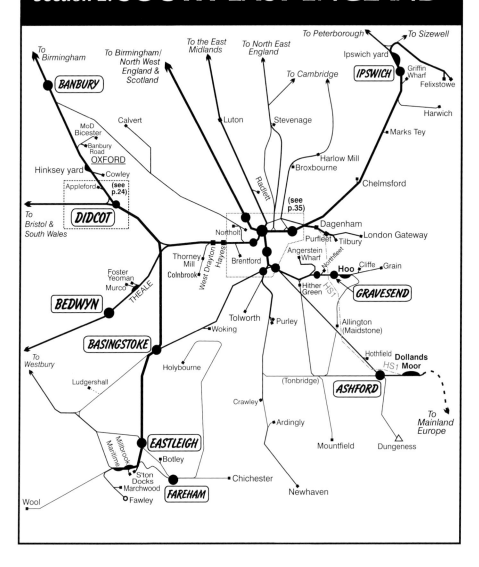

BANBURY

[06:00-21:00]

Mondays-Fridays:

North	South	H'code	Runs		Train	Traction	Type of train
-	06:10	1H06			Banbury-London Marylebone	DRS 68	Passenger
-	06c55	4015	MO	03:32	Crewe Basford Hall-Southampton	F.Liner 66	Freightliner
07:40	-	6M44	MO	04:50	Southampton E.Docks-Halewood	EWS 66	empty car carriers
-	07:40	1H15		06:09	Kidderminster-London Marylebone	DRS 68	Passenger
-	08T03	1H17		06:38	Stourbridge Junc.-London Marylebone	DRS 68	Passenger
08:15	-	6M21	T/ThO	07:29	Didcot yard-Kineton	EWS 66	MoD stores
08:15	-	6M66	MWFO	05:04	Southampton W.Docks-Garston	EWS 66	loaded car carriers
-	08:40	1H22		07:05	Kidderminster-London Marylebone	DRS 68	Passenger
-	08:55	4043	MX	06:43	Birch Coppice-Southampton	EWS 66	Intermodal
-	09:15	4015	MX	07:43	Hams Hall-Southampton	F.Liner 66	Freightliner
-	09:25	4018	MO	07:24	Lawley Street-Southampton	F.Liner 66	Freightliner
-	09:25	4014	MX	05:36	Garston-Southampton	F.Liner 70	Freightliner
09T46	-	1R15		08:41	Marylebone-Birmingham(Moor Street)	DRS 68	Passenger
-	10:05	6V03	T/ThO	09:29	Kineton-Didcot yard	EWS 66	MoD stores
11T07	-	1R21		10:10	Marylebone-Birmingham(Moor Street)	DRS 68	Passenger
11:15	-	6M26	(Q)	08:50	Eastleigh VQ-Mountsorrel	GBRf 66	empty ballast wagons
-	11:15	4090		06:12	Leeds-Southampton	F.Liner 66/70	Freightliner
11:20	-	4M55		08:55	Southampton-Lawley Street	F.Liner 66	Freightliner
-	11T40	1H33		10:55	Birmingham(Moor Street)-Marylebone	DRS 68	Passenger
-	11:55	4049	MX	09:22	Crewe Basford Hall-Southampton	F.Liner 66/70	Freightliner
12:20	-	4M28		09:32	Southampton-Ditton	F.Liner 66	Freightliner
12:50	-	6M50	FX	07:55	Westbury VQ-Bescot VQ	Colas 70	Departmental
-	12c55	4048	MO	11:26	Hams Hall-Southampton	F.Liner 66	Freightliner
13:15	-	4E69	TFO	09:32	Southampton-Wakefield Europort	EWS 66	Intermodal
13:15	-	4Z69	MThO	09:32	Southampton-Rotherham S.T.	EWS 66	Intermodal
13:20	-	4M18	MWFOQ	09:47	Fairwater yard-Washwood Heath	F.Liner 66	Departmental
-	13:20	4021		09:15	Trafford Park-Southampton	EWS 66	Intermodal
-	13T40	1H45		12:55	Birmingham(Moor Street)-Marylebone	DRS 68	Passenger
14T10	-	1R33		13:10	Marylebone-Birmingham(Moor Street)	DRS 68	Passenger
14:15	-	6M48		10:34	Southampton E.Docks-Halewood	EWS 66	empty car carriers
14:25	-	6M40		11:56	Westbury-Stud Farm	GBRf 66	empty ballast boxes
15:15	-	4M61		12:54	Southampton-Trafford Park	F.Liner 66/70	Freightliner
-	15:35	6042		11:31	Halewood-Southampton E.Docks	EWS 66	loaded car carriers
-	16:05	6V16	WO-Q	11:24	Stud Farm-Hinksey VQ	GBRf 66	loaded ballast boxes
16:20	-	4M52		11:32	Southampton E.Docks-Castle Bromwich	EWS 66	empty car carriers
-	16:25	6X01	TThO	10:17	Scunthorpe-Eastleigh	EWS 66	loaded rails
-	16T40	1H62		15:55	Birmingham(Moor Street)-Marylebone	DRS 68	Passenger
16:55	-	4M68		13:53	Southampton-Garston	F.Liner 70	Freightliner
17T08	-	1K45		16:15	London Marylebone-Kidderminster	DRS 68	Passenger
-	17:50	4095	MX	12:12	Leeds-Southampton	F.Liner 66/70	Freightliner

North	South	H'code	Runs	Train		Traction		Type of train
18T08	–	1K50		17:15 London Marylebone-Kidderminster		DRS	68	Passenger
–	18:10	4O17		15:48 Lawley Street-Southampton		F.Liner	66	Freightliner
18:36	–	1U50		17:21 London Marylebone-Banbury		DRS	68	Passenger
18:55	–	6M28		18:16 Hinksey VQ-Bescot VQ		F.Liner	66	Departmental
19T10	–	1K54		18:15 London Marylebone-Kidderminster		DRS	68	Passenger
19:20	–	4M99		16:57 Southampton-Trafford Park		F.Liner	70	Freightliner
–	19:40	4O76		17:01 Burton on Trent-Southampton		EWS	66	Intermodal
–	19:50	4O29		15:18 Trafford Park-Southampton		F.Liner	66	Freightliner
20:15	–	4M66		16:40 Southampton-Birch Coppice		EWS	66	Intermodal
20:25	–	4M97		17:32 Southampton-Hams Hall		F.Liner	66	Freightliner

Saturdays:

North	South	H'code	Runs	Train		Traction		Type of train
07:10	–	4M62		04:31 Southampton-Lawley Street		F.Liner	66	Freightliner
–	07:40	4O18		05:03 Lawley Street-Southampton		F.Liner	66	Freightliner
–	08:40	4O43		06:31 Birch Coppice-Eastleigh yard		EWS	66	Intermodal
–	08T44	1H10		07:12 Kidderminster-London Marylebone		DRS	68	Passenger
–	09:15	4O14		07:37 Hams Hall-Southampton		F.Liner	66	Freightliner
–	10:00	4O27		05:21 Garston-Southampton		F.Liner	70	Freightliner
–	10:40	4O54		05:27 Leeds-Southampton		F.Liner	66/70	Freightliner
–	10T43	1H17		09:10 Kidderminster-London Marylebone		DRS	68	Passenger
–	11:45	4O29		08:20 Crewe Basford Hall-Southampton		F.Liner	66	Freightliner
12T10	–	1R25		11:10 Marylebone-Birmingham(Moor Street)		DRS	68	Passenger
12:15	–	6M48		09:28 Southampton E.Docks-Halewood		EWS	66	empty car carriers
–	14T40	1H37		13:55 Birmingham(Moor Street)-Marylebone		DRS	68	Passenger
–	16:20	6O42	(Q)	11:33 Halewood-Southampton		EWS	66	loaded car carriers
18T07	–	1G49		17:10 Marylebone-Birmingham(Snow Hill)		DRS	68	Passenger
19T09	–	1G53		18:10 Marylebone-Birmingham(Snow Hill)		DRS	68	Passenger

Sundays:

North	South	H'code	Runs	Train		Traction		Type of train
–	12T40	1H27		11:55 Birmingham(Moor Street)-Marylebone		DRS	68	Passenger
19T05	–	1R53		18:10 Marylebone-Birmingham(Moor Street)		DRS	68	Passenger

DIDCOT PARKWAY
[24-hour]

Mondays-Fridays:

North	station	avoider	code	Runs	Train	Traction	Type of train
06:00	#	06:05	4018	MX	03:50 Lawley Street-Southampton	F.Liner 70	Freightliner
-	06:55	-	6015	MX	06:54 Didcot yard-Eastleigh yard	EWS 66	wagonload
07:15	07:10	-	6M66	MWFO	05:04 Southampton W.Docks-Garston	EWS 66	loaded car carriers
07:35(WC)		-	7A15	(Q)	05:04 Whatley-Appleford	MendipRail 59	loaded bogie boxes
-	07:35	-	6A49	T/ThO	07:32 Didcot yard-Bicester	EWS 66/67	MoD stores
07:50	07:55	-	4015	MO	03:32 Crewe Basford Hall-Southampton	F.Liner 66	Freightliner
-	08:10	-	6L35	MX	08:08 Didcot yard-Dagenham	EWS 66	empty car carriers
09:30	#	09:35	4043	MX	06:43 Birch Coppice-Southampton	EWS 66	Intermodal
10:00	#	10:05	4015	MX	07:43 Hams Hall-Southampton	F.Liner 66	Freightliner
10:00	#	10:05	4018	MO	07:24 Lawley Street-Southampton	F.Liner 70	Freightliner
10:05	#	10:10	4014	MX	05:36 Garston-Southampton	F.Liner 70	Freightliner
10:15(WC)		-	6M50	FX	07:55 Westbury VQ-Bescot VQ	Colas 70	Departmental
10:20	#	10:15	6M26	(Q)	08:50 Eastleigh VQ-Mountsorrel	GBRf 66	empty ballast wagons
-	10c35	-	6Z47	ThO-Q	08:49 Wembley-Cardiff Docks	EWS 66	empty bogie hoppers
10:35	10c45	-	6026	MX	10:19 Hinksey VQ-Eastleigh yard	F.Liner 66	Departmental
10:45	#	10:40	4M55		08:55 Southampton-Lawley Street	F.Liner 66	Freightliner
-	10:45	-	4L31		09:03 Bristol FLT-Felixstowe	F.Liner 66	Freightliner
11:05	11:10	-	4039	MX	09:43 Cowley(Oxford)-Southampton	EWS 66	car carriers
11:05	11:10	-	4040	MO	09:43 Cowley(Oxford)-Southampton	EWS 66	car carriers
11:30	11R35	-	6V03	T/ThO	09:29 Kineton-Didcot yard	EWS 66	MoD stores
11:45	#	11:40	4M28		09:32 Southampton-Ditton	F.Liner 66	Freightliner
11:55	#	12:00	4090		06:12 Leeds-Southampton	F.Liner 66/70	Freightliner
-	11:50	-	6B35	MWFOQ	10:46 Hayes-Moreton on Lugg	EWS 66	empty bogie hoppers
12:00	11:55	-	6V43	MX-Q	07:28 Cricklewood-Appleford	GBRf 66	spoil(in box wagons)
12:20	#	12:15	4E69	TFO	09:32 Southampton-Wakefield Europort	EWS 66	Intermodal
12:20	#	12:15	4Z69	MThO	09:32 Southampton-Rotherham S.T.	EWS 66	Intermodal
-	12:30	-	4070		09:58 Wentloog(Cardiff)-Southampton	F.Liner 70	Freightliner
12:55	#	13:00	4049	MX	09:22 Crewe Basford Hall-Southampton	F.Liner 66/70	Freightliner
13:10	13:05	-	6V43	MO-Q	10:15 Cricklewood-Appleford	GBRf 66	spoil(in box wagons)
13:15	#	13:10	6M48		10:34 Southampton E.Docks-Halewood	EWS 66	empty car carriers
-	13:15	-	4L32		11:00 Bristol FLT-Tilbury/Gateway	F.Liner 66	Freightliner
-	13c25	-	6V47	ThO	10:26 Tilbury-Margam	EWS 66	empty cargowagons
13:35(WC)		-	7C48	(Q)	13:30 Appleford-Westbury yard	MendipRail 59	empty box wagons
13:45(WC)		-	6M40		11:56 Westbury-Stud Farm	GBRf 66	empty ballast boxes
13:55	#	14:00	4048	MO	11:26 Hams Hall-Southampton	F.Liner 66	Freightliner
-	13:55	-	4M52	MX	11:32 Southampton E.Docks-Castle Bromwich	EWS 66	empty car carriers
-	14:15	-	6B33	MX-Q	13:00 Theale-Robeston	EWS 60	empty bogie tanks
14:25	#	14:30	4021		09:15 Trafford Park-Southampton	EWS 66	Intermodal
14:50	#	14:45	4M61		12:54 Southampton-Trafford Park	F.Liner 66/70	Freightliner
15:15	15c10	-	6V27		13:30 Eastleigh yard-Hinksey VQ	F.Liner 66	Departmental
-	15:35	-	6X38		13:50 Eastleigh yard-Didcot yard	EWS 66	wagonload
15:45	#	15:40	4M52	MO	13:35 Southampton E.Docks-Castle Bromwich	EWS 66	empty car carriers
15:45	^	-	4M52	MX	11:32 Southampton E.Docks-Castle Bromwich	EWS 66	empty car carriers
-	15:50	-	6V79	FO-Q	11:56 Angerstein-Avonmouth	GBRf 66	empty bogie hoppers
16:10	#	16:05	4M68		13:53 Southampton-Garston	F.Liner 70	Freightliner
-	16:20	-	6A48	WFX-Q	13:29 Bicester-Didcot yard	EWS 66/67	MoD stores
-	16:25	-	4057	MO	13:29 Wentloog(Cardiff)-Southampton	F.Liner 66	Freightliner
16:35	#	16:40	6042	FX	11:31 Halewood-Southampton E.Docks	EWS 66	loaded car carriers
16:55	#	17:00	6042	FO	11:31 Halewood-Southampton E.Docks	EWS 66	loaded car carriers

- These trains normally use the station avoiding line, but can easily be seen/photographed from the east end of the station.

North	station	avoider	code	Runs	Train	Traction	Type of train
-	17:15	-	6X44		14:38 Dagenham-Didcot yard	EWS 66	loaded car carriers
17:15	#	17:20	6M45	(Q)	17:09 Appleford-Cricklewood	GBRf 66	empty box wagons
17:55	#	18:00	6X01	TTh0	10:17 Scunthorpe-Eastleigh	EWS 66	loaded rails
18:00	#	18:05	4L40	TX	16:42 Cowley(Oxford)-Purfleet	EWS 66	enclosed car carriers
18:15(YN)		-	6E03	WO-Q	18:09 Appleford-Milford	EWS 66	empty flyash
-	18c15	-	4025	Th0-Q	16:25 Bristol FLT-Southampton	F.Liner 66	Freightliner
18:50	#	18:45	4M99		16:57 Southampton-Trafford Park	F.Liner 70	Freightliner
18:55	#	19:00	4017		15:48 Lawley Street-Southampton	F.Liner 66	Freightliner
19:25	#	19:20	4M66		16:40 Southampton-Birch Coppice	EWS 66	Intermodal
19:40	#	19:35	4M97		17:32 Southampton-Hams Hall	F.Liner 66	Freightliner
19:55	#	20:00	4095	MX	12:12 Leeds-Southampton	F.Liner 66/70	Freightliner
20:20	#	20:15	4V39		17:36 Southampton-Cowley(Oxford)	EWS 66	empty car carriers
20:30(YN)		-	6X65		20:28 Didcot yard-Mossend	EWS 66	wagonload
20:35	#	20:40	4076		17:01 Burton on Trent-Southampton	EWS 66	Intermodal
20:50	20:45	-	4E76		19:02 Southampton Millbrook-Leeds	F.Liner 66/70	Freightliner
-	20c50	-	6017	FO-Q	16:32 Barry Docks-Dollands Moor	EWS 66	Intermodal/covhops
21:15	#	21:20	4029		15:18 Trafford Park-Southampton	F.Liner 66	Freightliner
-	21R30	-	6A29		18:58 Newport ADJ-Didcot yard	EWS 66	wagonload
22:20(YN)		-	6E03	WO-Q	18:09 Appleford-Milford	EWS 66	empty containers
22:35	#	22:30	4M40		19:59 Southampton-Trafford Park	F.Liner 70	Freightliner
22:45	#	22:40	6E15	WFX-Q	21:06 Eastleigh yard-Scunthorpe	EWS 66	empty rail carriers
-	23:10	-	6V31		19:48(20:43 Mon) Dagenham-Didcot yard	EWS 66	wagonload
00:35	#	00:30	4M78		21:50 Southampton-Trafford Park	EWS 66	Intermodal
00:45	#	00:40	4M79		22:08 Southampton-Lawley Street	F.Liner 70	Freightliner
00:45	#	00:50	6027	TWO-Q	20:38 Mountsorrel-Eastleigh VQ	GBRf 66	ballast(in box wagons)
00:50(WC)		-	6V46	SX	19:00 Bescot VQ-Westbury VQ	Colas 70	Departmental
-	00R55	-	6B14		00:48 Didcot yard-Newport ADJ	EWS 66	wagonload
01:05	#	01:10	4052	Th0	18:27(Wed)Wakefield Europort-Southampton	EWS 66	Intermodal
01:15	#	01:10	4E48		23:01 Southampton Maritime-Leeds	F.Liner 66/70	Freightliner
-	01:15	-	6L31		01:15 Didcot yard-Dagenham	EWS 66	wagonload
01:25	#	01:20	6M38		23:38 Southampton E.Docks-Halewood	EWS 66	empty car carriers
01:30	#	01:35	4007		20:18 Leeds-Southampton Millbrook	F.Liner 66	Freightliner
01:40	#	01:45	4Z52	TFO-Q	20:15 Rotherham S.T.-Southampton	EWS 66	Intermodal
-	01:50	-	6A35	Th0	21:40 Moreton on Lugg-Hayes	EWS 66	loaded bogie hoppers
02:05	#	02:10	6V14		22:33 Stud Farm-Westbury VQ	GBRf 66	ballast(in box wagons)
02:10	#	02:15	6046		22:26 Halewood-Southampton Eastern Docks	EWS 66	loaded car carriers
-	02c40	-	6003	FO	22:32 Cardiff Docks-Crawley	EWS 66	loaded bogie hoppers
-	02c50	-	6L63	WSO-Q	21:25 Margam-Tilbury	EWS 66	loaded steel
-	03:00	-	4V30	SX	23:32 Tilbury-Bristol FLT	F.Liner 66	Freightliner
03:20	#	03:25	4011		00:23 Crewe Basford Hall-Southampton	F.Liner 66	Freightliner
03:45	#	03:40	4E01	SX	01:30 Southampton Millbrook-Leeds	F.Liner 66	Freightliner
03:45	#	03:40	4M46	SO	02:13 Southampton-Garston	F.Liner 66	Freightliner
04:20	#	04:25	4020		02:40 Castle Bromwich-Southampton E.Docks	EWS 66	loaded car carriers
-	04:30	-	4V26	MTX-Q	02:54 Southampton-Bristol FLT	F.Liner 66	Freightliner
04:45	#	04:40	4M69		02:39 Southampton-Burton on Trent	EWS 66	Intermodal
04:50	#	04:55	6066	TTh0	23:31 Garston-Southampton Western Docks	EWS 66	empty car carriers
-	04:55	-	4V51		03:12 Southampton-Wentloog(Cardiff)	F.Liner 70	Freightliner
-	05:00	-	4V36		23:34 Felixstowe-Bristol FLT	F.Liner 66	Freightliner
-	05c15	-	6V10	FO-Q	02:04 Dollands Moor-Barry Docks	EWS 66	Intermodal/covhops
05:20	#	05:15	4V40		02:56 Purfleet-Cowley(Oxford)	EWS 66	empty car carriers
05:45(YN)		-	6V15		17:27 Mossend-Didcot yard	EWS 66	wagonload
05:50	#	05:55	4022		01:47 Trafford Park-Southampton	F.Liner 70	Freightliner

Saturdays:

North	station	avoider	code	Runs	Train	Traction	Type of train
06:05	#	06:00	4M62		04:31 Southampton-Lawley Street	F.Liner 66	Freightliner
-	06:35	-	4V50		05:08 Millbrook-Wentloog(Cardiff)	F.Liner 66	Freightliner
08:05	08c10	-	4018		05:03 Lawley Street-Southampton	F.Liner 66	Freightliner
-	08:20	-	6L35		08:19 Didcot yard-Dagenham	EWS 66	empty car carriers
09:35	09c40	-	4043		06:31 Birch Coppice-Eastleigh yard	EWS 66	Intermodal
10:05	10:10	-	4014		07:37 Hams Hall-Southampton	F.Liner 66	Freightliner
10:55	#	11:00	4027		05:21 Garston-Southampton	F.Liner 70	Freightliner
11:00	#	11:05	6026	(Q)	10:50 Hinksey VQ-Eastleigh yard	F.Liner 66	Departmental
11:25	#	11:20	6M48		09:28 Southampton E.Docks-Halewood	EWS 66	empty car carriers
-	11:45	-	4V52	(Q)	10:00 Southampton-Wentloog(Cardiff)	F.Liner 70	Freightliner
11:55	#	12:00	4054		05:27 Leeds-Southampton	F.Liner 66/70	Freightliner
12:10	12:15	-	4040		10:44 Cowley(Oxford)-Southampton	EWS 66	enclosed car carriers
-	12:25	-	6B33		11:25 Theale-Margam	EWS 60	empty bogie tanks
12:35	12:40	-	4029		08:20 Crewe Basford Hall-Southampton	F.Liner 66	Freightliner
-	13:40	-	4059	(Q)	11:06 Wentloog(Cardiff)-Southampton	F.Liner 66	Freightliner
18:00	#	18:05	6042	(Q)	11:33 Halewood-Southampton	EWS 66	loaded car carriers
-	20:20	-	4V42		18:25 Southampton-Cowley(Oxford)	EWS 66	empty car carriers

Sundays: NO BOOKED TRAINS

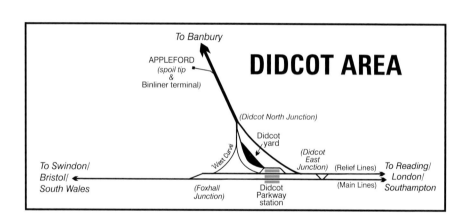

BEDWYN
(Berks and Hants)

[06:00-21:00]

Mondays-Fridays:

West	East	H'code	Runs	Train	Traction	Type of train
07:15	-	6C81	ThO	03:48 Colnbrook-Merehead	MendipRail 59	empty bogie hoppers
08:20	-	7C29	MX	06:22 Acton yard-Merehead	MendipRail 59	empty bogie box wagons
09:35	-	6V33	WO-Q	07:15 Wembley-Whatley	EWS 66	empty bogie hoppers
09:35	-	6Z28	FO-Q	05:52 Hither Green-Whatley	MendipRail 59	empty bogie hoppers
-	09:45	7A09		07:12 Merehead-Acton yard	MendipRail 59	loaded 'jumbo' train
10:20	-	7C31	WFO	08:40 Theale-Merehead	MendipRail 59	empty bogie hoppers
10:20	-	7C31	MO	09:55 Theale-Merehead	MendipRail 59	empty bogie hoppers
11:40	-	6V42	MX-Q	08:13 Wellingborough-Whatley	GBRf 66	empty bogie boxes
-	11:55	6M20	WX-Q	10:37(08:30 Tues) Whatley-St.Pancras	EWS 59	stone(in bogie hoppers)
-	11:55	6A26	WO-Q	10:37 Whatley-Hayes	EWS 66	stone(in bogie hoppers)
-	14:10	6A77	TThO	11:42 Merehead-Theale	MendipRail 59	loaded bogie hoppers
14:20	-	7C77		12:40 Acton yard-Merehead	MendipRail 59	empty 'jumbo' train
15:15	-	6V18		11:20 Allington-Whatley	class 59	empty bogie hoppers
-	15:50	6L21		13:30 Whatley-Dagenham	MendipRail 59	loaded bogie hoppers
-	15:55	6A83	WFO-Q	13:30 Avonmouth-West Drayton	class 59	loaded bogie hoppers
-	16:00	6A83	MO-Q	13:30 Avonmouth-Theale	EWS 66	loaded bogie hoppers
16:20	-	6C76		14:40 Acton yard-Whatley	MendipRail 59	empty bogie hoppers
17:20	-	7C64		15:24 Acton yard-Merehead	MendipRail 59	empty bogie hoppers
-	18:20	6M41	MX-Q	16:39 Whatley-Wellingborough	GBRf 66	empty bogie boxes
-	18:50	7A15		16:16 Merehead-Acton yard	MendipRail 59	loaded bogie boxes
-	19:10	6A97	WFO	17:05 Merehead-Colnbrook	MendipRail 59	loaded bogie hoppers
20:55	-	6C79	TThO	19:22 Theale-Whatley	MendipRail 59	empty bogie hoppers

Saturdays:

West	East	H'code	Runs	Train	Traction	Type of train
06:05	-	6C81		03:48 Colnbrook-Merehead	EWS 59	empty bogie hoppers
07:35	-	7C29		06:32 Acton yard-Merehead	MendipRail 59	empty bogie box wagons

Sundays: NO BOOKED TRAINS

BASINGSTOKE

[06:00-21:00]

Mondays-Fridays:

West	East	H'code	Runs	Train		Traction	Type of train
-	06:15	6M66	MWFO	05:04 Southampton W.Docks-Garston		EWS 66	loaded car carriers
06:50	-	4022	MX	01:47 Trafford Park-Southampton		F.Liner 70	Freightliner
07:00	-	4018	MX	03:50 Lawley Street-Southampton		F.Liner 70	Freightliner
07:05W	-	7Y44		04:22 Hoo Junction-Eastleigh yard		Colas 70	Departmental
A07:10W	-	6Z11	T/ThO	10:00 Dowlow-Southampton Up Yard		EWS 66	loaded box wagons
07:25	-	4020	MO	04:11 Castle Bromwich-Southampton E.Docks		EWS 66	loaded car carriers
07:50	-	6015	MX	06:54 Didcot yard-Eastleigh yard		EWS 66	wagonload
08:25	-	4050	MO	05:08 Daventry-Southampton		F.Liner 66	Freightliner
08:50	-	4015	MO	03:32 Crewe Basford Hall-Southampton		F.Liner 66	Freightliner
-	A09:05W	6012	ThX	03:26 Merehead-Woking		MendipRail 59	loaded box wagons
-	09:30	6M26	(Q)	08:50 Eastleigh VQ-Mountsorrel		GBRf 66	empty ballast wagons
-	09:35W	6Y48		09:01 Eastleigh yard-Hoo Junction		Colas 66/70	Departmental
-	10:00	4M55		08:55 Southampton-Lawley Street		F.Liner 66	Freightliner
10:20	-	4043	MX	06:43 Birch Coppice-Southampton		EWS 66	Intermodal
10:50	-	4015	MX	07:43 Hams Hall-Southampton		F.Liner 66	Freightliner
10:50	-	4018	MO	07:24 Lawley Street-Southampton		F.Liner 70	Freightliner
-	11:00	4M28		09:32 Southampton-Ditton		F.Liner 66	Freightliner
-	11:25	4Z69	MThO	09:32 Southampton-Rotherham S.T.		EWS 66	Intermodal
-	11:25	4E69	TFO	09:32 Southampton-Wakefield Europort		EWS 66	Intermodal
11:25	-	4014	MX	05:36 Garston-Southampton		F.Liner 70	Freightliner
11:45	-	6026	MX	10:19 Hinksey VQ-Eastleigh yard		F.Liner 66	Departmental
12:20	-	4039	MX	09:43 Cowley(Oxford)-Southampton		EWS 66	enclosed car carriers
12:20	-	4040	MO	09:43 Cowley(Oxford)-Southampton		EWS 66	enclosed car carriers
-	12:30	6M48		10:34 Southampton E.Docks-Halewood		EWS 66	empty car carriers
12:50	-	4090		06:12 Leeds-Southampton		F.Liner 66/70	Freightliner
-	13:15	4M52	MX	11:32 Southampton E.Docks-Castle Bromwich		EWS 66	empty car carriers
13:15	-	4070		09:58 Wentloog(Cardiff)-Southampton		F.Liner 70	Freightliner
13:45	-	4049	MX	09:22 Crewe Basford Hall-Southampton		F.Liner 66/70	Freightliner
-	14:00	4M61		12:54 Southampton-Trafford Park		F.Liner 66/70	Freightliner
-	14:25	6V27		13:30 Eastleigh yard-Hinksey VQ		F.Liner 66	Departmental
-	14:30	6X38		13:50 Eastleigh yard-Didcot yard		EWS 66	wagonload
14:50	-	4048	MO	11:26 Hams Hall-Southampton		F.Liner 66	Freightliner
-	15:00	4M52	MO	13:35 Southampton E.Docks-Castle Bromwich		EWS 66	empty car carriers
-	A15c20	4M68		13:53 Southampton-Garston		F.Liner 70	Freightliner
15:20	-	4021		09:15 Trafford Park-Southampton		EWS 66	Intermodal
-	15:30W	6Z14	T/ThO	14:48 Southampton up yard-Dowlow		EWS 66	empty box wagons
15:35W	-	4Y19		12:19 Mountfield-Southampton W.Docks		GBRf 66	empty gypsum containers
16:10	-	4013	FX	12:06 Daventry-Southampton		F.Liner 66	Freightliner
A16:15W	-	6V12	ThX	13:54 Merehead		MendipRail 59	empty box wagons
17:15W	-	6Y42		13:54 Hoo Junction-Eastleigh yard		Colas 66/70	Departmental
17:25	-	4057	MO	13:29 Wentloog(Cardiff)-Southampton		F.Liner 66	Freightliner
17:40	-	6042		11:31 Halewood-Southampton E.Docks		EWS 66	loaded car carriers

'Route Knowledge':   **(blank)** = Eastleigh to/from Reading;
             W = to/from Woking;
             A = to/from Andover (at Worting Junction)

West	East	H'code	Runs	Train	Traction	Type of train
-	18:30	4M66		16:40 Southampton-Birch Coppice	EWS 66	Intermodal
18:50	-	6X01	TTh0	10:17 Scunthorpe-Eastleigh	EWS 66	loaded rails
-	A18c55	4M97		17:32 Southampton-Hams Hall	F.Liner 66	Freightliner
19:20	-	4025	Th0-Q	16:25 Bristol FLT-Southampton	F.Liner 66	Freightliner
-	19:25	4V39		17:36 Southampton-Cowley(Oxford)	EWS 66	empty car carriers
19:55	-	4017		15:48 Lawley Street-Southampton	F.Liner 66	Freightliner
-	20:00	4E76		19:02 Southampton Millbrook-Leeds	F.Liner 66/70	Freightliner
20:40	-	4095	MX	12:12 Leeds-Southampton	F.Liner 66/70	Freightliner
-	20:40W	7Y43		19:57 Eastleigh yard-Hoo Junction	Colas 70	Departmental

Saturdays:

West	East	H'code	Runs	Train	Traction	Type of train
06:30	-	4022		01:23 Trafford Park-Southampton	F.Liner 70	Freightliner
09:15	-	4018		05:03 Lawley Street-Southampton	F.Liner 66	Freightliner
-	10:35	6M48		09:28 Southampton E.Docks-Halewood	EWS 66	empty car carriers
10:55	-	4043		06:31 Birch Coppice-Eastleigh yard	EWS 66	Intermodal
-	11:05	4V52	(Q)	10:00 Southampton-Wentloog(Cardiff)	F.Liner 70	Freightliner
11:15	-	4014		07:37 Hams Hall-Southampton	F.Liner 66	Freightliner
11:45	-	4027		05:21 Garston-Southampton	F.Liner 70	Freightliner
11:55	-	6026	(Q)	10:50 Hinksey VQ-Eastleigh yard	F.Liner 66	Departmental
12:55	-	4054		05:27 Leeds-Southampton	F.Liner 66/70	Freightliner
13:20	-	4040		10:44 Cowley(Oxford)-Southampton	EWS 66	enclosed car carriers
13:45	-	4029		08:20 Crewe Basford Hall-Southampton	F.Liner 66	Freightliner
14:45	-	4059	(Q)	11:06 Wentloog(Cardiff)-Southampton	F.Liner 66	Freightliner
-	15:30W	6Z14	(Q)	14:48 Southampton up yard-Wembley	EWS 66	empty box wagons
15:40W	-	4Y19	(Q)	12:02 Mountfield-Southampton W.Docks	GBRf 66	empty gypsum containers
18:55	-	6042	(Q)	11:33 Halewood-Southampton	EWS 66	loaded car carriers
-	19:30	4V42		18:25 Southampton-Cowley(Oxford)	EWS 66	empty car carriers

Sundays: NO BOOKED TRAINS

[06:00-midnight]

Mondays-Fridays:

West	East	H'code	Runs	Train	Traction	Type of train
-	S06:45	7052	Th0-Q	02:38 Merehead-Chichester	MendipRail 59	stone(in box wagons)
-	08:20	7035	MX-Q	06:05 Westbury yard-Fareham	MendipRail 59	stone(in box wagons)
-	S09:45	6Y32	MWO-Q	08:24 Fawley-Holybourne	EWS 66	bogie oil tanks
12:47	-	7V16	MX-Q	12:47 Fareham-Westbury yard	MendipRail 59	empty box wagons
13:15S	-	7V07	Th0-Q	12:41 Chichester-Merehead	MendipRail 59	empty box wagons
22:05	-	6Y34	MWO-Q	20:03 Holybourne-Eastleigh yard	EWS 66	bogie oil tanks

Saturdays & Sundays: NO BOOKED TRAINS

EASTLEIGH (Station)

[24-hour]

Mondays-Fridays:

North	South	H'code	Runs	Train	Traction	Type of train
-	06c20	4020	MX	02:40 Castle Bromwich-Eastern Docks	EWS 66	loaded car carriers
-	07:00	6B41	TO	06:57 Eastleigh yard-Fawley	EWS 66	loaded bogie tanks
-	07:00	6B93	ThO	06:55 Eastleigh yard-Fawley	EWS 66	empty bogie tanks
-	07c20	4022	MX	01:47 Trafford Park-Southampton	F.Liner 70	Freightliner
-	R07:50F	7035	MX-Q	06:05 Westbury yard-Fareham	MendipRail 59	stone(in box wagons)
-	08:00	6066	TThO	23:31 Garston-Western Docks	EWS 66	empty car carriers
-	08:05	4020	MO	04:11 Castle Bromwich-Eastern Docks	EWS 66	loaded car carriers
-	08c10	4018	MX	03:50 Lawley Street-Southampton	F.Liner 70	Freightliner
-	08c55	4050	MO	05:08 Daventry-Southampton	F.Liner 66	Freightliner
09c20	-	4M55		08:55 Southampton-Lawley Street	F.Liner 66	Freightliner
-	09c20	4015	MO	03:32 Crewe Basford Hall-Southampton	F.Liner 66	Freightliner
-	09:20	6B45	TO-Q	09:14 Eastleigh yard-Marchwood	EWS 66	MoD stores
-	09:40	6B43	MX-Q	09:38 Eastleigh yard-Western Docks	EWS 66	Intermodal
09c55	-	4M28		09:32 Southampton Maritime-Ditton	F.Liner 66	Freightliner
10c25	-	4E69	TFO	09:32 Western Docks-Wakefield Europort	EWS 66	Intermodal
10c25	-	4Z69	MThO	09:32(0947 Mon) Western Docks-Rotherham S.T.	EWS 66	Intermodal
11c00	-	6M48		10:34 Eastern Docks-Halewood	EWS 66	empty car carriers
-	11c25	4018	MO	07:24 Lawley Street-Southampton	F.Liner 70	Freightliner
-	11c25	4015	MX	07:43 Hams Hall-Southampton	F.Liner 66/70	Freightliner
11:35	-	6B38	MTO-Q	11:00 Marchwood-Eastleigh yard	EWS 66	MoD stores
-	11:55	4014	MX	05:36 Garston-Southampton	F.Liner 70	Freightliner
11:55	-	6041		10:14 Westbury yard-Eastleigh yard	EWS 66	Departmental
12:00	-	4M52	MX	11:32 Eastern Docks-Castle Bromwich	EWS 66	empty car carriers
-	12:15	4043	MX	06:43 Birch Coppice-Western Docks	EWS 66	Intermodal
-	12:15	4B53	MO	12:12 Eastleigh yard-Western Docks	EWS 66	Intermodal
12:35	-	6B44	MX-Q	12:07 Western Docks-Eastleigh yard	EWS 66	wagonload
-	12:50	4039	MX	09:43 Cowley(Oxford)-Eastern Docks	EWS 66	enclosed car carriers
13:05FR	-	7V16	MX-Q	12:47 Fareham-Westbury yard	MendipRail 59	empty box wagons
13c20	-	4M61		12:54 Southampton-Trafford Park	F.Liner 66/70	Freightliner
-	13c30	4090		06:12 Leeds-Southampton Maritime	F.Liner 66/70	Freightliner
-	13:45	4040	MO	09:43 Cowley(Oxford)-Southampton	EWS 66	enclosed car carriers
-	13c50	4070		09:58 Wentloog(Cardiff)-Maritime	F.Liner 70	Freightliner
14c00	-	4M52	MO	13:35 Eastern Docks-Castle Bromwich	EWS 66	empty car carriers
-	14c15	4049	MX	09:22 Crewe Basford Hall-Southampton	F.Liner 66/70	Freightliner
-	14:50	6V41	(Q)	14:47 Eastleigh-Westbury yard	EWS 66	Departmental
15c00	-	6Z14	TO-Q	14:48 Southampton up yard-Dowlow	EWS 66	empty box wagons
-	15c15	4048	MO	11:26 Hams Hall-Southampton	F.Liner 66	Freightliner
15:25	-	4B90	TThO	14:58 Maritime-Eastleigh works	F.Liner 66	Freightliner flats
-	16:05	4Y19		12:19 Mountfield-Southampton W.Docks	GBRf 66	empty gypsum containers
-	16c40	4021		09:15 Trafford Park-Western Docks	EWS 66	Intermodal
-	R16:55F	7040	FO-Q	13:35 Merehead-Eastleigh F.Y.	MendipRail 59	loaded bogie hoppers
-	17:05	4013	FX	12:06 Daventry-Southampton	F.Liner 66	Freightliner
17:20	-	4M99		16:57 Southampton-Trafford Park	F.Liner 70	Freightliner
17c35	-	4M66		16:40 Southampton-Birch Coppice	EWS 66	Intermodal
18:00	-	4V39		17:36 Eastern Docks-Cowley(Oxford)	EWS 66	empty car carriers
-	18:05	4B91	TThO	17:17 Eastleigh works-Maritime	F.Liner 66	Freightliner flats
-	18c15	4057	MO	13:29 Wentloog(Cardiff)-Southampton	F.Liner 66	Freightliner
-	18c20	6042		11:31 Halewood-Eastern Docks	EWS 66	loaded car carriers
19:10	-	6031	WX-Q	17:34 Westbury yard-Eastleigh yard	Colas 70	Departmental
19c20	-	4E76		19:02 Millbrook FLT-Leeds	F.Liner 66/70	Freightliner
-	20c05	4025	ThO-Q	16:25 Bristol FLT-Southampton	F.Liner 66	Freightliner
-	20:15	6V31	WX-Q	20:13 Eastleigh yard-Westbury yard	Colas 70	Departmental

North	South	H'code	Runs	Train	Traction	Type of train
20c20	-	4M40		19:59 Southampton-Trafford Park	F.Liner 70	Freightliner
20:25	-	4Y81		19:55 Western Docks-Tonbridge	GBRf 66	containerised gypsum
-	20c35	4017		15:48 Lawley Street-Southampton	F.Liner 66	Freightliner
-	21c10	4095	MX	12:12 Leeds-Southampton	F.Liner 66/70	Freightliner
21c40R	-	4M78	FX	21:08 Western Docks-Trafford Park	EWS 66	Intermodal
-	22c00	4076	FO	17:01 Burton on Trent-Western Docks	EWS 66	Intermodal
22c35R	-	4M79		22:13 Southampton Maritime-Lawley Street	F.Liner 70	Freightliner
22:35F	-	6Y34	MWO-Q	20:03 Holybourne-Eastleigh yard	EWS 66	bogie oil tanks
-	22c40	4029	FO	15:18 Trafford Park-Southampton	F.Liner 66	Freightliner
-	R22:55F	7044	FX	21:12 Westbury yard-Botley	MendipRail 59	loaded bogie hoppers
23c00	-	4M78	FO	21:50 Western Docks-Trafford Park	EWS 66	Intermodal
-	R23c05	4076	FX	17:01 Burton on Trent-Western Docks	EWS 66	Intermodal
23c10R	-	6M38	FX	Eastern Docks-Halewood	EWS 66	empty car carriers
23c15R	-	4M79	FO	22:57 Southampton Maritime-Lawley Street	F.Liner 70	Freightliner
23c40	-	4E48	FX	23:01 Southampton Maritime-Leeds	F.Liner 66/70	Freightliner
-	23c55	4013	FO	19:07 Daventry-Southampton	F.Liner 66	Freightliner
00c05R	-	4M13	SX	23:44 Southampton Maritime-Daventry	F.Liner 66	Freightliner
00c50	-	6M38	SO	00:23 Eastern Docks-Halewood	EWS 66	empty car carriers
00c50	-	4M13	SO	00:36 Southampton Maritime-Daventry	F.Liner 66	Freightliner
01c50R	-	4E01	SX	01:30 Southampton Millbrook-Leeds	F.Liner 66	Freightliner
02c35	-	4M46	SO	02:13 Southampton-Garston	F.Liner 66	Freightliner
02c50R	-	4V51	SX	02:27 Southampton-Wentloog(Cardiff)	F.Liner 70	Freightliner
-	R02c40	4052	ThO	18:27(Wed) Wakefield Europort-Western Docks	EWS 66	Intermodal
03c10R	-	4M69		02:39 Western Docks-Burton on Trent	EWS 66	Intermodal
03c35FR	-	7V97	SX	02:59 Botley-Merehead	MendipRail 59	empty bogie hoppers
-	R05c05	6046		22:26 Halewood-Eastern Docks	EWS 66	loaded car carriers
-	R03c50	4Z52	TFO	20:15 Rotherham S.T.-Western Docks	EWS 66	Intermodal
04c50	-	4M62	SO	04:31 Southampton-Lawley Street	F.Liner 66	Freightliner
-	R05:30	4011		00:23 Crewe-Southampton Maritime	F.Liner 66	Freightliner
05c30	-	4V50	SO	05:08 Millbrook-Wentloog(Cardiff)	F.Liner 70	Freightliner
05c35	-	6M66	MWFO	05:04 Western Docks-Garston	EWS 66	loaded car carriers

Saturdays:

North	South	H'code	Runs	Train	Traction	Type of train
-	07c00	4022		01:23 Trafford Park-Southampton	F.Liner 70	Freightliner
-	07:05	6066		00:46 Garston-Western Docks	EWS 66	empty car carriers
-	09c55	4018		05:03 Lawley Street-Southampton	F.Liner 66	Freightliner
09c55	-	6M48		09:28 Southampton E.Docks-Halewood	EWS 66	empty car carriers
10c25	-	4V52	(Q)	10:00 Southampton-Wentloog(Cardiff)	F.Liner 70	Freightliner
-	11:45	4014		07:37 Hams Hall-Southampton	F.Liner 66	Freightliner
-	12c15	4027		05:21 Garston-Southampton Maritime	F.Liner 70	Freightliner
-	13c35	4054		05:27 Leeds-Southampton	F.Liner 66/70	Freightliner
-	13:55	4040		10:44 Cowley(Oxford)-Eastern Docks	EWS 66	enclosed car carriers
-	14c15	4029		08:20 Crewe Basford Hall-Southampton	F.Liner 66	Freightliner
14c55	-	6Z14	(Q)	14:48 Southampton up yard-Wembley	EWS 66	empty box wagons
-	15c30	4059	(Q)	11:06 Wentloog(Cardiff)-Southampton	F.Liner 66	Freightliner
-	16:05	4Y19	(Q)	12:02 Mountfield-Western Docks	GBRf 66	empty gypsum
18:55	-	4V42		18:25 Eastern Docks-Cowley(Oxford)	EWS 66	empty car carriers
-	19:45	6042	(Q)	11:33 Halewood-Southampton	EWS 66	loaded car carriers
20:15	-	4Y81	(Q)	19:50 Western Docks-Tonbridge	GBRf 66	containerised gypsum

Sundays: NO BOOKED TRAINS

'Route Knowledge': Trains are routed 'main line' (Winchester-Southampton) apart from:

R = to/from Romsey(via Chandlers Ford); **F** = to/from Fareham line.

(See the Basingstoke table for details of trains from Eastleigh yard to the North)

DARTFORD
and
GRAVESEND

[06:00-21:00]

Mondays-Fridays:

Dartford	Gravesend	code	Runs	Train	Traction	Type of train
B06:40	07:00	6O35	MX	01:38 Whitemoor-Hoo Junction	GBRf 66	Departmental
10:20	10:10	6L37		09:58 Hoo Junction-Whitemoor	Colas 66/70	Departmental
10:40	10:25	7Y23	TO	10:22 Hoo Junction-Hither Green	EWS 66	Departmental
11:00	10:40	6V92	MO-Q	09:40 Grain-Brentford	GBRf 66	loaded bogie hoppers
11:00	10:40	6E40	TWO-Q	09:40 Grain-Ferme Park	GBRf 66	loaded ballast boxes
11:15	11:00	7Y36	TO-Q	10:31 Cliffe-Crawley	EWS 66	loaded box wagons
11:40	11:25	6M95	WFO-Q	10:57 Cliffe-Neasden	EWS 66	sand(in bogie hoppers)
12:15	11:55	6V18		11:20 Allington-Whatley	class 59	empty bogie hoppers
12:20	12:00	6V69	MO	11:00 East Peckham-Acton yard	EWS 66	empty bogie boxes
12:25	12:05	6V69	WO-Q	11:09 East Peckham-Southall yard	EWS 66	empty bogie boxes
12:35	12:45	6Y48		09:01 Eastleigh yard-Hoo Junction	Colas 66/70	Departmental
13:10	13:25	6Y08	MThO	11:30 Tolworth-Cliffe	EWS 66	empty Brett hoppers
14:15	14:00	7U71		13:31 Cliffe-Stewarts Lane	EWS 66	sand(in bogie box wagons)
14:25	14:10	6Y42		13:54 Hoo Junction-Eastleigh yard	Colas 66/70	Departmental
14:25	14:35	7O75	MO-Q	12:42 Acton yard-Grain	EWS 66	empty bogie boxes
15:20	15:35	6Z12	MO-Q	14:30 Angerstein wharf-Grain	GBRf 66	empty bogie hoppers
19:55	19:35	7M60	MO-Q	18:40 Grain-West Ruislip LUL	EWS 66	loaded box wagons
20:15	20:05	6L36		19:52 Hoo Junction-Whitemoor	GBRf 66	Departmental

Saturdays:

11:05	10:50	7Z71	(Q)	10:26 Cliffe-Stewarts Lane	EWS 66	sand(in bogie box wagons)
13:15	13:30	6Y08		11:30 Tolworth-Cliffe	EWS 66	empty Brett hoppers
14:05	14:25	6O10	(Q)	12:42 Wembley-Cliffe	EWS 66	empty bogie hoppers

Sundays: NO BOOKED TRAINS

'Route knowledge' (west of Dartford):

(blank) = via Sidcup;   **B** = via Bexleyheath;   **W** = via Woolwich

30

ASHFORD INTERNATIONAL
[06:00-midnight]

Mondays-Fridays:

West	East	H'code	Runs	Train	Traction	Type of train
-	T06:00	4028	MX	22:40 Scunthorpe-Dollands Moor	EWS 66	loaded steel(to Ebange)
07:25	-	6M45		07:07 Dollands Moor-Daventry	EWS 66	water(in cargowagons)
08:25	-	4E26		08:13 Dollands Moor-Scunthorpe	EWS 66	empty steel(ex Ebange)
-	T09:10	6062	Th0-Q	02:08 Crewe-Dungeness p.s.	2 DRS 37s	flask(s)
-	14:40	6B45	FO-Q	12:13 Wembley-Dollands Moor	EWS 66	empty china clay tanks
17:35	-	6M95	Th0-Q	16:35 Dungeness p.s.-Crewe	2 DRS 37s	flask(s)
-	T21:10	6D63	WTh0	18:53 Wembley-Dollands Moor	EWS 66	empty cargowagons
-	#21:35	6023	WX	20:52 Ripple Lane-Dollands Moor	EWS 92	Transfesa 'blue train'
-	T22:10	6D71	TFO	19:54 Wembley-Dollands Moor	EWS 66	empty cargowagons

Saturdays:

West	East	H'code	Runs	Train	Traction	Type of train
09:25	-	4E26		09:14 Dollands Moor-Scunthorpe	EWS 66	empty steel(ex Ebange)

Sundays:

West	East	H'code	Runs	Train	Traction	Type of train
12:20	-	4E32		12:05 Dollands Moor-Scunthorpe	EWS 66	empty steel(ex Ebange)
22:40#	-	6L21		22:32 Dollands Moor-Ripple Lane	EWS 92	Transfesa 'blue train'
23:25	-	6M13		23:11 Dollands Moor-Ditton	EWS 66	loaded steel

'**Route Knowledge**':   (**blank**) = via Maidstone;   **T** = via Tonbridge;

= these trains take the HS1 avoiding line, immediately north of the station.

KENSINGTON OLYMPIA
CLAPHAM JUNCTION
and
WANDSWORTH ROAD

[06:00-midnight]

Mondays-Fridays:

Kenny O Junction	Clapham Junction	Wandsworth Road	code	Runs	Train	Traction	Type of train
06:10	–	06:00	6E35	TTh0 04:01	Grain-Ferme Park	EWS 66	sand(in bogie hoppers)
06:45	–	07:05	6062	Th0-Q 02:08	Crewe-Dungeness p.s.	2 DRS 37s	flask(s)
07:35	–	07:20	6V63	MX 05:15	Angerstein-Acton(-St.Pancras)	EWS 66	loaded bogie hoppers
09:25	–	09:10	6M45	07:07	Dollands Moor-Daventry	EWS 66	water(in cargowagons)
10:15	–	10:05	4E26	08:13	Dollands Moor-Scunthorpe	EWS 66	empty steel(ex Ebange)
–		10:25	7U40	TTh0 09:45	Hither Green-Stewarts Lane	EWS 66	loaded bogie hoppers
11c10		11:20	6Z92	F0-Q 10:13	Bow-Tonbridge	GBRf 66	empty bogie hoppers
11:20	11:05	–	6V60	TWO-Q 09:23	Ardingly-Acton yard	class 59	empty bogie boxes
11:30		11:20	6L37	09:58	Hoo Junction-Whitemoor	Colas 66/70	Departmental
–	W11:25	11:35	6Y48	09:01	Eastleigh yard-Hoo Junction	Colas 66/70	Departmental
11:45	–	11:35	7V75	TTh0 09:57	Angerstein-Acton yard	EWS 66	empty bogie hoppers
12:00	12:10	–	7079	F0-Q 11:42	Acton yard-Crawley	EWS 66	loaded box wagons
12:05		11:50	6V92	MO-Q 09:40	Grain-Brentford	GBRf 66	loaded bogie hoppers
12:05		11:50	6E40	TWO-Q 09:40	Grain-Ferme Park	GBRf 66	loaded ballast boxes
–	12:05	12:15	6Y08	MTh0 11:30	Tolworth-Cliffe	EWS 66	empty Brett hoppers
12:20	12:05	–	6Z88	T0-Q 11:30	Tolworth-Wembley yard	EWS 66	empty Brett hoppers
	12:15	–	7V50	MFX-Q 11:08	Crawley-Acton yard	class 59	empty box wagons
	12:25	12:20	7Y36	T0-Q 10:31	Cliffe-Crawley	EWS 66	loaded box wagons
12:35	–		6Z58	WO-Q 10:44	Harlow Mill-Tonbridge	GBRf 66	empty bogie hoppers
12:35	–		6B45	F0-Q 12:13	Wembley-Dollands Moor	EWS 66	empty china clay tanks
12:45			6M49	FO	11:08 Crawley-Wembley	EWS 66	empty bogie hoppers
12:45	12:15	–	7V50	MFX-Q 11:08	Crawley-Acton yard	EWS 66	empty box wagons
–	W12:40	12:35	6M95	WFO-Q 10:57	Cliffe-Neasden	EWS 66	sand(in bogie hoppers)
12:50	13:05	–	7068	TWFO 12:34	Acton yard-Purley	class 59	loaded bogie hoppers
12:50	13:05	–	7069	MTh0 12:34	Acton yard-Crawley	class 59	loaded bogie boxes
13:00	–	12:45	6V65	T0-Q 11:07	Angerstein-Acton yard	EWS 66	loaded bogie hoppers
13:00	–	12:45	6Z66	MO-Q 11:07	Angerstein-Woking	EWS 66	loaded bogie boxes
	–	12:55	6B45	F0-Q 12:13	Wembley-Dollands Moor	EWS 66	empty china clay tanks
13:00	–	13:15	6098	WFO	12:05 Park Royal-Angerstein	EWS 66	empty bogie hoppers
13:00	–	13:15	7075	MO-Q 12:42	Acton yard-Grain	EWS 66	empty bogie boxes
13:15	–	13:05	6V18		11:20 Allington-Whatley	class 59	empty bogie hoppers
–	W13:45	13:35	6M79	MWO-Q 11:56	Angerstein-Bardon Hill	GBRf 66	empty bogie hoppers
13:30	13:45	–	7002	MWO	13:10 Acton yard-Tolworth	EWS 66	loaded bogie hoppers
13:45		13:35	6V79	F0-Q 11:56	Angerstein-Avonmouth	GBRf 66	empty bogie hoppers
	–	13:40	6V69	MO	11:00 East Peckham-Acton yard	EWS 66	empty bogie boxes
	–	13:40	6V69	WO	11:09 East Peckham-Southall yard	EWS 66	empty bogie boxes
–	W13:50	14:00	6080	T0-Q 12:15	Luton-Angerstein	EWS 66	empty bogie hoppers
14:00	–		6V69	MO	11:10 East Peckham-Acton yard	EWS 66	empty bogie boxes
14:00	–		6V69	WO	11:09 East Peckham-Southall yard	EWS 66	empty bogie boxes
–	W14:10	14:00	4Y19		12:19 Mountfield-Southampton W.Docks	GBRf 66	empty gypsum containers
14:20	14:10	–	6V00	TX-Q 12:15	Newhaven-Acton yard	class 59	empty box wagons
14:35	14:45	–	6Z79	WO-Q 09:10	Marks Tey-Crawley	EWS 66	loaded hoppers

at Clapham Junction: (blank) = via Main platforms; **W** = via Windsor line platforms

Kenny	Clapham	Wandsworth						
O	Junction	Road	code	Runs	Train		Traction	Type of train
-	-	15:05	7U71		13:31	Cliffe-Stewarts Lane	EWS 66	sand(in bogie box wagons)
-	W15:30	15:20	6Y42		13:54	Hoo Junction-Eastleigh yard	Colas 66/70	Departmental
-	-	15:25	6U41	TThO	14:47	Stewarts Lane-Angerstein	EWS 66	empty bogie hoppers
-	W15:40	15:45	6062	TO	14:33	St.Pancras-Hither Green	EWS 66	empty bogie hoppers
-	W15:40	15:45	6063	WFO	14:33	St.Pancras-Hither Green	EWS 66	empty bogie hoppers
18:00	W17:50	-	7Z50	ThO-Q	16:33	Woking-Wembley yard	EWS 66	empty bogie boxes
19:15	-	I	6D63	WThO	18:53	Wembley-Dollands Moor	EWS 66	empty cargowagons
19:20	-	19:05	6M95	ThO-Q	16:35	Dungeness p.s.-Crewe	2 DRS 37s	flask(s)
-	W19:10	19:20	6070	WFO-Q	18:37	Neasden-Grain	GBRf 66	empty bogie hoppers
^	-	19:25	6D63	WThO	18:53	Wembley-Dollands Moor	EWS 66	empty cargowagons
-	-	19:45	7U72		19:00	Stewarts Lane-Cliffe	EWS 66	empty bogie boxes
20:15	-	20:25	6D71	TFO	19:54	Wembley-Dollands Moor	EWS 66	empty cargowagons
20:45	20:30	-	7V67	TWFO	19:50	Purley-Acton yard	class 59	empty Yeoman hoppers
21:00	-	20:45	6L36		19:52	Hoo Junction-Whitemoor	GBRf 66	Departmental
21:05	20:55	-	7V17	MWO	20:21	Tolworth-Acton yard	EWS 66	empty bogie hoppers
21:15	21:05	-	7Z50	TO-Q	20:02	Crawley-Wembley yard	EWS 66	empty box wagons
21:15	21:05	-	7V69	MThO	20:02	Crawley-Acton yard	class 59	empty bogie boxes
-	W22:20	22:30	7Y43		19:57	Eastleigh yard-Hoo Junction	Colas 70	Departmental
22:35	-	-	7O55	MWThO	22:14	Acton yard-Stewarts Lane	EWS 66	loaded box wagons
-	W22:55	23:00	4Y81		19:55	Southampton W.Docks-Tonbridge	GBRf 66	containerised gypsum
23:05	23:15	-	6017	FO-Q	16:32	Barry Docks-Dollands Moor	EWS 66	Intermodal/covhops
23:45	-	23:55	6034	MWO-Q	23:22	Acton yard-Grain	EWS 66	empty bogie hoppers

Saturdays:

11:30	-	11:05	4E26		09:14	Dollands Moor-Scunthorpe	EWS 66	empty steel(ex Ebange)
-	-	12:15	7Z71	(Q)	10:26	Cliffe-Stewarts Lane	EWS 66	sand(in bogie box wagons)
-	12:05	12:15	6Y08		11:30	Tolworth-Cliffe	EWS 66	empty Brett hoppers
12:55	-	12:35	5X89	(Q)	11:30	Slade Green-Doncaster works	GBRf 66	EMU for overhaul
13:00	-	13:15	6010	(Q)	12:42	Wembley-Cliffe	EWS 66	empty bogie hoppers
-	W13:45	13:35	4Y19	(Q)	12:02	Mountfield-Southampton W.Docks	GBRf 66	empty gypsum containers
14:30	-	-	6M84	(Q)	13:30	Stewarts Lane-Barrow Hill	F.Liner 66	empty box wagons
-	-	17:45	7Z72	(Q)	17:00	Stewarts Lane-Cliffe	EWS 66	empty bogie boxes

Sundays:

14:00	-	13:45	4E32	(Q)	12:05	Dollands Moor-Scunthorpe	EWS 66	empty steel(ex Ebange)
14:00	W14:10	-	6038	(Q)	08:58	Halewood-Southampton E.Docks	EWS 66	loaded car carriers

33

WEST EALING

[06:00-midnight]

Mondays-Fridays:

West	East	H'code	Runs	Train	Traction	Type of train
06:50	-	6V76	MWFO	02:51 Stud Farm-Hayes	EWS 66	loaded bogie hoppers
06:50	-	6Z76	ThO-Q	02:51 Stud Farm-West Drayton	EWS 66	loaded bogie hoppers
07:45	-	6Z28	WFO-Q	05:52 Hither Green-Whatley	MendipRail 59	empty bogie hoppers
09:20	-	6A62	MWFO	09:10 Acton yard-Theale	EWS 66	sand(in bogie hoppers)
09:20	-	6Z47	ThO-Q	08:49 Wembley-Cardiff Docks	EWS 66	empty bogie hoppers
-	09:40	6L35	MX	08:08 Didcot yard-Dagenham	EWS 66	empty car carriers
-	09:45	4M68	T/ThO	09:14 Hayes-Acton yard	EWS 66	empty bogie hoppers
09:50	-	6M48	MO	09:32 Wembley yard-Calvert	EWS 66	spoil(in box wagons)
09:50	-	6M48	MX	08:51 Bow East/09:40 Acton yard-Calvert	EWS 66	spoil(in box wagons)
10:15	-	6V42	MX-Q	08:13 Wellingborough-Whatley	GBRf 66	empty bogie boxes
10:45	-	6V43	MX-Q	07:28 Cricklewood-Appleford	GBRf 66	spoil(in box wagons)
11:10	-	6M22	TX	08:55 Cricklewood-Calvert	EWS 66	loaded 'binliner'
-	11:15	7F43	MO	10:55 Colnbrook-Acton yard	EWS 66	empty bogie boxes
-	11:20	7A09		07:12 Merehead-Acton yard	MendipRail 59	YEOMAN 'jumbo' train
-	11:45	6A18	TFX-Q	10:39 Brentford-Acton yard	EWS 66	empty hoppers
-	11:50	4L31		09:03 Bristol FLT-Felixstowe	F.Liner 66	Freightliner
11:50	-	6V43	MO-Q	10:15 Cricklewood-Appleford	GBRf 66	spoil(in box wagons)
-	12:05	6Z57		10:06 Calvert-Willesden E.T.	DCR 56	empty bogie boxes
12:10	-	6V47	ThO	10:26 Tilbury-Margam	EWS 66	empty cargowagons
-	12:20	6M91		11:13 Theale-Earles	F.Liner 66	empty cement tanks
-	12:25	6098	WFO	12:05 Park Royal-Angerstein	EWS 66	empty bogie hoppers
12:45	-	6V92	MO-Q	09:40 Grain-Brentford	GBRf 66	loaded bogie hoppers
12:50	-	7C77		12:40 Acton yard-Merehead	MendipRail 59	empty 'jumbo' train
-	12:50	6M54	TO-Q	12:20 Colnbrook-Bardon Hill	GBRf 66	empty bogie hoppers
-	12:50	6M52	WO-Q	12:20 Colnbrook-Neasden	GBRf 66	empty bogie hoppers
-	13:05	6A25	Th/FO	11:55 West Drayton-Acton yard	EWS 66	empty bogie hoppers
-	13:10	6V01	(Q)	11:04 Oxford Banbury Road-Acton	EWS 66	empty bogie boxes
13:30	-	6Z89	WO-Q	09:10 Marks Tey-Brentford	EWS 66	loaded hoppers
13:30	-	7A18	TThO	13:24 Acton yard-Brentford	MendipRail 59	loaded bogie hoppers
-	13:35	6M20	WX-Q	10:37 Whatley-St.Pancras	EWS 59	stone(in bogie hoppers)
-	13:45	4L26	WO	12:44 Theale-Dagenham Dock	EWS 66	empty bogie hoppers
-	13:45	6A69	MFO	12:44 Theale-Acton yard	EWS 66	empty bogie hoppers
13:50	-	6V18		11:20 Allington-Whatley	class 59	empty bogie hoppers
-	14:10	6M70	WO-Q	12:25 Brentford-Neasden	GBRf 66	empty bogie hoppers
14:20	-	6V79	FO-Q	11:56 Angerstein-Avonmouth	GBRf 66	empty bogie hoppers
-	14:30	1Q19	FO-Q	10:28 Plymouth-Paddington	-	HST(measurement train)
14:35	-	4013	FX	12:06 Daventry-Southampton	F.Liner 66	Freightliner
-	14:40	6E38	MWFOQ	13:54 Colnbrook-Lindsey	Colas 60	empty bogie tanks
14:50	-	6C76		14:40 Acton yard-Whatley	MendipRail 59	empty bogie hoppers
15:30	-	7C64		15:24 Acton yard-Merehead	MendipRail 59	empty bogie hoppers
15:50	-	6V07	WFO-Q	12:00 Ipswich Griffin Wharf-Theale	EWS 66	loaded hoppers
-	15:55	4L32	(Q)	11:00 Bristol FLT-Tilbury	F.Liner 66	Freightliner
-	15:55	4L32	(Q)	11:00 Bristol FLT-London Gateway	F.Liner 66	Freightliner
16:05	-	6X44		14:38 Dagenham-Didcot yard	EWS 66	Ford cars
16:30	-	6V69	WO	11:09 East Peckham-Southall yard	EWS 66	empty bogie boxes
-	16:40	7V73	TO-Q	15:55 West Ruislip LUL-Acton yard	EWS 66	empty box wagons
-	18:10	6L21		13:30 Whatley-Dagenham	MendipRail 59	loaded bogie hoppers
-	18:50	6M45	(Q)	17:05 Appleford-Cricklewood	GBRf 66	empty box wagons
-	19:20	4L40	TX	16:42 Cowley(Oxford)-Purfleet	EWS 66	enclosed car carriers

34

West	East	H'code	Runs	Train		Traction	Type of train
19:35	–	6V11	TWO-Q	10:00	Dowlow-Theale	EWS 66	loaded box wagons
–	19:50	7A20	TThO	18:44	Brentford-Acton yard	MendipRail 59	empty bogie hoppers
19:50	–	6V51	WX-Q	18:34	St.Pancras-Whatley	EWS 66	empty bogie hoppers
–	20:05	6M49		18:32	Calvert-Wembley yard	EWS 66	empty box wagons
–	20:25	7A15	FX	16:16	Merehead-Acton yard	MendipRail 59	loaded bogie boxes
–	21:05	6M23	TX	19:17	Calvert-Cricklewood	EWS 66	empty 'binliner'
–	21:25	6M41	MX-Q	16:39	Whatley-Wellingborough	GBRf 66	empty bogie boxes
22:00	–	6V31		19:48(20:43 Mon)	Dagenham-Didcot yard	EWS 66	wagonload
–	22:30	7A48		22:23	West Drayton-Acton yard	EWS 66	empty bogie hoppers
22:40	–	7C23		22:32	Acton yard-Merehead	MendipRail 59	empty 'jumbo' train

Saturdays:

West	East	H'code	Runs	Train		Traction	Type of train
06:30	–	6V90		04:28	Dagenham-West Drayton	EWS 66	loaded bogie hoppers
06:35	–	7C29		06:32	Acton yard-Merehead	MendipRail 59	empty bogie box wagons
08:45	–	6Z22	(Q)	08:31	Acton yard-Hayes	EWS 66	loaded bogie hoppers
–	08:30	6M68		08:19	Hayes-Stud Farm	EWS 66	empty bogie hoppers
–	09:50	6L35		08:19	Didcot yard-Dagenham	EWS 66	empty car carriers
–	10:50	6M91	(Q)	09:16	Theale-Earles	F.Liner 66	empty cement tanks
–	13:30	6Z51	(Q)	13:23	Hayes-Acton yard	EWS 66	empty bogie hoppers
–	16:45	6Z52	(Q)	15:05	Oxford Banbury Road-Dagenham	EWS 66	empty bogie boxes

Sundays: NO BOOKED TRAINS

35

ACTON MAINLINE

[06:00-midnight]

Mondays-Fridays:

West	East	H'code	Runs	Train	Traction	Type of train
07:55	–	6V63	MX	05:15 Angerstein-Acton(-St.Pancras)	EWS 66	loaded bogie hoppers
09c05	–	6Z47	ThO-Q	08:49 Wembley-Cardiff Docks	EWS 66	empty bogie hoppers
–	09:55	6L35	MX	08:08 Didcot yard-Dagenham	EWS 66	empty car carriers
09:55	–	6M48	MO	09:32 Wembley yard-Calvert	EWS 66	spoil(in box wagons)
09:55	–	6M48	MFX-Q	08:51 Bow East-Calvert	EWS 66	spoil(in box wagons)
10:05	–	6V42	MX-Q	08:13 Wellingborough-Whatley	GBRf 66	empty bogie boxes
10:30	–	6V43	MX-Q	07:28 Cricklewood-Appleford	GBRf 66	spoil(in box wagons)
10:40	–	7Z30	MO-Q	09:35 Bow-Acton yard	EWS 66	loaded hoppers
–	10:45	6M62	TWFO	10:44 Acton yard-St.Pancras	EWS 66	loaded bogie hoppers
10c55	–	6M22	TX	08:55 Cricklewood-Calvert	EWS 66	loaded 'binliner'
11:30	–	7V57	ThX-Q	09:50 Harlow Mill-Acton yard	class 59	empty bogie boxes
11:40	–	7V53	WO-Q	10:34 Watford-Acton yard	class 59	empty bogie hoppers
11:45	–	6V60	TWO-Q	09:23 Ardingly-Acton yard	class 59	empty bogie boxes
–	11:45	7079	FO-Q	11:42 Acton yard-Crawley	EWS 66	loaded box wagons
11:55	–	6V47	ThO	10:26 Tilbury-Margam	EWS 66	empty cargowagons
12:00	–	6V28	WX-Q	10:38 Dagenham-Acton yard	class 59	empty bogie hoppers
12:00	–	6Z89	WO-Q	09:10 Marks Tey-Brentford	EWS 66	loaded hoppers
–	12:00	4L31		09:03 Bristol FLT-Felixstowe	F.Liner 66	Freightliner
–	12:10	6Z57		10:06 Calvert-Willesden E.T.	DCR 56	empty bogie boxes
12:10	–	7V75	TThO	09:57 Angerstein-Acton yard	EWS 66	empty bogie hoppers
12:20	–	7V36	FO	11:32 Ferme Park-Acton yard	EWS 66	empty bogie hoppers
12:30	–	6V92	MO-Q	09:40 Grain-Brentford	GBRf 66	loaded bogie hoppers
–	12:30	6M91		11:13 Theale-Earles	F.Liner 66	empty cement tanks
–	12:35	7068	TWFO	12:34 Acton yard-Purley	class 59	loaded bogie hoppers
–	12:35	7069	MThO	12:34 Acton yard-Crawley	class 59	loaded bogie boxes
–	12c40	6098	WFO	12:05 Park Royal-Angerstein	EWS 66	empty bogie hoppers
–	12:45	7075	MO-Q	12:42 Acton yard-Grain	EWS 66	empty bogie boxes
–	12:55	6M54	TO-Q	12:20 Colnbrook-Bardon Hill	GBRf 66	empty bogie hoppers
–	12:55	6M52	WO-Q	12:20 Colnbrook-Neasden	GBRf 66	empty bogie hoppers
–	13:10	7002	MWO	13:10 Acton yard-Tolworth	EWS 66	loaded bogie hoppers
13:10	–	7V50	MFX-Q	11:08 Crawley-Acton yard	class 59	empty box wagons
13:20	–	6V28	WO-Q	10:38 Dagenham-Acton yard	class 59	empty bogie hoppers
13:20	–	6V12	TThFO	10:54 Chelmsford-Acton yard	class 59	empty bogie boxes
–	13:25	6M11	T/WO	11:08 Acton yard-Wellingborough	GBRf 66	Departmental
13:35	–	6V18		11:20 Allington-Whatley	class 59	empty bogie hoppers
–	13c50	6M20	WX-Q	10:37 Whatley-St.Pancras	EWS 59	stone(in bogie hoppers)
13:50	–	6V65	TO-Q	11:07 Angerstein-Acton yard	EWS 66	sand(in bogie hoppers)
14:05	–	6V79	FO-Q	11:56 Angerstein-Avonmouth	GBRf 66	empty bogie hoppers
14:20	–	4013	FX	12:06 Daventry-Southampton	F.Liner 66	Freightliner
–	14:20	6L26	MFO	14:17 Acton yard-Dagenham	EWS 66	empty bogie hoppers
14:35	–	6V69	MO	11:00 East Peckham-Acton yard	EWS 66	empty bogie boxes
14:35	–	6V69	WO	11:09 East Peckham-Southall yard	EWS 66	empty bogie boxes
14:50	–	6V00	TX-Q	12:15 Newhaven-Acton yard	class 59	empty box wagons
–	14:55	4L26	WO	12:44 Theale-Dagenham Dock	EWS 66	empty bogie hoppers
–	15c10	6E38	MWFOQ	13:54 Colnbrook-Lindsey	Colas 60	empty bogie tanks
15:30	–	6V07	WFO-Q	12:00 Ipswich Griffin Wharf-Theale	EWS 66	loaded hoppers
15:50	–	6X44		14:38 Dagenham-Didcot yard	EWS 66	Ford cars
–	16:05	4L32		11:00 Bristol FLT-Tilbury/Gateway	F.Liner 66	Freightliner

36

West	East	H'code	Runs	Train	Traction	Type of train
-	18:35	6L21		13:30 Whatley-Dagenham	MendipRail 59	loaded bogie hoppers
-	19:00	6M45	(Q)	17:05 Appleford-Cricklewood	GBRf 66	empty box wagons
-	19:05	6M68	TWThO	19:01 Acton yard-Stud Farm	EWS 66	empty bogie hoppers
19c10	-	6V51	WX-Q	18:34 St.Pancras-Whatley	EWS 59	empty bogie hoppers
19:15	-	6M70	WFO-Q	19:03 Neasden-Wembley yard	EWS 66	empty bogie hoppers
19:25	-	6V11	TWO-Q	10:00 Dowlow-Theale	EWS 66	loaded box wagons
-	19c35	4L40	TX	16:42 Cowley(Oxford)-Purfleet	EWS 66	enclosed car carriers
-	19:45	6M70	WFO-Q	19:03 Neasden-Wembley yard	EWS 66	empty bogie hoppers
-	20:15	6M49		18:32 Calvert-Wembley yard	EWS 66	empty box wagons
20:15	-	6V35	(Q)	18:43 Dagenham-Acton yard	EWS 66	sand(in bogie hoppers)
21:05	-	7V67	MThX	19:50 Purley-Acton yard	class 59	empty Yeoman hoppers
21:20	-	6V08	ThO-Q	13:27 Tunstead-Brentford	F.Liner 66	loaded bogie hoppers
21:20	-	4013	FO	19:07 Daventry-Southampton	F.Liner 66	Freightliner
-	21c20	6M23	TX	19:17 Calvert-Cricklewood	EWS 66	empty 'binliner'
21:30	-	7V17	MWO	20:21 Tolworth-Acton yard	EWS 66	empty bogie hoppers
21:40	-	7V69	MThO	20:02 Crawley-Acton yard	class 59	empty bogie boxes
21:45	-	6V31		19:48(20:43 Mon) Dagenham-Didcot yard	EWS 66	wagonload
-	21:45	6E21	ThO-Q	21:00 West Ruislip-Peterborough	4 GBRf 20s	barrier wagons
-	21c50	6M41	MX-Q	16:39 Whatley-Wellingborough	GBRf 66	empty bogie boxes
-	22c25	6017	FO-Q	16:32 Barry Docks-Dollands Moor	EWS 66	Intermodal/covhops

Saturdays:

West	East	H'code	Runs	Train	Traction	Type of train
-	09c40	6M68		08:19 Hayes-Stud Farm	EWS 66	empty bogie hoppers
-	10:00	6L35		08:19 Didcot yard-Dagenham	EWS 66	empty car carriers
-	10c10	6M20		02:37 Whatley-St.Pancras	EWS 59/66	stone(in bogie hoppers)
-	11:00	4M34		11:04 Acton yard-Peak Forest	EWS 66	empty bogie hoppers
-	11:10	6M91	(Q)	09:16 Theale-Earles	F.Liner 66	empty cement tanks
12c50	-	6V62	(Q)	10:51 Tilbury-Margam	EWS 66	empty steel carriers
15:05	-	6V51		14:35 St.Pancras-Acton yard	EWS 59/66	empty bogie hoppers
-	16c50	6Z52	(Q)	15:05 Oxford Banbury Road-Dagenham	EWS 66	empty bogie boxes
17:50	-	6V10		12:02 West Burton p.s.-Acton	EWS 66	flyash(in bogie boxes)

Sundays: NO BOOKED TRAINS

WILLESDEN JUNCTION
(all lines)
[24-hour]

Mondays-Fridays:

From	Time	To	H'code	Runs	Train	Traction	Type of train
K	06c25	H	6E35	TTh0	04:01 Grain-Ferme Park	EWS 66	sand(in bogie hoppers)
	06:25		4M21	MX	03:10 Felixstowe-Trafford Park	GBRf 66	Intermodal
K	06c25	H	6E35	TTh0	04:01 Grain-Ferme Park	EWS 66	sand(in bogie hoppers)
	06:35	K	6062	Th0-Q	02:08 Crewe-Dungeness p.s.	2 DRS 37s	flask(s)
	06:35		1M11		23:40(23:15 Sun) Glasgow Central-Euston	F.Liner 90	Caledonian Sleeper
K	07:10	A	6Z28	WF0-Q	05:52 Hither Green-Whatley	MendipRail 59	empty bogie hoppers
	07:10		4M86		03:00 Felixstowe-Lawley Street	F.Liner 66	Freightliner
	07:15		4M07	MX	04:18 Felixstowe-Burton on Trent	EWS 66	Intermodal
	07:25		4L91	MX	02:10 Trafford Park-Felixstowe	F.Liner 90	Freightliner
	07:40		1M16		20:44(20:26 Sun) Inverness-Euston	F.Liner 90	Caledonian Sleeper
K	07:45	A	6V63	MX	05:15 Angerstein-Acton(-St.Pancras)	EWS 66	loaded bogie hoppers
	08:35		5M11		08:27 Euston-Wembley	GBRf 86	empty sleeper stock
	09:25		4L89	MX	22:01 Coatbridge-Felixstowe	2 F.Liner 86s	Freightliner
	09:30		6L04	(Q)	09:10 Wembley yard-Barrington(Foxton)	EWS 66	spoil(in box wagons)
K	09:35		6M45		07:07 Dollands Moor-Daventry	EWS 66	water(in cargowagons)
H	09:40	A	6M48	MFX-Q	08:51 Bow East-Calvert	EWS 66	spoil(in box wagons)
	09:40		5M16		09:27 Euston-Wembley	GBRf 86	empty sleeper stock
	10:15(KG)		6L35	MX	08:08 Didcot yard-Dagenham	EWS 66	empty car carriers
H	10:30	A	7Z30	MO-Q	09:35 Bow-Acton yard	EWS 66	empty bogie boxes
K	10c30	H	4E26		08:13 Dollands Moor-Scunthorpe	EWS 66	empty steel(ex Ebange)
	10:40		4L41	MX	06:04 Crewe Basford Hall-Felixstowe	F.Liner 66	Freightliner
	10:40		4L37	MO	06:24 Lawley Street-Felixstowe	F.Liner 66	Freightliner
	10:50		6X43	TO	09:45 Dagenham-Garston	GBRf 92	Ford cars
	10:50(KG)		4M94		07:39 Felixstowe-Lawley Street	F.Liner 66	Freightliner
H	11:00	K	6Z92	FO-Q	10:13 Bow-Tonbridge	GBRf 66	empty bogie hoppers
	11:20		4L89	MO	07:18 Crewe-Felixstowe	F.Liner 70	Freightliner
H	11c20	A	7V57	ThX-Q	09:50 Harlow Mill-Acton yard	class 59	empty bogie boxes
K	11:30	A	6V60	TWO-Q	09:23 Ardingly-Acton yard	class 59	empty bogie boxes
	11:35(KG)		6Z79	WO-Q	09:10 Marks Tey-Crawley	EWS 66	loaded hoppers
K	11:40	H	6L37		09:58 Hoo Junction-Whitemoor	Colas 66/70	Departmental
H	11:50	A	6V47	Th0	10:26 Tilbury-Margam	EWS 66	empty cargowagons
H	11:55	A	6V28	WX-Q	10:38 Dagenham-Acton yard	class 59	empty bogie hoppers
H	11:55	A	6Z89	WO-Q	09:10 Marks Tey-Brentford	EWS 66	loaded hoppers
A	11:55	K	7079	FO-Q	11:42 Acton yard-Crawley	EWS 66	loaded box wagons
K	11:55	A	7V75	TTh0	09:57 Angerstein-Acton yard	EWS 66	empty bogie hoppers
H	12:10	A	7V36	FO	11:32 Ferme Park-Acton yard	EWS 66	empty bogie hoppers
A	12:10	H	4L31		09:03 Bristol FLT-Felixstowe	F.Liner 66	Freightliner
	12:10		4L97	MX	05:01 Trafford Park-Felixstowe	F.Liner 70	Freightliner
K	12:20	A	6V92	MO-Q	09:40 Grain-Brentford	GBRf 66	loaded bogie hoppers
	12:25	K	6B45	FO-Q	12:13 Wembley-Dollands Moor	EWS 66	empty china clay tanks
K	12:25	H	6E40	TWO-Q	09:40 Grain-Ferme Park	GBRf 66	loaded ballast boxes
A	12R25		6Z57		10:06 Calvert-Willesden E.T.	DCR 56	empty bogie boxes
H	12c30	K	6Z58	WO-Q	10:44 Harlow Mill-Tonbridge	GBRf 66	empty bogie hoppers

'Route Knowledge':   (blank) = 'West Coast Main Line' (Wembley-Primrose Hill);

K = to/from Kensington Olympia;   **H** = to/from Gospel Oak **via High Level platforms**

A = to/from Acton Wells Junction;   **KG** = to/from Gospel Oak **via "Kensal Green chord"**

From	Time	To	H'code	Runs	Train	Traction	Type of train
K	12:30		6Z88	TO-Q	11:30 Tolworth-Wembley yard	EWS 66	empty Brett hoppers
	12:40		4M63		09:12 Felixstowe-Ditton	F.Liner 90	Freightliner
A	12:45	K	7068	TWFO	12:34 Acton yard-Purley	class 59	loaded bogie hoppers
A	12:45	K	7069	MThO	12:34 Acton yard-Crawley	class 59	loaded bogie boxes
A	12:50	K	7075	MO-Q	12:42 Acton yard-Grain	EWS 66	empty bogie boxes
A	12:50	K	6098	WFO	12:05 Park Royal-Angerstein	EWS 66	empty bogie hoppers
K	13:00	A	6M49	FO	11:08 Crawley-Wembley	EWS 66	empty bogie hoppers
K	13:00	A	7V50	MFX-Q	11:08 Crawley-Acton yard	class 59	empty box wagons
H	13:10	A	6V28	WO-Q	10:38 Dagenham-Acton yard	class 59	empty bogie hoppers
H	13:10	A	6V12	TThFO	10:54 Chelmsford-Acton yard	class 59	empty bogie boxes
K	13:15	A	6V65	TO-Q	11:07 Angerstein-Acton yard	EWS 66	sand(in bogie hoppers)
K	13:15	A	6Z66	MO-Q	11:07 Angerstein-Woking	EWS 66	loaded bogie boxes
	13:15		4M88		09:32 Felixstowe-Crewe	F.Liner 90	Freightliner
	13:20		4L93	MX	10:08 Lawley Street-Felixstowe	F.Liner 90	Freightliner
A	13:20	K	7002	MWO	13:10 Acton yard-Tolworth	EWS 66	loaded bogie hoppers
K	13:30	A	6V18		11:20 Allington-Whatley	class 59	empty bogie hoppers
	13:45		4M23		10:46 Felixstowe-Hams Hall	GBRf 66	Intermodal
K	13:55	A	6V79	FO-Q	11:56 Angerstein-Avonmouth	GBRf 66	empty bogie hoppers
K	14:10	A	6V69	MO	11:00 East Peckham-Acton yard	EWS 66	empty bogie boxes
K	14:10	A	6V69	WO	11:09 East Peckham-Southall yard	EWS 66	empty bogie boxes
	14:25	K	6Z79	WO-Q	09:10 Marks Tey-Crawley	EWS 66	loaded hoppers
A	14:30	H	6L26	MFO	14:17 Acton yard-Dagenham	EWS 66	empty bogie hoppers
K	14:40	A	6V00	TX-Q	12:15 Newhaven-Acton yard	class 59	empty box wagons
	14:40		6M05		11:23 Barrington(Foxton)-Wembley yard	EWS 66	empty box wagons
	14:50		4M87		11:13 Felixstowe-Trafford Park	2 F.Liner 86s	Freightliner
A	15:05	H	4L26	WO	12:44 Theale-Dagenham Dock	EWS 66	empty bogie hoppers
	15:15		6M57	MO	12:00 Ipswich Griffin Wharf-Watford	EWS 66	loaded hoppers
H	15:20	A	6V07	WFO-Q	12:00 Ipswich Griffin Wharf-Theale	EWS 66	loaded hoppers
	15:35(KG)		4L48		12:37 Daventry-Purfleet	DRS 66	Intermodal
H	15c40	A	6X44		14:38 Dagenham-Didcot yard	EWS 66	Ford cars
A	16:15	H	4L32	(Q)	11:00 Bristol FLT-Tilbury	F.Liner 66	Freightliner
A	16:15	H	4L32	(Q)	11:00 Bristol FLT-London Gateway	F.Liner 66	Freightliner
	16:20		4M93	MX	13:34 Felixstowe-Lawley Street	F.Liner 70	Freightliner
	17:10		4M93	MO	14:32 Felixstowe-Lawley Street	F.Liner 70	Freightliner
K	18:15		7Z50	ThO-Q	16:33 Woking-Wembley yard	EWS 66	empty bogie boxes
A	18:45	H	6L21		13:30 Whatley-Dagenham	MendipRail 59	loaded bogie hoppers
	19:05	K	6D63	WThO	18:53 Wembley-Dollands Moor	EWS 66	empty cargowagons
	19:10		4L90	MX	12:30 Crewe Basford Hall-Felixstowe	F.Liner 90	Freightliner
	19:10		4L90	MO	11:17 Trafford Park-Felixstowe	F.Liner 90	Freightliner
	19:15(KG)		4S83		17:35 London Gateway-Coatbridge	F.Liner 70	Freightliner
	19:20		4L18		14:18 Trafford Park-Felixstowe	GBRf 66	Intermodal
K	19:25		6M95	ThO-Q	16:35 Dungeness p.s.-Crewe	2 DRS 37s	flask(s)
	19:30		5S95		19:17 Wembley-Euston	F.Liner 90	empty sleeper stock
	19:30(KG)		4L56	MWFO	13:17 Trafford Park-London Gateway	EWS 66	Intermodal
A	19:40	H	4L40	TX	16:42 Cowley(Oxford)-Purfleet	EWS 66	enclosed car carriers
	19:50(KG)		6Z11	ThO-Q	09:35 Dowlow-Bow East	EWS 66	loaded box wagons
	19:50		6M07	(Q)	16:30 Barrington(Foxton)-Wembley yard	EWS 66	empty box wagons
	20:05	K	6D71	TFO	19:54 Wembley-Dollands Moor	EWS 66	empty cargowagons
H	20:05	A	6V35	(Q)	18:43 Dagenham-Acton yard	EWS 66	sand(in bogie hoppers)
	20R10	A	6Z56	(Q)	19:40 Willesden E.T.-Calvert	DCR 56	spoil(in box wagons)
	20:15		4L92		14:03 Ditton-Felixstowe	F.Liner 70	Freightliner
	20:20		4S88		16:13 Felixstowe-Coatbridge	F.Liner 70	Freightliner
	20:45		4M02		17:34 Felixstowe-Hams Hall	GBRf 66	Intermodal
K	20:55	A	7V67	TWFO	19:50 Purley-Acton yard	class 59	empty Yeoman hoppers
A	21:05	K	6072	MO-Q	19:52 Brentford-Grain	GBRf 66	empty bogie hoppers
A	21:10	K	6098	T/ThO	20:55 Acton yard-Angerstein	EWS 66	empty bogie hoppers
	21:15		4M89		14:33(14:46 Mon) Felixstowe-Ditton	F.Liner 66	Freightliner
K	21c15	H	6L36		19:52 Hoo Junction-Whitemoor	GBRf 66	Departmental
	21:20		5S96		21:04 Wembley-Euston	GBRf 86	empty sleeper stock

From	Time	To	H'code	Runs	Train	Traction	Type of train
K	21:20	A	7V17	MWO	20:21 Tolworth-Acton yard	EWS 66	empty bogie hoppers
	21:23		1S25		21:15 Euston-Inverness	F.Liner 90	Caledonian Sleeper
K	21:25	A	7Z50	TO-Q	20:02 Crawley-Wembley yard	EWS 66	empty box wagons
K	21:25	A	7V69	MThO	20:02 Crawley-Acton yard	class 59	empty bogie boxes
	21:35		4M92		18:33 Felixstowe-Lawley Street	F.Liner 66	Freightliner
	21:45		6L48		15:49 Garston-Dagenham	GBRf 92	empty car carriers
H	21:45	A	6V31		19:48(20:43 Mon) Dagenham-Didcot yard	EWS 66	wagonload
	22:00(KG)		4M60		20:42 Tilbury-Garston	F.Liner 70	Freightliner
A	22c00	H	6E21	ThO-Q	21:00 West Ruislip-Peterborough	4 GBRf 20s	barrier wagons
	22:05		4L96	FO	16:18 Trafford Park-Felixstowe	F.Liner 66	Freightliner
A	22:25	K	7055	(Q)	22:14 Acton yard-Stewarts Lane	EWS 66	loaded box wagons
	22:35		4L43		19:35 Lawley Street-Tilbury	F.Liner 66	Freightliner
	22:40		4L73	FO	18:30 Lawley Street-Felixstowe	F.Liner 66	Freightliner
A	22c45	H	7L46	MTO	22:39 Acton yard-Bow	EWS 66	loaded bogie hoppers
	22:55		1E06		22:45 Willesden PRDC-Low Fell RMT	-	Mail(325 unit)
A	22:55		6017	FO-Q	16:32 Barry Docks-Dollands Moor	EWS 66	Intermodal/covhops
A	23:10	H	7L46	MTX-Q	23:02 Acton yard-Bow	EWS 66	loaded bogie hoppers
A	23:15	K	6034	MWO-Q	23:03 Acton yard-Grain	EWS 66	empty bogie hoppers
A	23:40	H	6Z85	TFX-Q	23:30 Acton yard-Dagenham	EWS 66	empty bogie hoppers
	23:45		4M53		20:35 Felixstowe-Trafford Park	F.Liner 90	Freightliner
	23:50		4L71		18:41 Ditton-Felixstowe	F.Liner 90	Freightliner
	23:57		1S26		23:50 Euston-Glasgow Central	F.Liner 90	Caledonian Sleeper
A	00:10	H	6E02		22:58 Brentford-Scunthorpe	EWS 66	loaded 'binliner'
	00:20		4M59		21:31 Felixstowe-Ditton	F.Liner 66	Freightliner
	00:25		4L60		19:46 Garston-Felixstowe	F.Liner 90	Freightliner
H	00:35	A	6V04		18:59 Scunthorpe-Southall yard	EWS 66	empty 'binliner'
	00:40		4M73		21:41(Fri) Felixstowe-Ditton	F.Liner 66	Freightliner
H	00:40	A	6V09	WO-Q	13:00(Tues) West Burton p.s.-Acton yard	EWS 66	flyash(in box wagons)
H	00:45	A	6V22		23:44 Dagenham-Whatley	class 59	empty bogie hoppers
H	00:50	K	6036		22:01 Whitemoor-Hoo Junction	Colas 66	Departmental
	00:50		4M42		22:08 Felixstowe-Garston	F.Liner 70	Freightliner
	00:55(KG)		4M77		22:30 Purfleet-Daventry	DRS 66	Intermodal
	01:15	A	4V30		23:32 Tilbury-Bristol FLT	F.Liner 66	Freightliner
	01:30		6X41		00:32 Dagenham-Garston	GBRf 92/66	Ford cars
	01:30		4L28		22:35 Hams Hall-Felixstowe	GBRf 66	Intermodal
	01:45		1M80		21:43 Low Fell RMT-Willesden PRDC	-	Mail(325 unit)
	01:45	K	4016	FO	23:53 Daventry-Dollands Moor	EWS 66	Intermodal
	01:45	K	6016	TThSO	20:21 Ditton-Dollands Moor(-Neuss)	EWS 66	empty cargowagons
A	02:10	H	6L42	ThO	11:32(Wed) Trostre-Tilbury	EWS 66	Tinplate(covered wagons)
K	02:15		6M14	WFO	00:12 Dollands Moor(ex Neuss)-Ditton	EWS 66	aluminium(in cargowagons)
	02:15(KG)		4M72		00:57 Tilbury-Lawley Street	F.Liner 66	Freightliner
	02:30		4L77	SO	23:03(Fri) Lawley Street-Felixstowe	F.Liner 66	Freightliner
A	02:35	H	6L31		01:15 Didcot yard-Dagenham	EWS 66	wagonload
K	02:50		4M31	MSO	00:53 Dollands Moor-Hams Hall	EWS 66	Intermodal
	03:00		4L80		21:53 Garston-Tilbury	F.Liner 70	Freightliner
H	03:10	A	4V36		23:34 Felixstowe-Bristol FLT	F.Liner 66	Freightliner
A	03:10	K	6047	WThO	02:57 Acton yard-Ardingly	class 59	loaded bogie hoppers
A	03:25	K	6087		03:15 Acton yard-Allington	class 59	loaded bogie hoppers
A	03:30	H	6L30	TThO	03:25 Acton yard-Chelmsford	class 59	loaded bogie boxes
A	03:35	H	7L29	MWFO	03:25 Acton yard-Purfleet	class 59	loaded bogie boxes
	03:35		4L82		21:30 Ditton-Felixstowe	F.Liner 90	Freightliner
K	03:40	H	6L90	WO-Q	01:30 Grain-Harlow Hill	GBRf 66	loaded bogie hoppers
	03:40		6L47	WO-Q	22:03(Tue) Garston-Dagenham	GBRf 66	empty car carriers
H	03:55	A	4V40	WX	02:56 Purfleet-Cowley(Oxford)	EWS 66	empty car carriers
A	03:55	K	6001	TSX-Q	03:45 Acton yard-Newhaven	class 59	loaded box wagons

From	Time	To	H'code	Runs	Train	Traction	Type of train
	04:00		6L00		03:49 Wembley yard-Barrington(Foxton)	EWS 66	spoil(in box wagons)
K	04:15	A	6V10	FO-Q	02:04 Dollands Moor-Barry Docks	EWS 66	Intermodal/covhops
H	04c15	K	4028		22:40 Scunthorpe-Dollands Moor	EWS 66	loaded steel(to Ebange)
	04:15		4L69		01:06 Lawley Street-Felixstowe	F.Liner 70	Freightliner
H	04:25		6V53		03:50 Bow-Acton yard	EWS 66	empty bogie hoppers
	04:25(KG)		4M83	WFO	02:59 London Gateway-Trafford Park	EWS 66	Intermodal
A	04:25	K	6003	FO	22:32 Cardiff Docks-Crawley	EWS 66	loaded bogie hoppers
A	04:25	K	7074	TThO	04:14 Acton yard-Angerstein	EWS 59	loaded Yeoman hoppers
A	04:25	H	6L63	WSO-Q	21:25 Margam-Tilbury	EWS 66	loaded steel
K	04:30		6S94	WO-Q	02:21 Dollands Moor-Irvine	EWS 66	loaded china clay tanks
	04:30		4L81		19:26 Coatbridge-London Gateway	F.Liner 70	Freightliner
K	04:35	A	7V55	(Q)	03:52 Stewarts Lane-Acton yard	EWS 66	empty box wagons
A	04:35	H	7L54	(Q)	04:24 Acton yard-Harlow Mill	EWS 66	loaded box wagons
A	04:40	H	6Z56	MO	04:30 Acton yard-Ipswich Griffin Wharf	EWS 66	empty hoppers
A	04:45	K	6021	SO	02:00 Whatley-Hothfield	EWS 59	loaded HANSON hoppers
A	04c55	H	6L90	W/ThO	02:28 Grain-Bow	GBRf 66	loaded bogie hoppers
A	05:00	K	6044	W/ThO	01:40 Avonmouth-Crawley	GBRf 66	loaded bogie boxes
H	05c15	K	6035		01:38 Whitemoor-Hoo Junction	GBRf 66	Departmental
K	05:30	A	6V59	WFO	04:40 Angerstein-Park Royal	EWS 66	loaded bogie hoppers
H	05:35	A	6V90	SO	04:28 Dagenham-West Drayton	EWS 66	loaded bogie hoppers
A	05:35	H	6L28	SX	05:23 Acton yard-Dagenham	class 59	loaded bogie hoppers
	05:35		4M21		03:10 Felixstowe-Trafford Park	GBRf 66	Intermodal
	05:35		4M07	SO	02:27 Felixstowe-Burton on Trent	EWS 66	Intermodal
	05:35		4L95	SX	22:50 Ditton-Felixstowe	F.Liner 66	Freightliner
	05:50		4M45	SX	02:50 Felixstowe-Ditton	F.Liner 90	Freightliner

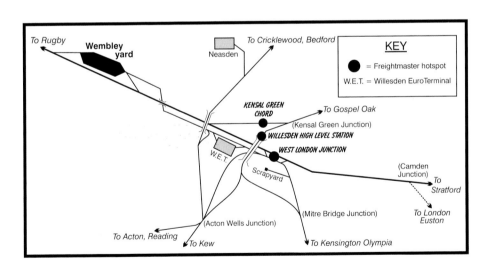

Saturdays:

From	Time	To	H'code	Runs	Train		Traction	Type of train
	06:35		1M11		23:40(Fri) Glasgow Central-Euston		F.Liner 90	Caledonian Sleeper
	06:40		4M45		02:57 Felixstowe-Ditton		F.Liner 90	Freightliner
	06:50		4M88		04:25 Felixstowe-Lawley Street		F.Liner 66	Freightliner
	07:05		4L95		22:50(Fri) Ditton-Felixstowe North		F.Liner 66	Freightliner
	07:35		1M16		20:44(Fri) Inverness-Euston		F.Liner 90	Caledonian Sleeper
	08:35		5M11		08:27 Euston-Wembley c.s.		GBRf 86	empty sleeper stock
	09:20		4L89		22:01(Fri) Coatbridge-Felixstowe	2	F.Liner 86s	Freightliner
	09:50		5M16		09:41 Euston-Wembley c.s.		GBRf 86	empty sleeper stock
	10:05(KG)		6M48		09:22 Bow East-Wembley yard		EWS 66	spoil(in box wagons)
A	10:10 H		6L35		08:19 Didcot yard-Dagenham		EWS 66	empty car carriers
	11:05		4L97		04:57 Trafford Park-Felixstowe		F.Liner 70	Freightliner
K	11c40 H		4E26		09:14 Dollands Moor-Scunthorpe		EWS 66	empty steel(ex Ebange)
	12:05		4M93		08:46 Felixstowe-Crewe		F.Liner 70	Freightliner
	12:35		4M87		09:46 Felixstowe-Crewe		F.Liner 90	Freightliner
A	12:50 K		6010	(Q)	12:42 Wembley-Cliffe		EWS 66	empty bogie hoppers
	12:45		4L93		08:21 Crewe-Felixstowe		F.Liner 66	Freightliner
	13:00		4M23		10:34 Felixstowe-Hams Hall		GBRf 66	Intermodal
K	13c10 H		5X89	(Q)	11:30 Slade Green-Doncaster works		GBRf 66	EMU for overhaul
	13:45		4L90		08:30 Lawley Street-Felixstowe		F.Liner 66	Freightliner
	14:05		4M20		10:14 Felixstowe-Lawley Street		F.Liner 66	Freightliner
	15:30(KG)		4M41	(Q)	13:57 London Gateway-Crewe Basford Hall		F.Liner 70	Freightliner
	16:05		4L20		12:44 Hams Hall-Harwich		GBRf 66	Intermodal
	16:45		4L96		12:32 Crewe Basford Hall-Ipswich yard		F.Liner 90	Freightliner
A	16:55 H		6Z52	(Q)	15:05 Oxford Banbury Road-Dagenham		EWS 66	empty bogie boxes
H	17:40 A		6V10		12:02 West Burton p.s.-Acton		EWS 66	flyash(in bogie boxes)
	19:55(KG)		6L48		13:36 Garston-Dagenham		GBRf 66	car carriers

Sundays:

From	Time	To	H'code	Runs	Train		Traction	Type of train
	13:50 K		6038	(Q)	08:58 Halewood-Southampton E.Docks		EWS 66	loaded car carriers
	14:00(KG)		4L48		12:09 Daventry-Purfleet		DRS 66	Intermodal
K	14c15 H		4E32	(Q)	12:05 Dollands Moor-Scunthorpe		EWS 66	empty steel(ex Ebange)
	18:55		5S95		18:43 Wembley-Euston		F.Liner 90	empty sleeper stock
	20:40		5S96		20:29 Wembley-Euston		F.Liner 90	empty sleeper stock
	21:05		1S25		20:57 Euston-Inverness		F.Liner 90	Caledonian Sleeper
	21:50(KG)		4M83		20:14 London Gateway-Trafford Park		EWS 66	Intermodal
	23:35		1S26		23:28 Euston-Glasgow Central		F.Liner 90	Caledonian Sleeper

WEST RUISLIP

[06:00-midnight]

Mondays-Fridays:

North	South	H'code	Runs	Train	Traction	Type of train
06:10	-	5T12		06:02 Wembley LMD-Oxford Parkway	DRS 68	empty stock
06:40	-	7M60	TO-Q	18:40(Mon)Grain-West Ruislip LUL	EWS 66	loaded box wagons
-	07:10	1H06		06:10 Banbury-London Marylebone	DRS 68	Passenger
-	08:05	1Y12		07:24 Oxford Parkway-London Marylebone	DRS 68	Passenger
-	08:20	1H15		06:09 Kidderminster-London Marylebone	DRS 68	Passenger
-	08:47	1H17		06:38 Stourbridge Junc.-London Marylebone	DRS 68	Passenger
08:55	-	1R15		08:41 Marylebone-Birmingham(Moor Street)	DRS 68	Passenger
-	09:20	1H22		07:05 Kidderminster-London Marylebone	DRS 68	Passenger
09:35	-	6A49	WFX-Q	07:32 Didcot yard-Bicester	EWS 66/67	MoD stores
10:23	-	1R21		10:10 Marylebone-Birmingham(Moor Street)	DRS 68	Passenger
10:35	-	6M48	MO	09:32 Wembley yard-Calvert	EWS 66	spoil(in box wagons)
10:35	-	6M48	MX	08:51 Bow East/09:40 Acton yard-Calvert	EWS 66	spoil(in box wagons)
11:40	-	6M22	TX	08:55 Cricklewood-Calvert	EWS 66	loaded 'binliner'
-	11:40	6Z57		10:06 Calvert-Willesden E.T.	DCR 56	empty bogie boxes
-	12:25	1H33		10:55 Birmingham(Moor Street)-Marylebone	DRS 68	Passenger
-	12:40	6V01	(Q)	11:04 Oxford Banbury Road-Acton	EWS 66	empty bogie boxes
13:23	-	1R33		13:10 Marylebone-Birmingham(Moor Street)	DRS 68	Passenger
-	14:20	1H45		12:55 Birmingham(Moor Street)-Marylebone	DRS 68	Passenger
-	14:40	6A48	WFX-Q	13:25 Bicester-Didcot yard	EWS 66/67	MoD stores
-	16:10	7V73	TO-Q	15:55 West Ruislip LUL-Acton yard	EWS 66	empty box wagons
16:28	-	1K45		16:15 London Marylebone-Kidderminster	DRS 68	Passenger
-	17:22	1H62		15:55 Birmingham(Moor Street)-Marylebone	DRS 68	Passenger
17:28	-	1K50		17:15 London Marylebone-Kidderminster	DRS 68	Passenger
17:35	-	1U50		17:21 London Marylebone-Banbury	DRS 68	Passenger
18:28	-	1K54		18:15 London Marylebone-Kidderminster	DRS 68	Passenger
18:30	-	1T54		18:18 London Marylebone-Oxford Parkway	DRS 68	Passenger
-	19:50	6M49		18:32 Calvert-Wembley yard	EWS 66	empty box wagons
-	19:55	5H74	FO	18:50 Banbury-Marylebone	DRS 68	empty stock
-	20:18	1Y75		19:29 Oxford Parkway-London Marylebone	DRS 68	Passenger
-	20:45	6M23	TX	19:17 Calvert-Cricklewood	EWS 66	empty 'binliner'

Saturdays:

North	South	H'code	Runs	Train	Traction	Type of train
-	09:25	1H10		07:12 Kidderminster-London Marylebone	DRS 68	Passenger
11:25	-	1R25		11:10 Marylebone-Birmingham(Moor Street)	DRS 68	Passenger
-	11:30	1H17		09:10 Kidderminster-London Marylebone	DRS 68	Passenger
-	15:25	1H37		13:55 Birmingham(Moor Street)-Marylebone	DRS 68	Passenger
-	16:25	6Z52	(Q)	15:05 Oxford Banbury Road-Dagenham	EWS 66	empty bogie boxes
17:25	-	1G49		17:10 Marylebone-Birmingham(Snow Hill)	DRS 68	Passenger
18:25	-	1G53		18:10 Marylebone-Birmingham(Snow Hill)	DRS 68	Passenger

Sundays:

North	South	H'code	Runs	Train	Traction	Type of train
-	13:25	1H27		11:55 Birmingham(Moor Street)-Marylebone	DRS 68	Passenger
18:25	-	1R53		18:10 Marylebone-Birmingham(Moor Street)	DRS 68	Passenger

43

HARROW & WEALDSTONE
(South Kenton)

[06:00-21:00]

Mondays-Fridays:

North	South	H'code	Runs	Train		Traction	Type of train
-	06:25	1M11		23:40	Glasgow Central-Euston	F.Liner 90	Caledonian Sleeper
06:45	-	6M46	MO	04:54	Ripple Lane-Peak Forest	EWS 66	empty bogie boxes
06:45	-	4M21	MX	03:10	Felixstowe-Trafford Park	GBRf 66	Intermodal
06:55	-	4M45	MX	02:50	Felixstowe-Ditton	F.Liner 66	Freightliner
-	07:35	1M16		20:44	Inverness-Euston	F.Liner 90	Caledonian Sleeper
07:35	-	4M86		03:00	Felixstowe-Lawley Street	F.Liner 66	Freightliner
07:55	-	4M07	MX	04:18	Felixstowe-Burton on Trent	EWS 66	Intermodal
-	08:45	4L89	MX	22:01	Coatbridge-Felixstowe	2 F.Liner 86s	Freightliner
-	09:05	6M76	FO	21:46	Mossend-Wembley(-Dollands Moor)	2 EWS 90s	wagonload
09:25	-	6M11	WO-Q	03:30	Theale-Dowlow	EWS 66	empty box wagons
-	09:40	4L41	MX	06:04	Crewe Basford Hall-Felixstowe	F.Liner 66	Freightliner
-	09:40	4L37	MO	06:24	Lawley Street-Felixstowe	F.Liner 66	Freightliner
10:00	-	6Z77	WX-Q	09:42	Willesden ET-Stud Farm	F.Liner 66	empty ballast
-	10:20	4L89	MO	07:18	Crewe-Felixstowe	F.Liner 70	Freightliner
-	10:40	6Z15	WO-Q	01:01	Dowlow-Bow East	EWS 66	loaded box wagons
-	10:50	7V53	WO-Q	10:34	Watford-Acton yard	class 59	empty bogie hoppers
10:55	-	6X43	TO	09:45	Dagenham-Garston	GBRf 92	Ford cars
-	11:10	4L97	MX	05:01	Trafford Park-Felixstowe	F.Liner 70	Freightliner
11:25	-	4M94		07:39	Felixstowe-Lawley Street	F.Liner 66	Freightliner
12:00	-	6M45		07:07	Dollands Moor-Daventry	EWS 66	water(in cargowagons)
-	12:35	4L93	MX	10:08	Lawley Street-Felixstowe	F.Liner 66	Freightliner
12:55	-	4M63		09:12	Felixstowe-Ditton	F.Liner 90	Freightliner
-	13:40	4013	FX	12:06	Daventry-Southampton	F.Liner 66	Freightliner
14:00	-	4M23		10:46	Felixstowe-Hams Hall	GBRf 66	Intermodal
14:25	-	4M88		09:32	Felixstowe-Crewe	F.Liner 90	Freightliner
-	14:40	4L48		12:37	Daventry-Purfleet	DRS 66	Intermodal
15:25	-	4M87		11:13	Felixstowe-Trafford Park	2 F.Liner 86s	Freightliner
15:45	-	1Q27	WO-Q	15:32	Euston-Derby	HST	measurement train
15:55	-	6M57	MO	12:00	Ipswich Griffin Wharf-Watford	EWS 66	loaded hoppers
16:35	-	1S96		16:22	Willesden PRDC-Shieldmuir	-	Mail(325 units)
-	16:35	6A42	MX	14:47	Daventry-Wembley	EWS 66	empty cargowagons
17:05	-	4M93	MX	13:34	Felixstowe-Lawley Street	F.Liner 70	Freightliner
-	17:30	4L90	MX	12:30	Crewe Basford Hall-Felixstowe	F.Liner 90	Freightliner
-	17:30	4L90	MO	11:17	Trafford Park-Felixstowe	F.Liner 90	Freightliner
-	17:40	6Z11	MFO-Q	10:00	Dowlow-Southampton	EWS 66	loaded box wagons
-	17:40	6V11	TWO-Q	10:00	Dowlow-Theale	EWS 66	loaded box wagons
-	17:40	6Z11	ThO-Q	09:35	Dowlow-Bow East	EWS 66	loaded box wagons
18:10	-	4M93	MO	14:32	Felixstowe-Lawley Street	F.Liner 70	Freightliner

44

North	South	H'code	Runs	Train	Traction	Type of train
-	18:40	4L92		14:03 Ditton-Felixstowe	F.Liner 70	Freightliner
-	18:45	4L18		14:18 Trafford Park-Felixstowe	GBRf 66	Intermodal
19:00	-	6Z14	T/ThO	14:48 Southampton up yard-Dowlow	EWS 66	empty box wagons
-	19:10	4L56	MWFO	13:17 Trafford Park-London Gateway	EWS 66	Intermodal
-	19:45	1A91		17:00 Warrington RMT-Willesden PRDC	-	Mail(325 units)
20:25	-	4S88		16:13 Felixstowe-Coatbridge	F.Liner 70	Freightliner
20:35	-	4S83		17:35 London Gateway-Coatbridge	F.Liner 70	Freightliner
-	20:45	6L48		15:49 Garston-Dagenham	GBRf 92	car carriers
21:00	-	4M02		17:34 Felixstowe-Hams Hall	GBRf 66	Intermodal

Saturdays:

North	South	H'code	Runs	Train	Traction	Type of train
06:55	-	4M45		02:57 Felixstowe-Ditton	F.Liner 90	Freightliner
07:10	-	4M88		04:25 Felixstowe-Lawley Street	F.Liner 66	Freightliner
-	07:30	1M16		20:44(Fri) Inverness-Euston	F.Liner 90	Caledonian Sleeper
-	07:40	4L89		22:01(Fri) Coatbridge-Felixstowe	2 F.Liner 86s	Freightliner
-	09:40	4L97		04:57 Trafford Park-Felixstowe	F.Liner 70	Freightliner
-	11:40	4L93		08:21 Crewe Basford Hall-Felixstowe	F.Liner 66	Freightliner
11:45	-	4M34		11:04 Acton yard-Peak Forest	EWS 66	empty bogie hoppers
-	12:10	4L90		08:30 Lawley Street-Felixstowe	F.Liner 66	Freightliner
12:40	-	6H50		12:18 Willesden-Tunstead	F.Liner 66	empty cement tanks
12:55	-	4M87		09:46 Felixstowe-Crewe	F.Liner 90	Freightliner
13:25	-	4M93		08:46 Felixstowe-Crewe	F.Liner 70	Freightliner
13:30	-	4M23		10:34 Felixstowe-Hams Hall	GBRf 66	Intermodal
14:30	-	4M20		10:14 Felixstowe-Lawley Street	F.Liner 66	Freightliner
15:25	-	6M84	(Q)	13:30 Stewarts Lane-Barrow Hill	F.Liner 66	empty box wagons
-	16:10	4L96		12:32 Crewe Basford Hall-Felixstowe	F.Liner 90	Freightliner
17:45	-	4M41	(Q)	13:57 London Gateway-Crewe Basford Hall	F.Liner 70	Freightliner
-	19:35	6L48		13:36 Garston-Dagenham	GBRf 66	car carriers

Sundays:

North	South	H'code	Runs	Train	Traction	Type of train
-	13:15	6038	(Q)	08:58 Halewood-Southampton E.Docks	EWS 66	loaded car carriers
-	14:40	4L48		13:09 Daventry-Purfleet	DRS 66	Intermodal

GOSPEL OAK
UPPER HOLLOWAY
and
CAMDEN ROAD

[06:00-22:00]

Mondays-Fridays:

Gospel Oak	Upper Holloway	Camden Road	code	Runs	Train	Traction	Type of train
06:20	06:25H	–	7E36	FO	05:54 Acton yard-Ferme Park	EWS 66	loaded bogie hoppers
06:40	06:45H	–	6E35	TThO	04:01 Grain-Ferme Park	EWS 66	sand(in bogie hoppers)
–	–	06:55	4M86		03:00 Felixstowe-Lawley Street	F.Liner 66	Freightliner
–	–	07:00	4M07	MX	04:18 Felixstowe-Burton on Trent	EWS 66	Intermodal
–	–	07:35	4L91	MX	02:10 Trafford Park-Felixstowe	F.Liner 90	Freightliner
09:25	–	09:20	6M48	MFX-Q	08:51 Bow East-Calvert	EWS 66	spoil(in box wagons)
–	–	09:45	6L04	(Q)	09:10 Wembley yard-Barrington(Foxton)	EWS 66	spoil(in box wagons)
–	–	09:50	4L89	MX	22:01 Coatbridge-Felixstowe	2 F.Liner 86s	Freightliner
10:10	–	10:05	7Z30	MO-Q	09:35 Bow-Acton yard	EWS 66	empty bogie boxes
10:25	10:30	–	6L35	MX	08:08 Didcot yard-Dagenham	EWS 66	empty car carriers
10:35	10:30	–	4M94		07:39 Felixstowe-Lawley Street	F.Liner 66	Freightliner
–	–	10:40	6X43	TO	09:45 Dagenham-Garston	GBRf 92	Ford cars
10:45	–	10:40	6Z92	FO-Q	10:13 Bow-Tonbridge	GBRf 66	empty bogie hoppers
10:45	–	10:50	4E26		08:13 Dollands Moor-Scunthorpe	EWS 66	empty steel(ex Ebange)
–	–	11:00	4L37	MO	06:24 Lawley Street-Felixstowe	F.Liner 66	Freightliner
–	–	11:00	4L41	MX	06:04 Crewe Basford Hall-Felixstowe	F.Liner 66	Freightliner
11:05	–	11:00	7V57	ThX-Q	09:50 Harlow Mill-Acton yard	class 59	empty bogie boxes
11:20	11:15	–	6Z79	WO-Q	09:10 Marks Tey-Crawley	EWS 66	loaded hoppers
–	–	11:20	4L89	MO	07:18 Crewe-Felixstowe	F.Liner 70	Freightliner
11:25	11:20	–	6V47	ThO	10:26 Tilbury-Margam	EWS 66	empty cargowagons
11:35	11:30	–	6Z89	WO-Q	09:10 Marks Tey-Brentford	EWS 66	loaded hoppers
11:35	11:30	–	6V28	WX-Q	10:38 Dagenham-Acton yard	class 59	empty bogie hoppers
11:55	11:50H	–	7V36	FO	11:32 Ferme Park-Acton yard	EWS 66	empty bogie hoppers
11:55	12:00H	–	6L37		09:58 Hoo Junction-Whitemoor	Colas 66/70	Departmental
12:05	–	12:00	6Z58	WO-Q	10:44 Harlow Mill-Tonbridge	GBRf 66	empty bogie hoppers
–	12:10	–	6M53	FO-Q	10:25 West Thurrock-Mountsorrel	EWS 66	empty box wagons
–	–	12:25	4L97	MX	05:01 Trafford Park-Felixstowe	F.Liner 70	Freightliner
12:25	–	12:30	4L31		09:03 Bristol FLT-Felixstowe	F.Liner 66	Freightliner
–	–	12:30	4M63		09:12 Felixstowe-Ditton	F.Liner 90	Freightliner
12:55	–	12:50	6V28	WO-Q	10:38 Dagenham-Acton yard	class 59	empty bogie hoppers
12:55	–	12:50	6V12	TThFO	10:54 Chelmsford-Acton yard	class 59	empty bogie boxes
–	–	13:00	4M88		09:32 Felixstowe-Crewe	F.Liner 90	Freightliner
–	–	13:20	4M23		10:46 Felixstowe-Hams Hall	GBRf 66	Intermodal
–	–	13:30	4L93	MX	10:08 Lawley Street-Felixstowe	F.Liner 66	Freightliner
–	14:30	–	6M92	FX-Q	13:18 West Thurrock-Tunstead	F.Liner 66	empty cement tanks
–	–	14:30	6M05		11:23 Barrington(Foxton)-Wembley yard	EWS 66	empty box wagons
–	–	14:40	4M87		11:13 Felixstowe-Trafford Park	2 F.Liner 86s	Freightliner
14:40	14:45	–	6L26	MFO	14:17 Acton yard-Dagenham	EWS 66	empty bogie hoppers
–	–	14:50	6M57	MO	12:00 Ipswich Griffin Wharf-Watford	EWS 66	loaded hoppers
15:05	–	15:00	6V07	WFO-Q	12:00 Ipswich Griffin Wharf-Theale	EWS 66	loaded hoppers
15:20	15:25	–	4L26	WO	12:44 Theale-Dagenham Dock	EWS 66	empty bogie hoppers
15:30	15:25	–	6X44		14:38 Dagenham-Didcot yard	EWS 66	Ford cars
15:55	16:05	–	4L48		12:37 Daventry-Purfleet	DRS 66	Intermodal

'Route Knowledge' (east of Upper Holloway):

(blank) = to/from South Tottenham;   H = to/from Ferme Park at Harringay Park Junction

Gospel Oak	Upper Holloway	code	Runs	Train		Traction	Type of train
-	-	16:05	4M93	MX	13:34 Felixstowe-Lawley Street	F.Liner 70	Freightliner
16:30	16:35	-	4L32	(Q)	11:00 Bristol FLT-Tilbury	F.Liner 66	Freightliner
-	16:35	-	4L32	(Q)	11:00 Bristol FLT-London Gateway	F.Liner 66	Freightliner
-	-	16:50	4M93	MO	14:32 Felixstowe-Lawley Street	F.Liner 70	Freightliner
19:00	18:55	-	4S83		17:35 London Gateway-Coatbridge	F.Liner 70	Freightliner
19:00	19:05	-	6L21		13:30 Whatley-Dagenham	MendipRail 59	loaded bogie hoppers
-	-	19:20	4L90	MO	11:17 Trafford Park-Felixstowe	F.Liner 90	Freightliner
-	-	19:20	4L90	MX	12:30 Crewe Basford Hall-Felixstowe	F.Liner 90	Freightliner
-	19:20	-	6L89	(Q)	11:49 Tunstead-West Thurrock	F.Liner 66	loaded cement tanks
-	-	19:35	6M07	(Q)	16:30 Barrington(Foxton)-Wembley yard	EWS 66	empty box wagons
-	-	19:45	4L18		14:18 Trafford Park-Felixstowe	GBRf 66	Intermodal
19:40	19:45	-	4L56	MWFO	13:17 Trafford Park-London Gateway	EWS 66	Intermodal
19:50	19:45	-	6V35	(Q)	18:43 Dagenham-Acton yard	EWS 66	sand(in bogie hoppers)
19:55	20:00	-	4L40	TX	16:42 Cowley(Oxford)-Purfleet	EWS 66	loaded car carriers
20:10	20:15	-	6Z15	WO-Q	01:01 Dowlow-Bow East	EWS 66	loaded box wagons
20:10	20:15	-	6Z11	ThO-Q	09:35 Dowlow-Bow East	EWS 66	loaded box wagons
-	-	20:10	4S88		16:13 Felixstowe-Coatbridge	F.Liner 70	Freightliner
-	-	20:30	4M02		17:34 Felixstowe-Hams Hall	GBRf 66	Intermodal
-	-	20:40	4L92		14:03 Ditton-Felixstowe	F.Liner 70	Freightliner
-	20:45	-	6M95	MX-Q	19:55 Ripple Lane-Peak Forest	EWS 66	empty bogie boxes
-	-	21:00	4M89		14:33(14:46 Mon) Felixstowe-Ditton	F.Liner 66	Freightliner
12:15	-	21:20	1S25	FO	20:18 Euston-Inverness(via ECML)	F.Liner 90	Caledonian Sleeper
-	-	21:25	4M92		18:13 Felixstowe-Lawley Street	F.Liner 66	Freightliner
21:25	21:20	-	6V31		19:48(20:43 Mon) Dagenham-Didcot yard	EWS 66	wagonload
21:35	-	21:40	6L36		19:52 Hoo Junction-Whitemoor	GBRf 66	Departmental
21:45	21:35	-	4M60		20:42 Tilbury-Garston	F.Liner 70	Freightliner

Saturdays:

-	-	07:20	4L91		02:08 Trafford Park-Felixstowe	F.Liner 90	Freightliner
-	-	09:35	4L89		22:01(Fri) Coatbridge-Felixstowe	2 F.Liner 86s	Freightliner
09:50	-	09:45	6M48		09:22 Bow East-Wembley yard	EWS 66	spoil(in box wagons)
10:25	10:30	-	6L35		08:19 Didcot yard-Dagenham	EWS 66	empty car carriers
-	-	11:20	4L97		04:57 Trafford Park-Felixstowe	F.Liner 70	Freightliner
-	-	11:50	4M93		08:46 Felixstowe-Crewe	F.Liner 70	Freightliner
11:55	-	12:00	4E26		09:14 Dollands Moor-Scunthorpe	EWS 66	empty steel(ex Ebange)
-	-	12:20	4M87		09:46 Felixstowe-Crewe	F.Liner 90	Freightliner
12:30	12:25	-	6V62		11:20 Tilbury-Margam	EWS 60	empty steel carriers
-	-	12:55	4M23		10:34 Felixstowe-Hams Hall	GBRf 66	Intermodal
-	-	12:55	4L93		08:21 Crewe-Felixstowe	F.Liner 66	Freightliner
13:25	-	13:30	5X89	(Q)	11:30 Slade Green-Doncaster works	GBRf 66	EMU for overhaul
-	-	13:50	4M20		10:14 Felixstowe-Lawley Street	F.Liner 66	Freightliner
-	-	14:00	4L90		08:30 Lawley Street-Felixstowe	F.Liner 66	Freightliner
14:00	13:55	-	6M92	(Q)	12:42 West Thurrock-Tunstead	F.Liner 66	empty cement tanks
15:20	15:15	-	4M41	(Q)	13:57 London Gateway-Crewe Bas.Hall	F.Liner 70	Freightliner
-	-	17:00	4L96		12:32 Crewe Basford Hall-Felixstowe	F.Liner 90	Freightliner
17:10	17:15	-	6Z52	(Q)	15:05 Oxford Banbury Road-Dagenham	EWS 66	empty bogie boxes
17:25	-	17:20	6V10		12:02 West Burton p.s.-Acton	EWS 66	flyash(in bogie boxes)
20:10	20:15	-	6L48		13:36 Garston-Dagenham	GBRf 66	car carriers

Sundays:

14:35	-	14:40	4E32	(Q)	12:05 Dollands Moor-Scunthorpe	EWS 66	empty steel(ex Ebange)
15:15	15:20	-	4L48		13:09 Daventry-Purfleet	DRS 66	Intermodal

STRATFORD

[06:00-midnight]

Mondays-Fridays:

West	East	H'code	Runs	Train	Traction	Type of train
06c20	-	4M07	MX	04:18 Felixstowe-Burton on Trent	EWS 66	Intermodal
06:30	-	4M86		03:00 Felixstowe-Lawley Street	F.Liner 66	Freightliner
-	08:30	4L91	MX	02:10 Trafford Park-Felixstowe	F.Liner 90	Freightliner
10:00	-	4M94		07:39 Felixstowe-Lawley Street	F.Liner 66	Freightliner
-	10:15	4L89	MX	22:01 Coatbridge-Felixstowe	2 F.Liner 86s	Freightliner
10:20	-	6X43	TO	09:45 Dagenham-Garston	GBRf 92	Ford cars
10:20	-	6Z79	WO-Q	09:10 Marks Tey-Crawley	EWS 66	loaded hoppers
10:20	-	6Z89	WO-Q	09:10 Marks Tey-Brentford	EWS 66	loaded hoppers
11:15	-	6V28	WO-Q	10:38 Dagenham-Acton yard	class 59	empty bogie hoppers
-	11:25	4L37	MO	06:24 Lawley Street-Felixstowe	F.Liner 66	Freightliner
-	11:25	4L41	MX	06:04 Crewe Basford Hall-Felixstowe	F.Liner 66	Freightliner
11c35	-	6M53	FO-Q	10:25 West Thurrock-Mountsorrel	EWS 66	empty self-dis train
11c40	-	6V12	TThFO	10:54 Chelmsford-Acton yard	class 59	empty bogie boxes
-	11:45	4L89	MO	07:18 Crewe-Felixstowe	F.Liner 70	Freightliner
12:00	-	4M63		09:12 Felixstowe-Ditton	F.Liner 66	Freightliner
-	12:05	6L36	TThO	11:17 Ferme Park-Dagenham	EWS 66	empty bogie hoppers
12:30	-	4M88		09:32 Felixstowe-Crewe	F.Liner 90	Freightliner
-	12:45	4L97	MX	05:01 Trafford Park-Felixstowe	F.Liner 70	Freightliner
13:00	-	4M23		10:46 Felixstowe-Hams Hall	GBRf 66	Intermodal
-	13:15	4L31		09:03 Bristol FLT-Felixstowe	F.Liner 66	Freightliner
-	14:15	4L93	MX	10:08 Lawley Street-Felixstowe	F.Liner 66	Freightliner
14:15	-	4M87		11:13 Felixstowe-Trafford Park	2 F.Liner 86s	Freightliner
14:30	-	6M57	MO	12:00 Ipswich Griffin Wharf-Watford	EWS 66	loaded hoppers
14:30	-	6V07	WFO-Q	12:00 Ipswich Griffin Wharf-Theale	EWS 66	loaded hoppers
15:35	-	4M93	MX	13:34 Felixstowe-Lawley Street	F.Liner 70	Freightliner
16:30	-	4M93	MO	14:32 Felixstowe-Lawley Street	F.Liner 70	Freightliner
-	19:45	4L90	MO	11:17 Trafford Park-Felixstowe	F.Liner 90	Freightliner
-	19:45	4L90	MX	12:30 Crewe Basford Hall-Felixstowe	F.Liner 90	Freightliner
19:45	-	4S88		16:13 Felixstowe-Coatbridge	F.Liner 66	Freightliner
20:00	-	4M02		17:34 Felixstowe-Hams Hall	GBRf 66	Intermodal
-	20:05	4L18		14:18 Trafford Park-Felixstowe	GBRf 66	Intermodal
20:35	-	4M89		14:33(14:46 Mon) Felixstowe-Ditton	F.Liner 66	Freightliner
-	21:00	4L92		14:03 Ditton-Felixstowe	F.Liner 70	Freightliner
21:00	-	4M92		18:13 Felixstowe-Lawley Street	F.Liner 66	Freightliner
22:15	-	4E66		21:13 London Gateway-Leeds	F.Liner 66	Freightliner
-	22:15	4L08	TThO	15:28 Wakefield Europort-London Gateway	EWS 66	Intermodal
-	22:20	6L48		15:49 Garston-Dagenham	GBRf 92	empty car carriers
-	22:55	4L96	FO	16:16 Trafford Park-Felixstowe	F.Liner 90	Freightliner
-	23:00	4L43		19:35 Lawley Street-Tilbury	F.Liner 66	Freightliner
23:05	-	4M53		20:46 Felixstowe-Trafford Park	F.Liner 90	Freightliner
-	23:15	4L73	FO	18:30 Lawley Street-Felixstowe	F.Liner 66	Freightliner

Saturdays:

West	East	H'code	Runs	Train	Traction	Type of train
-	06:25	4L95		22:50(Fri) Ditton-Felixstowe	F.Liner 66	Freightliner
-	07:45	4L91		02:08 Trafford Park-Felixstowe	F.Liner 90	Freightliner
-	09:55	4L89		22:01(Fri) Coatbridge-Felixstowe	2 F.Liner 86s	Freightliner
11:30	-	4M93		08:46 Felixstowe-Crewe	F.Liner 70	Freightliner
-	11:45	4L97		04:57 Trafford Park-Felixstowe	F.Liner 70	Freightliner
12:00	-	4M87		09:46 Felixstowe-Crewe	F.Liner 90	Freightliner
12:30	-	4M23		10:34 Felixstowe-Hams Hall	GBRf 66	Intermodal
13:15	-	4M20		10:14 Felixstowe-Lawley Street	F.Liner 66	Freightliner
-	13:45	4L93		08:21 Crewe Basford Hall-Felixstowe	F.Liner 66	Freightliner
-	14:25	4L90		08:30 Lawley Street-Felixstowe	F.Liner 66	Freightliner
-	17:25	4L96		12:32 Crewe Basford Hall-Felixstowe	F.Liner 90	Freightliner

Sundays: NO BOOKED TRAINS

IPSWICH STATION

[06:00-midnight]

Mondays-Fridays:

North	South	H'code	Runs	Train	Traction	Type of train
06c25	-	4L69	MX	01:06 Lawley Street-Felixstowe North	F.Liner 70	Freightliner
07:25	-	4L41	MO	01:55 Crewe-Ipswich yard	F.Liner 90	Freightliner
07:55	-	4L95	MX	22:50 Ditton-Felixstowe	F.Liner 66	Freightliner
-	08:35	4M94		07:39 Felixstowe-Lawley Street	F.Liner 66	Freightliner
09:55	-	4L91	MX	02:10 Trafford Park-Felixstowe	F.Liner 90	Freightliner
-	09:50	4C88	WO	09:45 Ipswich yard-Ilford	F.Liner 66	wagons for repair
-	10:50	4M63		09:12 Felixstowe-Ditton	F.Liner 90	Freightliner
-	11:15	4M88		09:32 Felixstowe-Crewe	F.Liner 90	Freightliner
-	11:30	4M23		10:46 Felixstowe-Hams Hall	GBRf 66	Intermodal
11c30	-	4L89	MX	22:01 Coatbridge-Felixstowe	2 F.Liner 86s	Freightliner
11:35	-	4R03	MO	11:02 Harwich-Felixstowe	GBRf 66	Intermodal
12:40	-	4L37	MO	06:24 Lawley Street-Felixstowe	F.Liner 66	Freightliner
12:40	-	4L41	MX	06:04 Crewe Basford Hall-Felixstowe	F.Liner 66	Freightliner
-	12:50	4M87		11:13 Felixstowe-Trafford Park	2 F.Liner 86s	Freightliner
13:05	-	4L89	MO	07:18 Crewe Basford Hall-Felixstowe	F.Liner 70	Freightliner
13:45	-	4Y88	WO	12:10 Ilford-Ipswich yard	F.Liner 66	wagons off repair
-	14:20	4M93	MX	13:34 Felixstowe-Lawley Street	F.Liner 70	Freightliner
14:30	-	4L31		09:03 Bristol FLT-Felixstowe	F.Liner 66	Freightliner
-	15:15	4M93	MO	14:32 Felixstowe-Lawley Street	F.Liner 70	Freightliner
15:35	-	4L93	MX	10:08 Lawley Street-Felixstowe	F.Liner 66	Freightliner
-	16:35	6A33	T/ThO	14:40 North Walsham-Harwich	GBRf 66	condensate tanks
17:30	-	4L97	MX	05:01 Trafford Park-Felixstowe	F.Liner 70	Freightliner
-	18:20	4S88		16:13 Felixstowe-Coatbridge	F.Liner 66	Freightliner
-	18c25	4M02		17:34 Felixstowe-Hams Hall	GBRf 66	Intermodal
-	18:50	4M89		14:33(14:46 Mon) Felixstowe-Ditton	F.Liner 66	Freightliner
-	19:50	4M92		18:13 Felixstowe-Lawley Street	F.Liner 66	Freightliner
20:55	-	6Y07	FX-Q	20:07 Harwich PQ-(as required)	2 F.Liner 66s	Departmental
21:05	-	4L90	MO	11:17 Trafford Park-Felixstowe	F.Liner 90	Freightliner
21:05	-	4L90	MX	12:30 Crewe Basford Hall-Felixstowe	F.Liner 90	Freightliner
21:35	-	4L18		14:18 Trafford Park-Felixstowe	GBRf 66	Intermodal
-	21:50	4M53		20:46 Felixstowe-Trafford Park	F.Liner 90	Freightliner
21:55	-	6H33	(Q)	23:23 Harwich PQ-Whitemoor	GBRf 66	Departmental
-	22:30	4M59		21:31 Felixstowe-Ditton	F.Liner 66	Freightliner
22:35	-	4L92		14:03 Ditton-Felixstowe	F.Liner 70	Freightliner
-	22:50	4M73		21:41 Felixstowe-Ditton	F.Liner 66	Freightliner
-	23:10	4M42		22:08 Felixstowe-Garston	F.Liner 70	Freightliner

Saturdays:

North	South	H'code	Runs	Train	Traction	Type of train
06c05	-	4L69		01:05 Lawley Street-Felixstowe	F.Liner 70	Freightliner
08:05	-	4L95		22:50(Fri) Ditton-Felixstowe	F.Liner 66	Freightliner
09:05	-	4L91		02:08 Trafford Park-Felixstowe	F.Liner 90	Freightliner
-	10:20	4M93		08:46 Felixstowe-Crewe Basford Hall	F.Liner 70	Freightliner
-	10:50	4M87		09:46 Felixstowe-Crewe Basford Hall	F.Liner 90	Freightliner
-	11:15	4M23		10:34 Felixstowe-Hams Hall	GBRf 66	Intermodal
11c25	-	4L89		22:01(Fri) Coatbridge-Felixstowe	2 F.Liner 86s	Freightliner
-	11:50	4M20		10:14 Felixstowe-Lawley Street	F.Liner 66	Freightliner
13c05	-	4L97		04:57 Trafford Park-Felixstowe	F.Liner 70	Freightliner
-	13:15	4A26		12:34 Felixstowe-Harwich	GBRf 66	empty flats
15:05	-	4L93		08:21 Crewe Basford Hall-Felixstowe	F.Liner 66	Freightliner
-	15:15	4M41		15:12 Ipswich yard-Crewe Basford Hall	F.Liner 66	Freightliner
15:50	-	4L90		08:30 Lawley Street-Felixstowe	F.Liner 66	Freightliner
-	18:15	4L20		12:44 Hams Hall-Harwich	GBRf 66	Intermodal

Sundays: NO BOOKED TRAINS

51

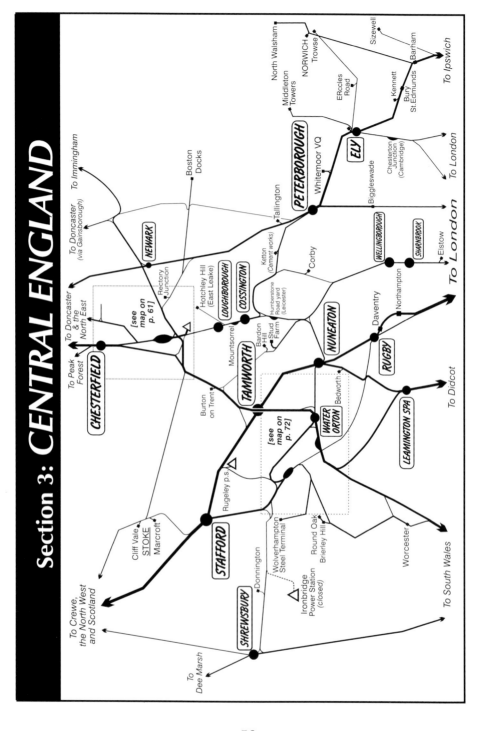

Section 3: **CENTRAL ENGLAND**

To Ipswich
Sizewell
Barham
North Walsham
NORWICH
Trowse
Kennett
Bury St.Edmunds
Middleton Towers
ERccles Road
To London
Chesterton Junction (Cambridge)
ELY
PETERBOROUGH
Whitemoor VQ
To Immingham
Boston Docks
Biggleswade
To Doncaster (via Gainsborough)
Tallington
Tallington
NEWARK
WELLINGBOROUGH
SHARNBROOK
Elstow
Ketton (Cement works)
Corby
Rectory Junction
Hotchley Hill (East Leake)
LOUGHBOROUGH
COSSINGTON
Humberstone Road yard (Leicester)
Northampton
To London
[see map on p. 61]
To Doncaster & the North East
Mountsorrel
Bardon Hill
Stud Farm
Daventry
NUNEATON
To Peak Forest
CHESTERFIELD
TAMWORTH
RUGBY
To Didcot
Burton on Trent
Bedworth
WATER ORTON
[see map on p. 72]
LEAMINGTON SPA
Rugeley p.s.
Cliff Vale
STOKE
Marcroft
STAFFORD
Donnington
Wolverhampton Steel Terminal
Round Oak
Brierley Hill
Worcester
To Crewe, the North West and Scotland
Ironbridge Power Station (closed)
To South Wales
SHREWSBURY
To Dee Marsh

52

[06:00-21:00]

Mondays-Fridays:

North	South	H'code	Runs	Train		Traction	Type of train
-	06:10	6L53	WFO-Q	03:36	Mountsorrel-Chesterton Junction	EWS 66	loaded box wagons
-	06:50	4L83	MX	01:42	Leeds-Felixstowe	F.Liner 66	Freightliner
-	07R25	6L85	TThO	00:51	Warrington Arpley-Middleton Towers	EWS 66	empty box wagons
07:45	-	4E62	MX	05:38	Felixstowe-Doncaster Railport	F.Liner 66	Freightliner
-	08:05	6L74	MThO	04:32	Mountsorrel-Harlow Mill	EWS 66	loaded box wagons
08:55	-	4E22	MX	05:50	Felixstowe-Leeds	F.Liner 66	Freightliner
09R05	-	6L85	TThO	00:51	Warrington Arpley-Middleton Towers	EWS 66	empty box wagons
-	09:05	6L41	MWX-Q	06:37	Mountsorrel-Barham	EWS 66	loaded hoppers
-	09:25	4L02	MX	03:54	Hams Hall-Felixstowe	GBRf 66	Intermodal
10R30	09R40	6L39	(Q)	06:37	Mountsorrel-Norwich Trowse	EWS 66	loaded hoppers
10:35	-	4M81		08:01	Felixstowe-Crewe	F.Liner 66/70	Freightliner
11:35	-	6E53	TO	10:27	Ipswich yard-Lindsey	F.Liner 66	empty TTA tanks
-	13:05	6L43	MWX-Q	08:55	Mountsorrel-Kennett	EWS 66	loaded hoppers
13:20	-	6M70	WFO-Q	12:36	Chesterton Junction-Mountsorrel	EWS 66	empty box wagons
-	13:35	4L93	MO	10:34	Lawley Street-Felixstowe	F.Liner 66	Freightliner
13:35	-	4M38		10:29	Felixstowe North-Birch Coppice	GBRf 66	Intermodal
13:50	-	4Z33		11:22	Felixstowe-Doncaster Railport	GBRf 66	Intermodal
-	14:10	4L45		09:36	Wakefield Europort-Felixstowe	EWS 66	Intermodal
14:20	-	6L37		09:58	Hoo Junction-Whitemoor	Colas 66	Departmental
-	15:10	4L85		12:13	Doncaster Railport-Felixstowe	F.Liner 66	Freightliner
16:00	-	6M45	MWX-Q	14:17	Barham-Mountsorrel	EWS 66	empty hoppers
-	16:10	4L87	MX	08:47	Leeds-Felixstowe	F.Liner 66	Freightliner
-	16:55	4Z79		12:00	Selby-Felixstowe	GBRf 66	Intermodal
-	17R00	4M86	FX-Q	16:58	Ely Potter Group-Peak Forest	EWS 66	empty bogie hoppers
-	17R00	4M86	FO	16:58	Ely-Doncaster Belmont	EWS 66	empty bogie hoppers
17:05	-	6M29	MThO	15:17	Harlow Mill-Mountsorrel	EWS 66	empty box wagons
17R30	-	4M86	FX-Q	16:58	Ely Potter Group-Peak Forest	EWS 66	empty bogie hoppers
17R30	-	4M86	FO	16:58	Ely-Doncaster Belmont	EWS 66	empty bogie hoppers
17:35	-	4E55		15:20(15:46 Mon)	Felixstowe-Doncaster	F.Liner 66	Freightliner
18:05	-	6M80	MFX-Q	17:31	Bury St.Edmunds-Barrow Hill	F.Liner 66	empty box wagons
-	18:15	4L07		11:38	Burton on Trent-Felixstowe	EWS 66	Intermodal
-	19:15	4L22		14:35	Hams Hall-Felixstowe	GBRf 66	Intermodal
-	20:05	4L55		16:20	Doncaster Railport-Felixstowe	F.Liner 66	Freightliner
20:05	-	4E50		17:45	Felixstowe-Leeds	F.Liner 66	Freightliner

Saturdays:

07:20	-	4E62		05:15	Felixstowe-Doncaster Railport	F.Liner 66	Freightliner
-	07:35	6L40	(Q)	04:52	Mountsorrel-Barham	EWS 66	loaded hoppers
08:20	-	4E22		06:14	Felixstowe-Leeds	F.Liner 66	Freightliner
-	09:10	4L02		04:50	Hams Hall-Felixstowe	GBRf 66	Intermodal
-	13:30	4L39		08:30	Birch Coppice-Felixstowe	GBRf 66	Intermodal
14:05	-	4M67		12:13	Felixstowe-Crewe	F.Liner 70	Freightliner
-	15:05	4L85		11:23	Leeds-Ipswich yard	F.Liner 66	Freightliner
15:55	-	6M44	(Q)	14:15	Barham-Mountsorrel	EWS 66	empty hoppers
-	16:45	4L20		12:44	Hams Hall-Harwich	GBRf 66	Intermodal

Sundays: NO BOOKED TRAINS

PETERBOROUGH(station)

[24 hour]

Mondays-Fridays:

North	South	H'code	Runs	Train	Traction	Type of train
-	S06c00M	4L83	MX	01:42 Leeds-Felixstowe	F.Liner 66	Freightliner
-	S06:15M	6L85	TTh0	00:51 Warrington Arpley-Middleton Towers	EWS 66	empty box wagons
M06:25	-	6E77	MFX-Q	05:52 Whitemoor-Tallington	GBRf 66	Departmental(sleepers)
06c50J	-	4E08	TTh0	03:41 London Gateway-Wakefield Europort	EWS 66	Intermodal
-	S06c55M	6L74	MTh0	04:32 Mountsorrel-Harlow Mill	EWS 66	loaded box wagons
-	07:40M	6L98	MWF0	04:52 Doncaster-Middleton Towers	GBRf 66	empty sand hoppers
-	S07c55M	6L39	(Q)	06:37 Mountsorrel-Norwich Trowse	EWS 66	loaded hoppers
-	S07c55M	6L41	MWX-Q	06:37 Mountsorrel-Barham	EWS 66	loaded hoppers
M08c30	-	4E62	MX	05:38 Felixstowe-Doncaster Railport	F.Liner 66	Freightliner
-	S08:40M	4L02	MX	03:54 Hams Hall-Felixstowe	GBRf 66	Intermodal
-	S08:45M	6L75	(Q)	04:15 Peak Forest-Ely	EWS 66	loaded bogie hoppers
-	09:55M	6L25	MFX-Q	09:39 Tallington-Whitemoor	GBRf 66	Departmental(sleepers)
M10c10	-	4E22	MX	05:50 Felixstowe-Leeds	F.Liner 66	Freightliner
M11c25S	-	4M81		08:01 Felixstowe-Crewe	F.Liner 66/70	Freightliner
M11c50S	-	6M60		11:12 Whitemoor-Mountsorrel	GBRf 66	empty ballast boxes
-	S11c55M	6L43	MWX-Q	08:55 Mountsorrel-Kennett	EWS 66	loaded hoppers
M12c10	-	6E84	MFX-Q	08:20 Middleton Towers-Monk Bretton	GBRf 66	loaded sand hoppers
M12c10	-	6E84	MFO	08:20 Middleton Towers-Barnby Dun	GBRf 66	loaded sand hoppers
M12c20S	-	6E53	TO	10:27 Ipswich yard-Lindsey	F.Liner 66	empty TTA tanks
12:45	-	4E26		08:13 Dollands Moor-Scunthorpe	EWS 66	empty steel(ex Ebange)
-	S12:50M	4L93	MO	10:34 Lawley Street-Felixstowe	F.Liner 66	Freightliner
-	J13:15M	4L45		09:36 Wakefield Europort-Felixstowe	EWS 66	Intermodal
M14c00S	-	6M20	TO-Q	12:15 Eccles Road-Dowlow	EWS 66	empty bogie boxes
M14c15S	-	4M38		10:29 Felixstowe North-Birch Coppice	GBRf 66	Intermodal
M14c30S	-	6M70	WF0-Q	12:36 Chesterton Junction-Mountsorrel	EWS 66	empty box wagons
-	J14c30M	4L85		12:13 Doncaster Railport-Felixstowe	F.Liner 66	Freightliner
M14c45J	-	4Z33		11:22 Felixstowe-Doncaster Railport	GBRf 66	Intermodal
15c15S	-	6M67	TO-Q	11:50 Broxbourne-Mountsorrel	EWS 66	empty hoppers
15c25J	-	4E25		11:25 Bow/14:36 Biggleswade-Heck	EWS 66	empty PLASMOR wagons
M15c30J	-	6E88	MWF0	12:39 Middleton Towers-Goole Glassworks	GBRf 66	loaded sand hoppers
-	15:30M	4L87	MX	08:47 Leeds-Felixstowe	F.Liner 66	Freightliner
-	J15:55M	4Z79	MWF0Q	12:00 Selby-Felixstowe	GBRf 66	Intermodal
-	16:55M	4Z34	WFOQ	13:58 Doncaster Wood yard-Whitemoor	F.Liner 66	Departmental
M17c05S	-	6M45	MWX-Q	14:17 Barham-Mountsorrel	EWS 66	empty hoppers
M17c15S	-	6M88	TTh0	14:35 Middleton Towers-Ellesmere Port	EWS 66	sand(in box wagons)
-	S17:30M	4L07		11:38 Burton on Trent-Felixstowe	EWS 66	Intermodal
M18c15S	-	4M86	FX-Q	16:58 Ely-Peak Forest	EWS 66	empty bogie hoppers
M18c20J	-	4M86	FO	16:58 Ely-Doncaster Belmont	EWS 66	empty bogie hoppers
M18c30S	-	6M29	MTh0	15:17 Harlow Mill-Mountsorrel	EWS 66	empty box wagons
-	S18:30M	4L22		14:35 Hams Hall-Felixstowe	GBRf 66	Intermodal
M18c40	-	4E55		15:20(15:46 Mon) Felixstowe-Doncaster	F.Liner 66	Freightliner
M19:10S	-	6M80	MFX-Q	17:31 Bury St.Edmunds-Barrow Hill	F.Liner 66	empty box wagons
M19c15S	-	6M58	WO	16:05 Norwich-Peak Forest	EWS 66	empty bogie boxes
-	19:15M	4L55	MX	16:20 Doncaster Railport-Felixstowe	F.Liner 66	Freightliner
-	J19c30	4L08	TTh0	15:28 Wakefield Europort-London Gateway	EWS 66	Intermodal
-	S19:55M	6L15		17:52 Toton-Whitemoor	GBRf 66	Departmental
M20c05S	-	6M43	(Q)	18:13 Norwich-Mountsorrel	EWS 66	empty hoppers
-	20:15M	4L55	MO	16:20 Doncaster Railport-Felixstowe	F.Liner 66	Freightliner
-	S20:25M	6L27		17:24 Mountsorrel-Whitemoor VQ	GBRf 66	loaded ballast boxes
M20:30	-	4E50		17:45 Felixstowe-Leeds	F.Liner 66	Freightliner
-	S21c10M	4L86	FX	16:18 Trafford Park-Felixstowe	F.Liner 66	Freightliner
M21c30S	-	6M44	MWX-Q	18:52 Kennett-Mountsorrel	EWS 66	empty hoppers
-	J21c30	6V09	TO	13:00 West Burton p.s.-Acton yard	EWS 66	flyash(in box wagons)
-	J21c55M	6L49	TO	17:49 Lindsey-Ipswich yard	F.Liner 66	fuel oil tanks

54

North	South	H'code	Runs		Train	Traction	Type of train
-	22:00M	4L79		15:55	Tees Dock-Felixstowe	F.Liner 66	Freightliner
-	22c05	6V04		18:59	Scunthorpe-Southall yard	EWS 66	empty 'binliner'
M22:20	-	4E60		18:21	Felixstowe-Tees Dock	F.Liner 66	Freightliner
M22c55S	-	6M15		22:34	Whitemoor-Toton	GBRf 66	Departmental
-	S23:10M	4L73	FX	18:30	Lawley Street-Felixstowe	F.Liner 66	Freightliner
-	23:30M	6L84		21:43	Doncaster Decoy-Whitemoor	GBRf 66	Departmental
23:55	-	6E21	Th0-Q	21:00	West Ruislip-Peterborough	4 GBRf 20s	barrier wagons
-	00:05	1M80		21:43	Low Fell RMT-Willesden PRDC	-	Mail(325 unit)
00:10	-	1E06		22:45	Willesden PRDC-Low Fell RMT	-	Mail(325 unit)
00c35	-	4E66		21:13	London Gateway-Leeds	F.Liner 66	Freightliner
-	S00:35M	4L23	SX	21:10	Birch Coppice-Felixstowe	GBRf 66	Intermodal
-	J01:20M	4Z35		20:43	Doncaster Railport-Felixstowe	GBRf 66	Intermodal
-	J01c55	4028		22:40	Scunthorpe-Dollands Moor	EWS 66	loaded steel(to Ebange)
-	S02c05M	4L58	SX	23:03	Lawley Street-Felixstowe	F.Liner 66	Freightliner
M02:05	-	6035		01:38	Whitemoor-Hoo Junction	GBRf 66	Departmental
M02c15J	-	4E45		22:49	Felixstowe-Wakefield	EWS 66	Intermodal
02c30J	-	6E02		22:58	Brentford-Scunthorpe	EWS 66	loaded 'binliner'
-	J02c30M	4L88		23:49	Leeds FLT-London Gateway	F.liner 66	Freightliner
-	J02:55M	6L31	SX	00:06	Doncaster-Middleton Towers	GBRf 66	empty 4-wheel hoppers
-	03:00	6035		01:38	Whitemoor-Hoo Junction	GBRf 66	Departmental
M03:00J	-	6E04		02:35	Whitemoor-Doncaster Decoy	GBRf 66	Departmental
M03c35J	-	4E83		00:36	Felixstowe-Doncaster Railport	F.Liner 66	Freightliner
-	S03c35M	6L38	T0-Q	01:58	Mountsorrel-Broxbourne	EWS 66	loaded hoppers
-	S03c45M	6Z59	T0-Q	21:39	Dowlow-Eccles Road	EWS 66	loaded bogie boxes
-	S03:50	6L99	TTh0	23:00	Peak Forest-Ripple Lane	EWS 66	stone(in box wagons)
-	04c25	6H93	SO	21:39(Fri)	Heck-Biggleswade	EWS 66	Blocks[PLASMOR]
-	S04c35M	6L80	MTX-Q	00:00	Tunstead-Bury St.Edmunds	F.Liner 66	loaded box wagons
-	J04:45M	4L45	SO-Q	02:15	Wakefield Europort-Felixstowe	EWS 66	Intermodal
-	J04:55M	4L42		03:05	Doncaster Railport-Felixstowe	F.Liner 66	Freightliner
M04c50J	-	4Z78		01:58	Felixstowe-Selby	GBRf 66	Intermodal
M05c05S	-	4M04		02:15	Felixstowe-Hams Hall	GBRf 66	Intermodal
-	S05c20M	6L53	WF0-Q	00:00	Mountsorrel-Chesterton Junction	EWS 66	loaded box wagons
M05:45	-	4Z33	WF0-Q	05:20	Whitemoor-Doncaster Wood yard	F.Liner 66	Departmental
-	05c45	6L70	SX	21:39	Heck-Bow	EWS 66	Blocks[PLASMOR]
-	05c55M	4L83	SO	01:46	Leeds-Felixstowe	F.Liner 66	Freightliner

Saturdays:

North	South	H'code	Runs		Train	Traction	Type of train
-	S07c25M	6L85		02:35	Warrington Arpley-Middleton Towers	EWS 66	empty box wagons
M08c05	-	4E62		05:15	Felixstowe-Doncaster Railport	F.Liner 66	Freightliner
-	S08:25M	4L02		04:50	Hams Hall-Felixstowe	GBRf 66	Intermodal
M09c05	-	4E22		06:14	Felixstowe-Leeds	F.Liner 66	Freightliner
-	S12:25M	4L39		08:30	Birch Coppice-Felixstowe	GBRf 66	Intermodal
12c30	-	4D56		11:32	Biggleswade-Heck	EWS 66	empty PLASMOR wagons
14:00	-	4E26		09:14	Dollands Moor-Scunthorpe	EWS 66	empty steel(ex Ebange)
-	J14c00	6V10		12:02	West Burton p.s.-Acton	EWS 66	flyash(in bogie boxes)
-	14:25M	4L85		11:23	Leeds-Ipswich yard	F.Liner 66	Freightliner
M14c55S	-	4M67		12:13	Felixstowe-Crewe	F.Liner 70	Freightliner
-	S15:55M	4L20		11:55	Hams Hall-Harwich	GBRf 66	Freightliner
M16c20S	-	6M89		13:39	Middleton Towers-Warrington Arpley	EWS 66	sand(in box wagons)
M16c55S	-	6M44	(Q)	14:15	Barham-Mountsorrel	EWS 66	empty hoppers
M18c25	-	4E45	(Q)	14:33	Felixstowe-Wakefield	EWS 66	Intermodal

Sundays:

North	South	H'code	Runs		Train	Traction	Type of train
-	08:50	6H67	(Q)	08:48	Peterborough yard-Stevenage	EWS 66	loaded self-dis train
16c55	-	4E32		12:05	Dollands Moor-Scunthorpe	EWS 66	empty steel(ex Ebange)
18c00S	-	6M33	(Q)	16:06	Stevenage-Mountsorrel	EWS 66	empty self-dis.train

'Route Knowledge': **(blank)** = ECML;   **M** = to/from March;

S = to/from Stamford line (at Helpston Junction);   **J** = to/from Sleaford (at Werrington Junction)

WELLINGBOROUGH AREA
(Sharnbrook and Harrowden Junctions)

[06:00 - 21:00]

Mondays-Fridays:

Harrowden	Sharnbrook	code	Runs	Train	Traction	Type of train
-	08:35	6V42	MX-Q	08:13 Wellingborough-Whatley	GBRf 66	empty bogie boxes
08:55	09:15	6M30	MO-Q	21:42(Sun) Moreton-on-Lugg-Radlett	EWS 66	loaded hoppers
09:45	09:25	6D32	TX	09:02 Elstow-Mountsorrel	EWS 66	empty 4-wheel hoppers
09:55	10:00	1Q52	ThO-Q	08:51 Derby RTC-St.Pancras	HST	measurement train
11:35	11:20	4H03	WFO	09:57 Bletchley-Peak Forest	EWS 66	empty bogie hoppers
12:35	12:20	6M32	MWFO	09:47 Neasden-Bardon Hill/Croft	GBRf 66	empty bogie hoppers
13:35	13:15	6F93	MX	11:05 St.Pancras-Ketton	EWS 66	empty cement tanks
14:00	13:40	6M53	FO-Q	10:25 West Thurrock-Mountsorrel	EWS 66	empty box wagons
14:20	-	6Z75	MO-Q	14:10 Wellingborough-Peak Forest	EWS 66	empty bogie boxes
14:35	14:15	6M91		11:13 Theale-Earles	F.Liner 66	empty cement tanks
14:40	14:20	6D31	MO-Q	13:27 Radlett-Toton	EWS 66	empty hoppers
14:40	14:20	6Z77	TWFO	13:39 Luton-Mountsorrel	EWS 66	empty bogie boxes
15:20	14:55	6M54	TO-Q	12:20 Colnbrook-Bardon Hill	GBRf 66	empty bogie hoppers
-	15:20	6M11	T/WO	11:08 Acton yard-Wellingborough	GBRf 66	Departmental
15:40	15:35	1Q52	ThO-Q	14:46 St.Pancras-Derby RTC	HST	measurement train
16:20	16:05	6M79	MWO-Q	11:56 Angerstein-Bardon Hill	GBRf 66	empty bogie hoppers
16:40	16:25	6M92	FX-Q	13:18 West Thurrock-Tunstead	F.Liner 66	empty cement tanks
17:05	17:20	6L89	(Q)	11:49 Tunstead-West Thurrock	F.Liner 66	loaded cement tanks
17:35	17:20	6E38	MWFOQ	13:54 Colnbrook-Lindsey	Colas 60	empty bogie tanks
19:05	17:50	6H74	MO-Q	17:09 Luton-Peak Forest	EWS 66	empty bogie boxes
19:05	19:20	6V08	ThO-Q	13:27 Tunstead-Brentford	F.Liner 66	loaded bogie hoppers

Saturdays:

07:10	06:55	6M90		04:45 West Thurrock-Tunstead	F.Liner 66	empty cement tanks
08:55	09:15	6C31		07:07 Mountsorrel-Radlett	EWS 66	loaded hoppers
11:40	11:15	6M68		08:19 Hayes-Stud Farm	EWS 66	empty bogie hoppers
13:10	12:55	6M91	(Q)	09:16 Theale-Earles	F.Liner 66	empty cement tanks
14:00	13:40	6H10		12:29 Bletchley-Peak Forest	EWS 66	empty bogie hoppers
14:20	13:55	6Z77	(Q)	13:09 Luton-Mountsorrel	EWS 66	empty bogie boxes
15:10	14:50	6D31		13:56 Radlett-Mountsorrel	EWS 66	empty hoppers
15:50	15:25	6M92	(Q)	12:42 West Thurrock-Tunstead	F.Liner 66	empty cement tanks
17:40	17:15	6M84	(Q)	13:30 Stewarts Lane-Barrow Hill	F.Liner 66	empty box wagons
17:55	18:15	6Z69		16:29 Stud Farm-Hither Green	EWS 66	loaded bogie hoppers

Sundays: NO BOOKED TRAINS

NEWARK *(North Gate)*
[06:00-midnight]

Mondays-Fridays:

North	South	H'code	Runs		Train	Traction	Type of train
E06:45G	-	4Z33	MWFOQ	05:20	Whitemoor-Doncaster Wood yard	F.Liner 66	Departmental
09:35G	-	4E62	MX	05:38	Felixstowe-Doncaster Railport	F.Liner 66	Freightliner
11:30	-	4E22	MX	05:50	Felixstowe-Leeds	F.Liner 66	Freightliner
13:25	-	6E84	MFX-Q	08:20	Middleton Towers-Monk Bretton	GBRf 66	loaded sand hoppers
13:25	-	6E84	MFO	08:20	Middleton Towers-Barnby Dun	GBRf 66	loaded sand hoppers
13:30	-	4E26		08:13	Dollands Moor-Scunthorpe	EWS 66	empty steel(ex Ebange)
14:25L	-	6E82	MWX-Q	12:16	Rectory Junction-Lindsey	Colas 60	empty bogie tanks
-	14:25	4L87	MX	08:47	Leeds-Felixstowe	F.Liner 66	Freightliner
-	15:55	4Z33	MWFOQ	13:58	Doncaster Wood yard-Whitemoor	F.Liner 66	Departmental
-	G17:45	4L55		16:20	Doncaster Railport-Felixstowe	F.Liner 66	Freightliner
19:35G	-	4E55		15:20	Felixstowe-Doncaster Railport	F.Liner 66	Freightliner
-	21:10	6V04		18:59	Scunthorpe-Southall yard	EWS 66	empty 'binliner'
-	21:15	4L79		15:55	Tees Dock-Felixstowe	F.Liner 66	Freightliner
21:35	-	6E86	FO-Q	18:21	Ketton-Doncaster Belmont	EWS 66	empty box wagons
21:50	-	4E50		17:45	Felixstowe-Leeds	F.Liner 66	Freightliner
-	22:25	6L84		21:43	Doncaster Decoy-Whitemoor	GBRf 66	Departmental
23:35	-	4E60		18:21	Felixstowe-Tees Dock	F.Liner 66	Freightliner
-	23:35	1M80		21:43	Low Fell RMT-Willesden PRDC	-	Mail(325 unit)

Saturdays:

North	South	H'code		Train	Traction	Type of train
09:05G	-	4E62	05:15	Felixstowe-Doncaster Railport	F.Liner 66	Freightliner
10:20	-	4E22	06:14	Felixstowe-Leeds	F.Liner 66	Freightliner
-	12:15	6H78	11:01	Doncaster Decoy-Peterborough yard	GBRf 66	empty sand hoppers
-	13:30	4L85	08:55	Leeds-Ipswich yard	F.Liner 66	Freightliner
13:35	-	4D56	11:32	Biggleswade-Heck	EWS 66	empty PLASMOR wagons
15:00	-	4E26	09:14	Dollands Moor-Scunthorpe	EWS 66	empty steel(ex Ebange)
-	20:25	6H86	18:12	Heck-Peterborough yard	EWS 66	Plasmor breeze blocks

Sundays:

North	South	H'code			Train	Traction	Type of train
17:15	-	4E32		12:05	Dollands Moor-Scunthorpe	EWS 66	empty steel(ex Ebange)
-	22:40	6L31	(Q)	21:48	Doncaster-Middleton Towers	GBRf 66	empty 4-wheel hoppers
-	22:45	6007		20:15	Scunthorpe-Dollands Moor	EWS 66	loaded steel(to Ebange)

'**Route knowledge**': (**blank**) = ECML
                      L = to/from Lincoln via Newark crossing avoiding curve
                      G = to/from Gainsborough via Newark crossing avoiding curve

CHESTERFIELD

[06:00-midnight]

Mondays-Fridays:

North	South	H'code	Runs		Train	Traction	Type of train
-	D06:05E	6L75	(Q)	04:15	Peak Forest-Ely	EWS 66	loaded bogie hoppers
-	D06:30E	6D80	MWX-Q	05:00	Tunstead-Ratcliffe p.s.	F.Liner 66	loaded bogie hoppers
-	07:05E	6M82	(Q)	05:02	Drax-Hotchley Hill	EWS 66	containerised gypsum
07:30	-	4E01	MX	01:30	Southampton Millbrook-Leeds	F.Liner 66	Freightliner
-	07:35E	4O90		06:12	Leeds-Southampton	F.Liner 66/70	Freightliner
-	08:00E	6M59	MX-Q	17:05	Hunterston-Ratcliffe p.s.	EWS 66	loaded EWS coal hoppers
08:30	-	4E01	MO	03:22	Southampton Maritime-Leeds	F.Liner 66	Freightliner
E08:45D	-	6M90	FO-Q	02:28	Brentford-Tunstead	F.Liner 66	empty bogie hoppers
E09:10D	-	6M88	MX-Q	03:48	West Thurrock-Tunstead	F.Liner 66	empty cement tanks
-	09:15	6M18	FO-Q	07:23	Doncaster Decoy-Toton	DRS 66	Departmental
-	D10:00E	6G65	(Q)	09:19	Earles-Walsall	F.Liner 66	loaded cement tanks
E10:20	-	6Z46	MWFOQ	07:15	Stud Farm-Doncaster Decoy	GBRf 66	loaded ballast
E11:05	-	6E88	MWFO	09:45	Mountsorrel-Tyne yard	F.Liner 66	loaded ballast
E11:30	-	6E62	MWX-Q	10:28	Ratcliffe p.s.-Barrow Hill	F.Liner 66	empty bogie hoppers
E11:40	-	4E12	FO-Q	04:02	London Gateway-Rotherham S.T.	EWS 66	Intermodal
-	12:00E	6X01	TThO	10:17	Scunthorpe-Eastleigh	EWS 66	loaded rails
12:15D	-	4M11	MWFO	10:00	Washwood Heath-Peak Forest	EWS 66	empty bogie hoppers
-	D12:15	6M83	(Q)	10:51	Tinsley-Bardon Hill	GBRf 66	empty bogie hoppers
-	12:30E	6M73		10:52	Doncaster Decoy-Toton	GBRf 66	Departmental
E12:35	-	4E54	MX-Q	11:46	Ratcliffe p.s.-Milford	EWS 66	empty EWS coal hoppers
E13:05	-	6E20	FO-Q	12:27	Toton-Doncaster Decoy	DRS 66	Departmental
13:15D	-	4M11	TThO	10:42	Washwood Heath-Peak Forest	EWS 66	empty HTA hoppers
-	D13:15E	6L89	(Q)	11:49	Tunstead-West Thurrock	F.Liner 66	loaded cement tanks
-	13:40E	4O95	MX	12:12	Leeds-Southampton	F.Liner 66/70	Freightliner
E14:10D	-	4H03	WFO	09:57	Bletchley-Peak Forest	EWS 66	empty bogie hoppers
E14:30	-	6E53	TO	10:27	Ipswich yard-Lindsey	F.Liner 66	empty TTA tanks
-	14:45E	6M23	MX-Q	12:57	Doncaster Decoy-Mountsorrel	GBRf 66	empty ballast wagons
-	15:15E	6M69	TO-Q	13:52	Heck-Dowlow	EWS 66	empty box wagons
15:15D	-	6M82	FX-Q	12:41	Walsall-Dowlow	EWS 66	empty box wagons
E15:30	-	6Z34	WO-Q	14:25	Chaddesden(Derby)-Stockton	DCR 56	empty box wagons
-	15:50E	4L10	FO-Q	15:18	Rotherham S.T.-London Gateway	EWS 66	Intermodal
-	16:00E	6V08	ThO-Q	13:27	Tunstead-Brentford	F.Liner 66	loaded bogie hoppers
16:00	-	6E08	MThO	13:03	Wolverhampton S.T.-Immingham	EWS 60	empty steel
-	16:15E	6M35	FX-Q	11:10	Rylstone-Small Heath	GBRf 66	loaded bogie boxes
-	16:35	6V80	FO-Q	14:08	Gascoigne Wood-Portbury	GBRf 66	gypsum(in box wagons)
E16:50D	-	6M91		11:13	Theale-Earles	F.Liner 66	empty cement tanks
17:00	-	6E08	TWFO	13:03	Wolverhampton-Immingham	EWS 60	empty steel
E17:05	-	4E69	TFO	09:32	Southampton-Wakefield Europort	EWS 66	Intermodal
E17:05	-	4Z69	MThO	09:32	Southampton-Rotherham S.T.	EWS 66	Intermodal
E17:10D	-	6M69	TO-Q	13:52	Heck-Dowlow	EWS 66	empty box wagons
-	17:55	6V35	ThO-Q	17:10	Rotherham-Cardiff Tidal	EWS 66	scrap(in bogie boxes)
E18:30	-	6E79	W/ThO	15:02	Wolverhampton-Rotherham S.T.	EWS 66	empty steel

'Route knowledge': (blank) = from Barrow Hill line to Derby and v.v.;
                    D = to/from Dore;   E = to/from Erewash Valley (at Clay Cross Junction)

58

North	South	H'code	Runs	Train	Traction	Type of train
-	18:35	6V35	MO-Q	17:44 Rotherham-Cardiff Tidal	EWS 66	empty steel
-	19:00	6V81	WFO	18:32 Rotherham-Cardiff Tidal	EWS 66	scrap(in bogie boxes)
E19:00	-	6E83	(Q)	15:37 Hotchley Hill-Milford sidings	EWS 66	empty gypsum containers
E19:10	-	6M92	FX-Q	13:18 West Thurrock-Tunstead	F.Liner 66	empty cement tanks
-	20:00E	4052	WO	18:27 Wakefield Europort-Southampton	EWS 66	Intermodal
-	20:20E	6M07	WO-Q	13:53 North Blyth-Ratcliffe p.s.	F.Liner 66	loaded FHH coal hoppers
-	20:50E	4Z52	MThO	20:15 Rotherham S.T.-Southampton	EWS 66	Intermodal
E20:50D	-	4M86	FX-Q	16:58 Ely-Peak Forest	EWS 66	empty bogie hoppers
E21:25	-	6M80	MFX-Q	17:31 Bury St.Edmunds-Barrow Hill	F.Liner 66	empty box wagons
-	D21:35E	6L10	FX-Q	20:00 Tunstead-West Thurrock	F.Liner 66	loaded cement tanks
-	21:40	4007		20:18 Leeds-Southampton Millbrook	F.Liner 66	Freightliner E22:05D -
6M58	WO	16:05 Norwich-Peak Forest			EWS 66	empty bogie boxes
-	22:15	6V02		18:37 Tees yard-Margam	EWS 66	empty steel/lime
-	22:35	6V19	ThFO	17:22 Immingham-Llanwern	EWS 66	steel/empties
E23:00	-	6E22	MX-Q	21:43 Mountsorrel-Doncaster Decoy	GBRf 66	loaded ballast
23:05D	-	6H66	(Q)	20:55 Walsall-Earles sidings	F.Liner 66	empty cement tanks
-	D23:05E	6V91	FX-Q	22:29 Earles-Theale	F.Liner 66	loaded cement tanks
-	23:05E	6092	FO-Q	19:53 Tunstead-Stewarts Lane	F.Liner 66	loaded bogie hoppers

Saturdays:

North	South	H'code	Runs	Train	Traction	Type of train
-	06:45	4054		05:27 Leeds-Southampton	F.Liner 66	Freightliner
E10:05D	-	6M90		04:45 West Thurrock-Tunstead	F.Liner 66	empty cement tanks
-	11:00E	4V52	(Q)	09:31 Wakefield Europort-Didcot yard	EWS 66	Intermodal
15:15D	-	6H64		12:07 Walsall-Dowlow	EWS 66	empty box wagons
E16:10D	-	6M91	(Q)	09:16 Theale-Earles	F.Liner 66	empty cement tanks
E17:35D	-	6H10		12:29 Bletchley-Peak Forest	EWS 66	empty bogie hoppers
E19:15D	-	6M92	(Q)	12:42 West Thurrock-Tunstead	F.Liner 66	empty cement tanks
E20:00	-	6M84	(Q)	13:30 Stewarts Lane-Barrow Hill	F.Liner 66	empty box wagons

Sundays:

North	South	H'code	Runs	Train	Traction	Type of train
12:50	-	6E68	(Q)	10:12 Kingsbury-Humber	EWS 60	empty bogie tanks
-	15:05E	6M57	(Q)	11:06 Lindsey-Kingsbury	EWS 60	loaded bogie tanks
21:50	-	6E47		13:45 Margam-Middlesbrough	EWS 66	loaded steel
-	D22:25E	6L10		21:02 Tunstead-West Thurrock	F.Liner 66	loaded cement tanks
-	D23:55E	6V91		23:16 Earles-Theale	F.Liner 66	loaded cement tanks

59

TOTON SOUTH
and
TROWELL JUNCTION
[06:00-21:00]

Mondays-Fridays:

Trowell Junc	Toton South	code	Runs	Train	Traction	Type of train
-	06:10	6X49	TWThO 06:05	Toton-Beeston	EWS 66/67	Departmental
06:30	06:50	6L75	(Q) 04:15	Peak Forest-Ely	EWS 66	loaded bogie hoppers
07:05	07:10	6D80	MWX-Q 05:00	Tunstead-Ratcliffe p.s.	F.Liner 66	loaded bogie hoppers
07:35	08:05	6M82	(Q) 05:02	Drax-Hotchley Hill	EWS 66	containerised gypsum
08:10	08:15	4O90	06:12	Leeds-Southampton	F.Liner 66/70	Freightliner
08:35	08:15	6M88	MX-Q 03:48	West Thurrock-Tunstead	F.Liner 66	empty cement tanks
08:35	08:45	6M59	MX-Q 17:05	Hunterston-Ratcliffe p.s.	EWS 66	loaded EWS coal hoppers
-	09:25	6D46	MX-Q 07:15	Stud Farm-Toton VQ	GBRf 66	loaded ballast
10:30	10:15	6E88	MWFO 09:45	Mountsorrel-Tyne yard	F.Liner 66	loaded ballast
10:35		6G65	ThX-Q 09:19	Earles-Walsall	F.Liner 66	loaded cement tanks
11:05	10:40	6E62	MWX-Q 10:28	Ratcliffe p.s.-Barrow Hill	F.Liner 66	empty bogie hoppers
11:20	11:10	4E12	FO-Q 04:02	London Gateway-Rotherham S.T.	EWS 66	Intermodal
	11:15	6G65	(Q) 09:19	Earles-Walsall	F.Liner 66	loaded cement tanks
12:10	12:00	4E54	MX-Q 11:46	Ratcliffe p.s.-Milford	EWS 66	empty EWS coal hoppers
12:25	12:35	6X01	TThO 10:17	Scunthorpe-Eastleigh	EWS 66	loaded rails
12:35	-	6E20	FO-Q 12:27	Toton-Doncaster Decoy	DRS 66	Departmental
13:05	-	6M73	10:52	Doncaster Decoy-Toton	GBRf 66	Departmental
13:35	13:05	4H03	WFO 09:57	Bletchley-Peak Forest	EWS 66	empty bogie hoppers
-	13:45	6D44	11:09	Bescot-Toton	EWS 66	Departmental
13:50	13:55	6L89	(Q) 11:49	Tunstead-West Thurrock	F.Liner 66	loaded cement tanks
14:00	13:55	6E53	TO 10:27	Ipswich yard-Lindsey	F.Liner 66	empty TTA tanks
14:20	14:30	4O95	MX 12:12	Leeds-Southampton	F.Liner 66/70	Freightliner
15:00	15:00	6Z34	WO-Q 14:25	Chaddesden(Derby)-Stockton	DCR 56	empty box wagons
-	15:15	6K50	15:13	Toton-Crewe	GBRf 66	Departmental
-	15:15	6X50	TWThO 14:51	Beeston-Toton	EWS 66/67	Departmental
15:20	15:25	6M23	MX-Q 12:57	Doncaster Decoy-Mountsorrel	GBRf 66	empty ballast wagons
16:20	16:10	6M91	11:13	Theale-Earles	F.Liner 66	empty cement tanks
-	16:15	6M20	TO-Q 12:05	Eccles Road-Dowlow	EWS 66	empty bogie boxes
-	16:15	6M88	ThO-Q 12:56	Immingham-Ketton	EWS 66	coal(in MEA box wagons)
16:35	16:20	4Z69	MThO 09:32	Southampton-Rotherham S.T.	EWS 66	Intermodal 16:35
16:20		4E69	TFO 09:32	Southampton-Wakefield Europort	EWS 66	Intermodal
-	16:25	6D31	MO-Q 13:27	Radlett-Toton	EWS 66	empty hoppers
-	16:45	6Z75	MO-Q 14:10	Wellingborough-Peak Forest	EWS 66	empty bogie boxes
-	16:45	6Z96	(Q) 14:40	Bescot VQ-Toton	DRS 66/68	Departmental
16:45		6V08	ThO-Q 13:27	Tunstead-Brentford	F.Liner 66	loaded bogie hoppers
-	16:55	6G45	16:53	Toton-Bescot	EWS 66	Departmental
-	17:00	6V08	ThO-Q 13:27	Tunstead-Brentford	F.Liner 66	loaded bogie hoppers
17:00	17:40	6V80	FO-Q 14:08	Gascoigne Wood-Portbury	GBRf 66	gypsum(in box wagons)
18:00	17:45	6E79	W/ThO 15:02	Wolverhampton-Rotherham S.T.	EWS 66/60	empty steel
-	17:55	6L15	17:52	Toton-Whitemoor	GBRf 66	Departmental
18:25	18:15	6E83	(Q) 15:37	Hotchley Hill-Milford sidings	EWS 66	empty gypsum containers
-	19:30	6K97	MX-Q 19:27	Toton-Crewe VQ	DRS 66/68	Departmental
20:20	19:40	4M86	FX-Q 16:58	Ely-Peak Forest	EWS 66	empty bogie hoppers
20:30	20:55	4O52	WO 18:27	Wakefield Europort-Southampton	EWS 66	Intermodal

Saturdays:

Trowell Junc	Toton South	code	Runs	Train	Faction	Type of train
09:40	09:30	6M90		04:45 West Thurrock-Tunstead	F.Liner 66	empty cement tanks
-	10:45	7F54	(Q)	07:45 Stud Farm-Toton	EWS 66	loaded bogie hoppers
11:30	|	4V52	(Q)	09:31 Wakefield Europort-Didcot yard	EWS 66	Intermodal
12:00	11:45	6E89		05:00 Portbury-Doncaster Hexthorpe	GBRf 66	empty box wagons
15:40	15:30	6M91	(Q)	09:16 Theale-Earles	F.Liner 66	empty cement tanks
17:05	15:45	6H10		12:29 Bletchley-Peak Forest	EWS 66	empty bogie hoppers
|	18:40	4V52	(Q)	09:31 Wakefield Europort-Didcot yard	EWS 66	Intermodal
18:45	18:40	6M92	(Q)	12:42 West Thurrock-Tunstead	F.Liner 66	empty cement tanks

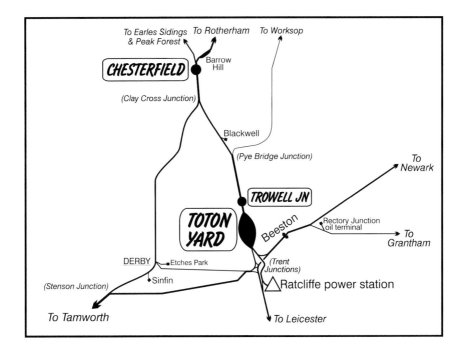

LOUGHBOROUGH
and
COSSINGTON *(Sileby)*

[06:00-21:00]

Mondays-Fridays:

Loughboro'	Sileby	code	Runs	Train	Traction	Type of train
-	06:45	6L39	(Q)	06:37 Mountsorrel-Norwich Trowse	EWS 66	loaded hoppers
-	06:45	6L41	MWX-Q	06:37 Mountsorrel-Barham	EWS 66	loaded hoppers
-	07:05	6M00	MX	23:25 Tyne yard-Mountsorrel	F.Liner 66	empty ballast boxes
07:15	07:25	6L75	(Q)	04:15 Peak Forest-Ely	EWS 66	loaded bogie hoppers
07:45	07:35	6M88	MX-Q	03:48 West Thurrock-Tunstead	F.Liner 66	empty cement tanks
08:40	08:50	6M82	(Q)	05:02 Drax-Hotchley Hill	EWS 66	containerised gypsum
09:10	09:00	6D46	MX-Q	07:15 Stud Farm-Toton VQ	GBRf 66	loaded ballast
-	09:00	6L43	MWX-Q	08:55 Mountsorrel-Kennett	EWS 66	loaded hoppers
09:20	09:25	1Q52	ThO-Q	08:51 Derby RTC-St.Pancras	HST	measurement train
09:50	-	6E88	MWFO	09:45 Mountsorrel-Tyne yard	F.Liner 66	loaded ballast
-	10:05	6M82	(Q)	05:02 Drax-Hotchley Hill	EWS 66	containerised gypsum
-	10:50	6U76		08:59 Crewe-Mountsorrel	DRS 66/68	empty ballast boxes
-	11:15	6D32	TX	09:02 Elstow-Mountsorrel	EWS 66	empty 4-wheel hoppers
12:45	12:35	4H03	WFO	09:57 Bletchley-Peak Forest	EWS 66	empty bogie hoppers
-	13:00	6E65	MO	12:55 Mountsorrel-Peterborough yard	EWS 66	loaded box wagons
-	13:00	6B30	TWFO	12:55 Mountsorrel-Northampton	EWS 66	loaded box wagons
-	13:20	6M60		11:12 Whitemoor-Mountsorrel	GBRf 66	empty ballast boxes
13:35	13:25	6E53	TO	10:27 Ipswich yard-Lindsey	F.Liner 66	empty TTA tanks
-	13:30	6M31	TO-Q	10:42 Banbury-Mountsorrel	EWS 66	empty box wagons
13:50	-	6U77		13:42 Mountsorrel-Crewe	DRS 66/68	loaded ballast boxes
14:00	14:10	6M96	FO-Q	05:51 Margam-Corby	EWS 66	loaded steel(coil)
-	14:20	6M64	WO-Q	12:29 Peterborough yard-Mountsorrel	EWS 66	empty box wagons
14:20	14:30	6L89	(Q)	11:49 Tunstead-West Thurrock	F.Liner 66	loaded cement tanks
-	15:15	6Z74	MO-Q	12:55 Luton-Mountsorrel	EWS 66	empty bogie boxes
-	15:15	6M53	FO-Q	10:25 West Thurrock-Mountsorrel	EWS 66	empty box wagons
15:45	15:40	6M91		11:13 Theale-Earles	F.Liner 66	empty cement tanks
15:45	15:50	6M23	MX-Q	12:57 Doncaster Decoy-Mountsorrel	GBRf 66	empty ballast wagons
16:00	15:50	6M20	TO-Q	12:15 Eccles Road-Dowlow	EWS 66	empty bogie boxes
16:00	15:50	6D31	MO-Q	13:27 Radlett-Toton	EWS 66	empty hoppers
-	15:55	6Z77	TWFO	13:39 Luton-Mountsorrel	EWS 66	empty bogie boxes
16:10	16:05	1Q52	ThO-Q	14:46 St.Pancras-Derby RTC	HST	measurement train
16:25	16:20	6Z75	MO-Q	14:10 Wellingborough-Peak Forest	EWS 66	empty bogie boxes
-	16:20	6M70	WFO-Q	12:36 Chesterton Junction-Mountsorrel	EWS 66	empty box wagons
-	16:25	6E83	(Q)	15:37 Hotchley Hill-Milford sidings	EWS 66	empty gypsum containers
-	16:50	6M26	(Q)	08:50 Eastleigh VQ-Mountsorrel	GBRf 66	empty ballast wagons
-	16:50	6M23	MX-Q	12:57 Doncaster Decoy-Mountsorrel	GBRf 66	empty ballast wagons
17:15		6M67	TO-Q	11:50 Broxbourne-Mountsorrel	EWS 66	empty hoppers
-	17:30	6L27		17:24 Mountsorrel-Whitemoor VQ	GBRf 66	loaded ballast boxes

62

Loughboro'	Sileby	code	Runs	Train	Traction	Type of train
-	09:00	6L43	MWX-Q	08:55 Mountsorrel-Kennett	EWS 66	loaded hoppers
09:20	09:25	1Q52	ThO-Q	08:51 Derby RTC-St.Pancras	HST	measurement train
09:50	-	6E88	MWFO	09:45 Mountsorrel-Tyne yard	F.Liner 66	loaded ballast
-	10:05	6M82	(Q)	05:02 Drax-Hotchley Hill	EWS 66	containerised gypsum
-	10:50	6U76		08:59 Crewe-Mountsorrel	DRS 66/68	empty ballast boxes

Saturdays:

-	07:15	6C31		07:07 Mountsorrel-Radlett	EWS 66	loaded hoppers
09:10	09:00	6M90		04:45 West Thurrock-Tunstead	F.Liner 66	empty cement tanks
10:30	10:25	7F54	(Q)	07:45 Stud Farm-Toton	EWS 66	loaded bogie hoppers
-	12:20	6M64	(Q)	10:26 Peterborough yard-Mountsorrel	EWS 66	empty box wagons
15:10	15:00	6M91	(Q)	09:16 Theale-Earles	F.Liner 66	empty cement tanks
-	15:45	6Z77	(Q)	13:09 Luton-Mountsorrel	EWS 66	empty bogie boxes
16:00	15:50	6H10		12:29 Bletchley-Peak Forest	EWS 66	empty bogie hoppers
-	16:45	6D31		13:56 Radlett-Mountsorrel	EWS 66	empty hoppers
-	17:15	6E67	(Q)	17:09 Mountsorrel-Peterborough yard	EWS 66	loaded box wagons
18:20	18:15	6M92	(Q)	12:42 West Thurrock-Tunstead	F.Liner 66	empty cement tanks
-	18:20	6M44	(Q)	14:15 Barham-Mountsorrel	EWS 66	empty hoppers

Sundays: NO BOOKED TRAINS

NUNEATON

[06:00-midnight]

Mondays-Fridays:

North	South	H'code	Runs	Train		Traction	Type of train
06:40	-	6M13	MO	23:11(Sun)	Dollands Moor-Ditton	EWS 66	aluminium(cargowagons)
-	06:40	4M30	MO	22:33(Sun)	Grangemouth-Daventry	EWS 66	Intermodal
-	06:40	6M76	FO	21:46(Thurs)	Mossend-Wembley	2 EWS 90s	empty china clay tanks
06:45	-	4S43		06:16	Daventry-Mossend	2 DRS 66s	'Tesco Express'
07:00	-	4M83	WFO	02:59	London Gateway-Trafford Park	EWS 66	Intermodal
-	W07:10	4L37	MO	06:24	Lawley Street-Felixstowe	F.Liner 66	Freightliner
-	07:15	4L41	MX	06:04	Crewe Basford Hall-Felixstowe	F.Liner 66	Freightliner
07:35	-	6X41	MO	03:30	Dagenham-Garston	GBRf 66	Ford cars
07:35	-	6S94	WO	02:21	Dollands Moor-Irvine	2 EWS 90s	loaded china clay tanks
-	07:40	4Z55	MX	00:54	Coatbridge-Daventry	F.Liner 70	Intermodal
-	W07:45C	6M03	MWFO	21:00	Robeston-Bedworth	EWS 66	loaded bogie tanks
L07:45W	-	4M04	MX	02:15	Felixstowe-Hams Hall	GBRf 66	Intermodal
-	07:55	6Z15	WO-Q	01:01	Dowlow-Bow East	EWS 66	loaded box wagons
-	08c10C	4014	MX	05:36	Garston-Southampton	F.Liner 70	Freightliner
-	W08:20C	4018	MO	07:24	Lawley Street-Southampton	F.Liner 66	Freightliner
-	08:35	4L89	MO	07:18	Crewe-Felixstowe	F.Liner 70	Freightliner
08:40	-	4M45	MX	02:50	Felixstowe-Ditton	F.Liner 90	Freightliner
08:40	-	6M46	MO	04:54	Ripple Lane-Peak Forest	EWS 66	empty bogie boxes
08:50W	-	4V38		08:20	Daventry-Wentloog	DRS 66	'Tesco Express'
C09c05	-	6M44	MO	04:50	Southampton E.Docks-Halewood	EWS 66	empty car carriers
09c05	-	4M21	MX	03:10	Felixstowe-Trafford Park	GBRf 66	Intermodal
-	09:35	4L97	MX	05:01	Trafford Park-Felixstowe	F.Liner 70	Freightliner
C09:35	-	4M86		03:00	Felixstowe-Lawley Street	F.Liner 66	Freightliner
-	10:20L	6U76		08:59	Crewe Basford Hall-Mountsorrel	DRS 66/68	empty ballast boxes
-	W10:45	4L93	MX	10:08	Lawley Street-Felixstowe	F.Liner 66	Freightliner
-	10:50C	4049	MX	09:22	Crewe Basford Hall-Southampton	F.Liner 66/70	Freightliner
-	W11:10L	4L93	MO	10:34	Lawley Street-Felixstowe	F.Liner 66	Freightliner
11:40	-	6M11	WO-Q	03:30	Theale-Dowlow	EWS 66	empty box wagons
-	11c50C	4021		09:15	Trafford Park-Southampton	EWS 66	Intermodal
-	W11:55L	4F30	ThO-Q	11:30	Washwood Heath-Wellingborough	GBRf 66	Departmental
-	W12:30L	6M31	TO-Q	10:42	Banbury-Mountsorrel	EWS 66	empty box wagons
L12:30W	-	6V92	(Q)	10:22	Corby-Margam	EWS 66	empty steel
12:40	-	4Z44		12:13	Daventry-Coatbridge	F.Liner 70	Intermodal
L12:55W	-	6G16	WX-Q	11:24	Stud Farm-Bescot VQ	GBRf 66	loaded ballast boxes
13:05	-	6X43	TO	09:45	Dagenham-Garston	GBRf 92	Ford cars
-	13:05	4Z27		05:25	Coatbridge-Daventry	F.Liner 70	Intermodal
L13:20W	-	6V16	WO-Q	11:24	Stud Farm-Hinksey VQ	GBRf 66	loaded ballast boxes
L13:30nc	-	4M81		08:01	Felixstowe-Crewe	F.Liner 66/70	Freightliner
-	W14:05L	6Z77	WFX-Q	09:42	Willesden ET-Stud Farm	F.Liner 66	empty ballast
13:45W	-	4M94		07:39	Felixstowe-Lawley Street	F.Liner 66	Freightliner
-	13:45	4L90	MX	12:30	Crewe Basford Hall-Felixstowe	F.Liner 90	Freightliner
-	14:00	4M25		06:06	Mossend-Daventry	2 EWS 90s	Intermodal
L14:00W	-	6B30	TWFO	12:55	Mountsorrel-Northampton	EWS 66	loaded box wagons
-	14c30C	6042		11:31	Halewood-Southampton E.Docks	EWS 66	loaded car carriers
C14:35W	-	6M50	FX	07:55	Westbury VQ-Bescot VQ	Colas 70	Departmental
14:40	-	4M63		09:12	Felixstowe-Ditton	F.Liner 90	Freightliner
-	14:45	4L90	MO	11:17	Trafford Park-Felixstowe	F.Liner 90	Freightliner

'Route knowledge': (blank) = Trent Valley (Rugby to Stafford);
C=to/from Coventry line; W= to/from Water Orton line; L= to/from Leicester line

North	South	H'code	Runs	Train	Traction	Type of train
-	W15:10L	4L22		14:35 Hams Hall-Felixstowe	GBRf 66	Intermodal
C15:15W	-	4M18	MWFOQ	09:47 Fairwater yard-Washwood Heath	F.Liner 66	Departmental
-	W15:30L	4L07		11:38 Burton on Trent-Felixstowe	EWS 66	Intermodal
-	W15c40	6B30	TWFO	12:55 Mountsorrel-Northampton	EWS 66	loaded box wagons
-	15:45	6Z11	MFO-Q	10:00 Dowlow-Southampton	EWS 66	loaded box wagons
-	15:45	6V11	TWO-Q	10:00 Dowlow-Theale	EWS 66	loaded box wagons
-	15:45	6Z11	ThO-Q	09:35 Dowlow-Bow East	EWS 66	loaded box wagons
15:50W	-	4M23		10:46 Felixstowe-Hams Hall	GBRf 66	Intermodal
-	W16:00L	6M26	(Q)	08:50 Eastleigh VQ-Mountsorrel	GBRf 66	empty ballast wagons
-	16:10	4L56	MWFO	13:17 Trafford Park-London Gateway	EWS 66	Intermodal
C16c20	-	4M61		12:54 Southampton-Trafford Park	F.Liner 66/70	Freightliner
L16:25W	-	4M38		10:29 Felixstowe North-Birch Coppice	GBRf 66	Intermodal
-	W16:35C	4017		15:48 Lawley Street-Southampton	F.Liner 66	Freightliner
16:40	-	4M88		09:32 Felixstowe-Crewe Basford Hall	F.Liner 90	Freightliner
-	16:45	4L92		14:03 Ditton-Felixstowe	F.Liner 70	Freightliner
-	W16:50L	6M40		11:56 Westbury-Stud Farm	GBRf 66	empty ballast boxes
-	16:55	4L18		14:18 Trafford Park-Felixstowe	GBRf 66	Intermodal
17:00	-	1Q27	WO-Q	15:32 Euston-Derby	HST	measurement train
17:10	-	4M87		11:13 Felixstowe-Trafford Park	2 F.Liner 86s	Freightliner
C17:35W	-	6V55	MWFO	16:08(15:30 Fri) Bedworth-Robeston	EWS 66	empty bogie tanks
18:05	-	1S96		16:22 Willesden PRDC-Shieldmuir	-	Mail(325 units)
-	18c20C	4029		15:18 Trafford Park-Southampton	F.Liner 66	Freightliner
-	18:25	1A91		17:00 Warrington RMT-Willesden PRDC	-	Mail(325 units)
C18c30	-	4M68		13:53 Southampton-Garston	F.Liner 70	Freightliner
-	18:50	6L48		15:49 Garston-Dagenham	GBRf 92	car carriers
18:55W	-	4M93	MX	13:34 Lawley-Lawley Street	F.Liner 70	Freightliner
19:05	-	4Z45		18:39 Daventry-Coatbridge	F.Liner 70	Intermodal
-	W19:30	4L73	FO	18:30 Lawley Street-Felixstowe	F.Liner 66	Freightliner
-	W19:30L	4L73	FX	18:30 Lawley Street-Felixstowe	F.Liner 66	Freightliner
-	19:40L	4L86	FX	16:18 Trafford Park-Felixstowe	F.Liner 66	Freightliner
-	19:40	4L96	FO	16:18 Trafford Park-Felixstowe	F.Liner 66	Freightliner
L19c40nc	-	6M88	TThO	14:35 Middleton Towers-Ellesmere Port	EWS 66	sand(in box wagons)
19:45	-	4S47		19:13 Daventry-Mossend	2 EWS 90s	Intermodal
L19:55W	-	6Z79	WFX-Q	18:45 Stud Farm-Willesden ET	F.Liner 66	loaded ballast
20:00W	-	4M93	MO	14:32 Lawley-Lawley Street	F.Liner 70	Freightliner
-	W20:10	4L43		19:35 Lawley Street-Tilbury	F.Liner 66	Freightliner
C20:30	-	4M99		16:57 Southampton-Trafford Park	F.Liner 70	Freightliner
-	20:55	1A97		19:18 Warrington RMT-Willesden PRDC	-	Mail(325 units)
C21:20W	-	4M98		17:32 Southampton-Hams Hall	F.Liner 70	Freightliner
L21:25W	-	6027	(Q)	20:38 Mountsorrel-Eastleigh VQ	GBRf 66	ballast(in box wagons)
-	W21:45L	6E81	TWO-Q	17:00 Portbury-West Burton	GBRf 66	empty box wagons
L21:50W	-	6V93	FO-Q	20:06 Corby-Margam	EWS 66	empty steel
-	21:50	4L71		18:41 Ditton-Felixstowe	F.Liner 90	Freightliner
-	22:10	4L60		19:46 Garston-Felixstowe	F.Liner 66	Freightliner
22:20	-	4S83		17:35 London Gateway-Coatbridge	F.Liner 70	Freightliner
22:25	-	4S49		21:58 Daventry-Grangemouth	EWS 66	Intermodal
C22c35	-	6X65		20:28 Didcot yard-Mossend	EWS 66	wagonload
-	W22:40	4L23	FX	21:10 Birch Coppice-Felixstowe	GBRf 66	Intermodal
22:45	-	1S25		21:15 Euston-Inverness	F.Liner 90	Caledonian Sleeper
22c55W	-	4M02		17:34 Felixstowe-Hams Hall	GBRf 66	Intermodal
23:00	-	4S88		16:13 Felixstowe-Coatbridge	F.Liner 90	Freightliner
-	W23:00	4L28		22:35 Hams Hall-Felixstowe	GBRf 66	Intermodal
23:10	-	6M95	ThO-Q	16:35 Dungeness p.s.-Crewe	2 DRS 37s	flask(s)
-	23:15	6016	MWFO	20:21 Ditton-Dollands Moor	EWS 92	empty cargowagons
23:35W	-	4M92		18:13 Felixstowe-Lawley Street	F.Liner 66	Freightliner
-	W23:35L	4L58	FX	23:03 Lawley Street-Felixstowe	F.Liner 66	Freightliner
-	W23:35	4L77	FO	23:03 Lawley Street-Felixstowe	F.Liner 66	Freightliner

Saturdays:

North	South	H'code	Runs	Train	Traction	Type of train
07:05	–	4S43		06:40 Daventry-Mossend	2 DRS 66s	'Tesco Express'
–	07:20	4Z55		00:55 Coatbridge-Daventry	F.Liner 70	Intermodal
–	07:40	4L97		04:57 Trafford Park-Felixstowe	F.Liner 70	Freightliner
L07:55W	–	4M04		02:16 Felixstowe-Hams Hall	GBRf 66	Intermodal
08:45	–	4M45		02:57 Felixstowe-Ditton	F.Liner 90	Freightliner
08:50W	–	4M88		04:25 Felixstowe-Lawley Street	F.Liner 66	Freightliner
09:10	–	4M21		03:15 Felixstowe-Trafford Park	GBRf 66	Intermodal
–	09:40	4L93		08:21 Crewe Basford Hall-Felixstowe	F.Liner 66	Freightliner
–	W09:45	4L90		08:30 Lawley Street-Felixstowe	F.Liner 66	Freightliner
–	W10:00L	4L39		08:30 Birch Coppice-Felixstowe	GBRf 66	Intermodal
11:40	–	4S49		11:12 Daventry-Grangemouth	EWS 66	Intermodal
12:30	–	4Z44		12:05 Daventry-Coatbridge	F.Liner 70	Intermodal
–	13:05	4Z27		05:25 Coatbridge-Daventry	F.Liner 70	Intermodal
–	W13:10L	4L20		12:44 Hams Hall-Harwich	GBRf 66	Intermodal
C13c20	–	6M48		09:28 Southampton E.Docks-Halewood	EWS 66	empty car carriers
13:35	–	4M34		11:04 Acton yard-Peak Forest	EWS 66	empty bogie hoppers
–	13:55	4L96		12:32 Crewe Basford Hall-Felixstowe	F.Liner 90	Freightliner
14:40	–	4M87		09:46 Felixstowe-Crewe Basford Hall	F.Liner 90	Freightliner
15:05	–	4M93		08:46 Felixstowe-Crewe	F.Liner 70	Freightliner
15:15	–	6H50		12:18 Willesden-Tunstead	F.Liner 66	empty cement tanks
15:35W	–	4M23		10:34 Felixstowe-Hams Hall	GBRf 66	Intermodal
L16:35nc	–	4M67		12:13 Felixstowe-Crewe	F.Liner 66	Freightliner
–	17:10	6L48		13:36 Garston-Dagenham	GBRf 66	car carriers
L18c30nc	–	6M89		13:39 Middleton Towers-Warrington Arpley	EWS 66	sand(in box wagons)
19:40	–	4M41	(Q)	13:57 London Gateway-Crewe Basford Hall	F.Liner 70	Freightliner

Sundays:

North	South	H'code	Runs	Train	Traction	Type of train
–	11:05	6038	(Q)	08:58 Halewood-Southampton E.Docks	EWS 66	loaded car carriers
19:10	–	4Z45		18:39 Daventry-Coatbridge	F.Liner 70	Intermodal
–	20:05	4Z55		14:05 Coatbridge-Daventry	F.Liner 70	Intermodal
–	21:05	4M48		14:43 Mossend-Daventry	2 DRS 66s	'Tesco Express'
21:40	–	4S49		21:16 Daventry-Grangemouth	EWS 66	Intermodal

[24 hour]

Mondays-Fridays:

North	South	H'code	Runs	Train	Traction	Type of train
06:25	-	4S43		06:16 Daventry-Mossend	2 DRS 66s	'Tesco Express'
06:35	-	4M83	WFO	02:59 London Gateway-Trafford Park	EWS 66	Intermodal
-	06:45	1M16		20:44 Inverness-Euston	F.Liner 90	Caledonian Sleeper
-	07c05	6M76	FO	21:46(Thurs) Mossend-Wembley	2 EWS 90s	empty china clay tanks
07:15	-	6X41	MO	03:30 Dagenham-Garston	GBRf 66	Ford cars
07:15	-	6S94	WO	02:21 Dollands Moor-Irvine	2 EWS 90s	loaded china clay tanks
-	07c35	4L37	MO	06:24 Lawley Street-Felixstowe	F.Liner 66	Freightliner
-	07c35	4L41	MX	06:04 Crewe Basford Hall-Felixstowe	F.Liner 66	Freightliner
-	08:05	4Z55	MX	00:54 Coatbridge-Daventry	F.Liner 70	Intermodal
-	08c20	6Z15	WO-Q	01:01 Dowlow-Bow East	EWS 66	loaded box wagons
08:20	-	4M45	MX	02:50 Felixstowe-Ditton	F.Liner 90	Freightliner
08:20	-	6M46	MO	04:54 Ripple Lane-Peak Forest	EWS 66	empty bogie boxes
08:35	-	4V38		08:20 Daventry-Wentloog	DRS 66	'Tesco Express'
08:50	-	4M21	MX	03:10 Felixstowe-Trafford Park	GBRf 66	Intermodal
-	08:50	4L89	MO	07:18 Crewe-Felixstowe	F.Liner 70	Freightliner
09:00C	-	4M86		03:00 Felixstowe-Lawley Street	F.Liner 66	Freightliner
-	09:50	4L97	MX	05:01 Trafford Park-Felixstowe	F.Liner 70	Freightliner
10:00C	-	4M07	MX	04:18 Felixstowe-Burton on Trent	EWS 66	Intermodal
10c55	-	6M11	WO-Q	03:30 Theale-Dowlow	EWS 66	empty box wagons
-	11:05	4L93	MX	10:08 Lawley Street-Felixstowe	F.Liner 66	Freightliner
11:55C	-	6Z77	WFX-Q	09:42 Willesden ET-Stud Farm	F.Liner 66	empty ballast
12:20	-	4Z44		12:13 Daventry-Coatbridge	F.Liner 70	Intermodal
12:35	-	6X43	TO	09:45 Dagenham-Garston	GBRf 92	Ford cars
12:55	-	4M94		07:39 Felixstowe-Lawley Street	F.Liner 66	Freightliner
-	13:20	4Z27		05:25 Coatbridge-Daventry	F.Liner 70	Intermodal
-	14:15	4M25		06:06 Mossend-Daventry	2 EWS 90s	Intermodal
14:25	-	4M63		09:12 Felixstowe-Ditton	F.Liner 90	Freightliner
-	15:15	4L90	MO	11:17 Trafford Park-Felixstowe	F.Liner 90	Freightliner
15:35	-	4M23		10:46 Felixstowe-Hams Hall	GBRf 66	Intermodal
-	15:35	4L90	MX	12:30 Crewe Basford Hall-Felixstowe	F.Liner 90	Freightliner
-	16:05	6Z11	MFO-Q	10:00 Dowlow-Southampton	EWS 66	loaded box wagons
-	16:05	6V11	TWO-Q	10:00 Dowlow-Theale	EWS 66	loaded box wagons
-	16:05	6Z11	ThO-Q	09:35 Dowlow-Bow East	EWS 66	loaded box wagons
-	16:10	6B30	TWFO	12:55 Mountsorrel-Northampton	EWS 66	loaded box wagons
16:25	-	4M88		09:32 Felixstowe-Crewe Basford Hall	F.Liner 90	Freightliner
16:50	-	4M87		11:13 Felixstowe-Trafford Park	2 F.Liner 86s	Freightliner
-	17c05	4L92		14:03 Ditton-Felixstowe	F.Liner 70	Freightliner
-	17:10	4L18		14:18 Trafford Park-Felixstowe	GBRf 66	Intermodal
-	17c35	4L56	MWFO	13:17 Trafford Park-London Gateway	EWS 66	Intermodal
17:50	-	1S96		16:22 Willesden PRDC-Shieldmuir	-	Mail(325 units)
-	18:30	1A91		17:00 Warrington RMT-Willesden PRDC	-	Mail(325 units)
18:30	-	4M93	MX	13:34 Felixstowe-Lawley Street	F.Liner 70	Freightliner
18:50	-	4Z45		18:39 Daventry-Coatbridge	F.Liner 70	Intermodal

'Route knowledge': **(blank)** = Trent Valley (Rugby to Stafford); **C**=to/from Coventry line

North	South	H'code	Runs	Train	Traction	Type of train
-	19:10	6L48		15:49 Garston-Dagenham	GBRf 92	car carriers
19:25	-	4S47		19:13 Daventry-Mossend	2 EWS 90s	Intermodal
19:40	-	4M93	MO	14:32 Felixstowe-Lawley Street	F.Liner 70	Freightliner
-	19:50	4L73	FO	18:30 Lawley Street-Felixstowe	F.Liner 66	Freightliner
-	20:00	4L96	FO	16:18 Trafford Park-Felixstowe	F.Liner 66	Freightliner
-	20c40	4L43		19:35 Lawley Street-Tilbury	F.Liner 66	Freightliner
21:00	-	6Z14	TO-Q	14:48 Southampton up yard-Dowlow	EWS 66	empty box wagons
-	21:10	1A97		19:18 Warrington RMT-Willesden PRDC	-	Mail(325 units)
-	C21:55	6Z79	WFX-Q	18:45 Stud Farm-Willesden ET	F.Liner 66	loaded ballast
22:00	-	4S83		17:35 London Gateway-Coatbridge	F.Liner 70	Freightliner
22:05	-	4S49		21:58 Daventry-Grangemouth	EWS 66	Intermodal
-	22:05	4L71		18:41 Ditton-Felixstowe	F.Liner 90	Freightliner
-	22c25	4L60		19:46 Garston-Felixstowe	F.Liner 66	Freightliner
22:25	-	1S25		21:15 Euston-Inverness	F.Liner 66	Caledonian Sleeper
22:30	-	4M02		17:34 Felixstowe-Hams Hall	GBRf 66	Intermodal
22:45	-	4S88		16:13 Felixstowe-Coatbridge	F.Liner 90	Freightliner
22:50	-	6M95	ThO-Q	16:35 Dungeness p.s.-Crewe	2 DRS 37s	flask(s)
23:00C	-	6D30	TWFO	22:37 Northampton-Mountsorrel	EWS 66	empty box wagons
23c15	-	4M92		18:13 Felixstowe-Lawley Street	F.Liner 66	Freightliner
-	C23:15	4M36		18:58 Wentloog-Daventry	DRS 66	'Tesco Express'
-	23:20	4L28		22:35 Hams Hall-Felixstowe	GBRf 66	Intermodal
-	23c35	6016	MWFO	20:21 Dollands Moor	EWS 66	empty cargowagons
-	00:05	4L77	SO	23:03(Fri) Lawley Street-Felixstowe	F.Liner 66	Freightliner
00c20	-	4M89		14:33(14:46 Mon) Felixstowe-Ditton	F.Liner 66	Freightliner
00c25	-	4M60		20:42 Tilbury-Garston	F.Liner 70	Freightliner
-	01:10	4L25	FX-Q	22:18 Trafford Park-London Gateway	EWS 66	Intermodal
-	01c15	4L80		21:53 Garston-Tilbury	F.Liner 70	Freightliner
-	01:20	4L82		21:30 Ditton-Felixstowe	F.Liner 66	Freightliner
01:20	-	1S26		23:50 Euston-Glasgow Central	F.Liner 90	Caledonian Sleeper
01c35	-	4M53		20:46 Felixstowe-Trafford Park	F.Liner 90	Freightliner
-	01:35	4M48		19:04 Mossend-Daventry	2 DRS 66s	'Tesco Express'
01:50	-	1F04		00:22 Willesden PRDC-Warrington RMT	-	Mail(325 units)
-	02:00	6L47	WO	22:03(Tue) Garston-Dagenham	GBRf 92	empty car carriers
-	02c15	4L69		01:06 Lawley Street-Felixstowe North	F.Liner 70	Freightliner
-	02:30	6V56	WSO	21:30 Peak Forest-Acton yard	EWS 66	loaded Cemex hoppers
-	02c40	4L81		19:26 Coatbridge-London Gateway	F.Liner 70	Freightliner
02:40	-	4M73		21:41 Felixstowe-Ditton	F.Liner 66	Freightliner
02:45	-	4M59		21:31 Felixstowe-Ditton	F.Liner 66	Freightliner
03c00	-	4M42		22:08 Felixstowe-Garston	F.Liner 70	Freightliner
03:05	-	6X41		00:32 Dagenham-Garston	GBRf 92	Ford cars
-	03:10	6A50	SO	22:57 Tunstead-Willesden	F.Liner 66	loaded cement tanks
-	03:15	4L95		22:50 Ditton-Felixstowe	F.Liner 66	Freightliner
-	03:45	6062	ThO-Q	02:08 Crewe-Dungeness p.s.	2 DRS 37s	flask(s)
-	03:55	4M30		19:10 Grangemouth-Daventry	EWS 66	Intermodal
03c55	-	6M14	WFO	00:12 Dollands Moor-Ditton	EWS 66	aluminium(cargowagons)
04:00	-	4M72		00:57 Tilbury-Lawley Street	F.Liner 66	Freightliner
04c05	-	6Z12	ThFO	23:56 Bow East-Dowlow	EWS 66	empty box wagons
-	04c05	6B10	WFO	23:03 Peak Forest-Bletchley	EWS 66	loaded Cemex hoppers
-	04:05	4L89	SO	22:01(Fri) Coatbridge-Felixstowe	2 F.Liner 86s	Freightliner
-	04:45	4L91	SX	02:12 Trafford Park-Felixstowe	F.Liner 90	Freightliner
-	05:25	1M11		23:40 Glasgow Central-Euston	F.Liner 90	Caledonian Sleeper
-	05:35	4L89	SX	22:01 Coatbridge-Felixstowe	2 F.Liner 86s	Freightliner

Saturdays:

North	South	H'code	Runs	Train		Traction	Type of train
-	06c15	6B10		02:19	Peak Forest-Bletchley stone term.	EWS 66	loaded bogie hoppers
06:45	-	4S43		06:40	Daventry-Mossend	2 DRS 66s	'Tesco Express'
-	06:45	1M16		20:44(Fri)	Inverness-Euston	class 90	Caledonian Sleeper
07:30C	-	4M07		02:27	Felixstowe-Burton on Trent	EWS 66	Intermodal
-	07:40	4Z55		00:55	Coatbridge-Daventry	F.Liner 70	Intermodal
-	08:00	4L97		04:57	Trafford Park-Felixstowe	F.Liner 70	Freightliner
08:25	-	4M45		02:57	Felixstowe-Ditton	F.Liner 90	Freightliner
08:40	-	4M88		04:25	Felixstowe-Lawley Street	F.Liner 66	Freightliner
08:45	-	4M21		03:15	Felixstowe-Trafford Park	GBRf 66	Intermodal
-	10:05	4L93		08:21	Crewe Basford Hall-Felixstowe	F.Liner 66	Freightliner
-	10c10	4L90		08:30	Lawley Street-Felixstowe	F.Liner 66	Freightliner
11:20	-	4S49		11:12	Daventry-Grangemouth	EWS 66	Intermodal
12:10	-	4Z44		12:05	Daventry-Coatbridge	F.Liner 70	Intermodal
13:10	-	4M34		11:04	Acton yard-Peak Forest	EWS 66	empty bogie hoppers
-	13:20	4Z27		05:25	Coatbridge-Daventry	F.Liner 70	Intermodal
14:25	-	4M87		09:46	Felixstowe-Crewe Basford Hall	F.Liner 90	Freightliner
14c30	-	6H50		12:18	Willesden-Tunstead	F.Liner 66	empty cement tanks
-	14c30	4L96		12:32	Crewe Basford Hall-Felixstowe	F.Liner 90	Freightliner
14:50	-	4M93		08:46	Felixstowe-Crewe	F.Liner 70	Freightliner
15:00	-	4M23		10:34	Felixstowe-Hams Hall	GBRf 66	Intermodal
15:55C	-	4M20		10:14	Felixstowe-Lawley Street	F.Liner 66	Freightliner
-	17:30	6L48		13:36	Garston-Dagenham	GBRf 66	car carriers
19:05	-	4M41	(Q)	13:57	London Gateway-Crewe Basford Hall	F.Liner 70	Freightliner
-	C23:25	4M30		10:15	Grangemouth-Daventry	EWS 66	Intermodal

Sundays:

North	South	H'code	Runs	Train		Traction	Type of train
09:15C	-	4V38	(Q)	09:06	Daventry-Wentloog	DRS 66	'Tesco Express'
-	11c30	6O38	(Q)	08:58	Halewood-Southampton E.Docks	EWS 66	loaded car carriers
18:50	-	4Z45		18:39	Daventry-Coatbridge	F.Liner 70	Intermodal
-	20:35	4Z55		14:05	Coatbridge-Daventry	F.Liner 70	Intermodal
-	C21:00	4M36		17:00	Wentloog-Daventry	DRS 66	'Tesco Express'
-	21:25	4M48		14:43	Mossend-Daventry	2 DRS 66s	'Tesco Express'
21:25	-	4S49		21:16	Daventry-Grangemouth	EWS 66	Intermodal
22:25	-	1S25		20:57	Euston-Inverness	F.Liner 90	Caledonian Sleeper

WATER ORTON

[24-hour]

Mondays-Fridays:

West	East	H'code	Runs	Train	Traction	Type of train
-	06:45W	4L37	MO	06:24 Lawley Street-Felixstowe	F.Liner 66	Freightliner
-	06:45W	6M70	WO-Q	02:54 Cardiff Tidal-Kingsbury	EWS 66	empty box wagons
07:05W	-	6V80	MFX-Q	22:56 Gasgoigne Wood-Portbury	GBRf 66	gypsum(in box wagons)
-	07:10W	4E01	MO	03:22 Southampton Maritime-Leeds	F.Liner 66	Freightliner
-	07:15W	6M03	MWFO	21:00 Robeston-Bedworth	EWS 66	loaded bogie tanks
07:20W	-	4043	MX	06:43 Birch Coppice-Southampton	EWS 66	Intermodal
-	07:45W	4M69	MX	02:35 Southampton-Burton on Trent	EWS 66	Intermodal
07:45W	-	4015	MX	07:43 Hams Hall-Southampton	F.Liner 66	Freightliner
07:50W	-	4G30	ThO-Q	05:59 Wellingborough-Washwood Heath	GBRf 66	Departmental
-	07:50W	4018	MO	07:24 Lawley Street-Southampton	F.Liner 66	Freightliner
08:45W	-	6V35	MO-Q	04:50 Rotherham-Cardiff Tidal	EWS 66	empty box wagons
09:15W	-	4V38		08:20 Daventry-Wentloog	DRS 66	'Tesco Express'
09:45W	-	4090		06:12 Leeds-Southampton	F.Liner 66/70	Freightliner
09:55W	-	4M86		03:00 Felixstowe-Lawley Street	F.Liner 66	Freightliner
-	S09:55W	4E12	MTX-Q	04:02 London Gateway-Rotherham S.T.	EWS 66	Intermodal
-	10:20W	4L93	MX	10:08 Lawley Street-Felixstowe	F.Liner 66	Freightliner
-	10:50W	4L93	MO	10:34 Lawley Street-Felixstowe	F.Liner 66	Freightliner
-	10:45	4M11	MWFO	10:00 Washwood Heath-Peak Forest	EWS 66	empty bogie hoppers
-	11:20	4M11	TThO	10:42 Washwood Heath-Peak Forest	EWS 66	empty bogie hoppers
11:30W	-	4048	MO	11:26 Hams Hall-Southampton	F.Liner 66	Freightliner
-	S11:50W	6D44		11:09 Bescot E.S.-Toton	EWS 66	Departmental
-	12:10W	6M31	TO-Q	10:42 Banbury-Mountsorrel	EWS 66	empty box wagons
-	S12:20	4D76	MO	11:38 Bescot yard-Burton on Trent	EWS 66	Intermodal
-	S12:20	4M07	MX	04:18 Felixstowe-Burton on Trent	EWS 66	Intermodal
S12:20	-	4L07		11:38 Burton on Trent-Felixstowe	EWS 66	Intermodal
-	12:35W	4F30	ThO-Q	11:30 Washwood Heath-Wellingborough	GBRf 66	Departmental
-	12:35W	6M96	FO-Q	05:51 Margam-Corby	EWS 66	loaded steel(coil)
12:50W	-	6V92		10:22 Corby-Margam	EWS 66	empty steel
-	S13:15	6M82	FX-Q	12:41 Walsall-Dowlow	EWS 66	empty box wagons
S13:20W	-	6G16	WX-Q	11:24 Stud Farm-Bescot VQ	GBRf 66	loaded ballast boxes
S13:35	-	6G65	(Q)	09:19 Earles-Walsall	F.Liner 66	loaded cement tanks
-	S13:40W	6Z77	WFX-Q	09:42 Willesden ET-Stud Farm	F.Liner 66	empty ballast
-	13:45	6Z34	TO-Q	09:46 Cardiff Tidal-Chaddesden(Derby)	DCR 56	empty box wagons
13:45W	-	6V16	WO-Q	11:24 Stud Farm-Hinksey VQ	GBRf 66	loaded ballast boxes
-	S14:15W	6E08	MThO	13:03 Wolverhampton S.T.-Immingham	EWS 60	empty steel
14:15W	-	4M94		07:39 Felixstowe-Lawley Street	F.Liner 66	Freightliner
14:20W	-	6X01	TThO	10:17 Scunthorpe-Eastleigh	EWS 66	loaded rails
-	14:50	4E69	TFO	09:32 Southampton-Wakefield Europort	EWS 66	Intermodal
-	14:50	4Z69	MThO	09:32 Southampton-Rotherham S.T.	EWS 66	Intermodal
S15:10W	-	6M50	FX	07:55 Westbury VQ-Bescot VQ	Colas 70	Departmental
-	S15:10W	4L07		11:38 Burton on Trent-Felixstowe	EWS 66	Intermodal
-	S15:15	6E08	TWFO	13:03 Wolverhampton-Immingham	EWS 60	empty steel
-	S15:25W	6Z96	(Q)	14:40 Bescot E.S.-Toton	DRS 66/68	Departmental
-	15:35W	6M26	(Q)	08:50 Eastleigh VQ-Mountsorrel	GBRf 66	empty ballast wagons
-	15:50	6E07		14:50 Washwood Heath-Boston	Colas 56	covered steel carriers
15:45W	-	4M18	MWFOQ	09:47 Fairwater yard-Washwood Heath	F.Liner 66	Departmental
-	16:10W	4017		15:48 Lawley Street-Southampton	F.Liner 66	Freightliner
-	S16:15	6E79	W/ThO	15:02 Wolverhampton-Rotherham S.T.	EWS 66	empty steel

'Route knowledge':   (blank) =Main Line (Washwood Heath to Tamworth and v.v.);
S=to/from Sutton Park line; W=to/from Whitacre Junction.

West	East	H'code	Runs	Train	Traction	Type of train
-	16:25W	6M40		11:56 Westbury-Stud Farm	GBRf 66	empty ballast boxes
16:35	-	4095	MX	12:12 Leeds-Southampton	F.Liner 66/70	Freightliner
-	17:25	1Z21	FO-Q	13:30 Paddington-Derby RTC	HST	measurement train
17:30	-	1Z16	ThO-Q	16:43 Derby Etches Park-Paddington	HST	measurement train
17:40W	-	4076		17:01 Burton on Trent-Southampton	EWS 66	Intermodal
S17:50W	-	4L10	MTX-Q	15:18 Rotherham S.T.-London Gateway	EWS 66	Intermodal
18:15W	-	6V55	MWFO	16:08(15:30 Fri) Bedworth-Robeston	EWS 66	empty bogie tanks
18:35	-	6M35	FX-Q	11:10 Rylstone-Small Heath	GBRf 66	loaded bogie boxes
S18:40W	-	6G45		16:53 Toton-Bescot E.S.	EWS 66	Departmental
19:10W	-	7X09	WO-Q	11:47 Old Dalby-West Ruislip	4 GBRf 20s	LUL tube stock
-	19:10W	4L73		18:30 Lawley Street-Felixstowe	F.Liner 66	Freightliner
19:20W	-	4M93	MX	13:34 Felixstowe-Lawley Street	F.Liner 70	Freightliner
-	19:50W	4L43		19:35 Lawley Street-Tilbury	F.Liner 66	Freightliner
S20:15W	-	6Z79	WFX-Q	18:45 Stud Farm-Willesden ET	F.Liner 66	loaded ballast
20:25W	-	4M93	MO	14:32 Felixstowe-Lawley Street	F.Liner 70	Freightliner
20:35W	-	6V04	WO-Q	19:59 Kingsbury-Cardiff Tidal	EWS 66	scrap(in bogie boxes)
20:35W	-	6V80	FO-Q	14:08 Gascoigne Wood-Portbury	GBRf 66	gypsum(in box wagons)
20:50W	-	6V81	WFO	18:32 Rotherham-Cardiff Tidal	EWS 66	scrap(in bogie boxes)
20:50W	-	6V35	MO-Q	17:44 Rotherham-Cardiff Tidal	EWS 66	empty steel
-	21:25W	6E81	MFX-Q	17:00 Portbury-West Burton	GBRf 66	empty box wagons
-	S21:35	6H66	(Q)	20:55 Walsall-Earles sidings	F.Liner 66	empty cement tanks
21:50W	-	6027	(Q)	20:38 Mountsorrel-Eastleigh VQ	GBRf 66	ballast(in box wagons)
-	21:50W	4M66		16:40 Southampton-Birch Coppice	EWS 66	Intermodal
22:10W	-	6V93	FO-Q	20:06 Corby-Margam	EWS 66	empty steel
22:30W	-	4052	WO	18:27 Wakefield Europort-Southampton	EWS 66	Intermodal
-	22:40	6E30	FX	16:21 Margam-Hartlepool	EWS 66	loaded steel(coil)
-	22:50	4E76		19:02 Southampton Millbrook-Leeds	F.Liner 66/70	Freightliner
23:05	-	4Z52	MThO	20:15 Rotherham S.T.-Southampton	EWS 66	Intermodal
-	23:15W	4L58	FX	23:03 Lawley Street-Felixstowe	F.Liner 66	Freightliner
-	23:15W	4L77	FO	23:03 Lawley Street-Felixstowe	F.Liner 66	Freightliner
23:20W	-	6M08		20:16 Boston-Washwood Heath	Colas 56	steel(in covered wagons)
23:35	-	4007		20:18 Leeds-Southampton	F.Liner 66	Freightliner
-	23:50	6E35	W/ThO	17:58 Cardiff Docks-Port Clarence	GBRf 66	empty bogie tanks
-	23:55	6E09	TO-Q	13:54 Onllwyn-Immingham	EWS 66	loaded EWS coal hoppers
23:55	-	6V02		18:37 Tees yard-Margam	EWS 66	empty steel/lime
00:00W	-	4M92		18:13 Felixstowe-Lawley Street	F.Liner 66	Freightliner
00:05W	-	6V14		22:33 Stud Farm-Westbury VQ	GBRf 66	ballast(in box wagons)
00:10	-	6V19	FSO	17:22 Immingham-Llanwern	EWS 66	steel/empties
-	00:15	6E03	ThO-Q	18:09 Appleford-Milford	EWS 66	empty flyash containers
-	S00:25W	6D30	WThSO	22:37 Northampton-Mountsorrel	EWS 66	empty self-dis.train
-	00:30	6E15	ThX-Q	21:06 Eastleigh yard-Scunthorpe	EWS 66	empty rail carriers
-	00:55	6E47	WFO	19:09 Margam-Middlesborough Goods	EWS 66	loaded steel
-	01:20W	4L69		01:06 Lawley Street-Felixstowe	F.Liner 70	Freightliner
01:25	-	6V85	FO-Q	22:11 Milford-Appleford	EWS 66	containerised flyash
02:10	-	6V00	WO-Q	19:30 Port Clarence-Cardiff Docks	GBRf 66	loaded bogie tanks
-	02:15	6E20	TSO	23:08 Llanwern-Immingham	EWS 66	loaded/empty steel
02:50	-	6V49	TThSO	19:34 Tees yard-Margam	EWS 66	empty steel
-	02:55	6E80	MWFO	23:20 Cardiff Tidal-Rotherham	EWS 66	empty bogie boxes
S03:05	-	6M99		20:53 Immingham-Wolverhampton S.T.	EWS 66	loaded steel
03:15W	-	6G32	TO-Q	02:07 Moutsorrel-Banbury	EWS 66	loaded box wagons
-	03:30	4E48		23:01 Southampton Maritime-Leeds	F.Liner 66/70	Freightliner
-	04:10W	4018		03:50 Lawley Street-Southampton	F.Liner 66	Freightliner
-	04:35W	6M94	SX	22:44 Margam-Corby	EWS 66	loaded steel(coil)
04:40W	-	6M10	SX	01:15 Peak Forest-Washwood Heath	EWS 66	loaded bogie hoppers
04:45W	-	4M72		00:57 Tilbury-Lawley Street	F.Liner 66	Freightliner
-	S05:35W	6F16	WX-Q	04:58 Bescot VQ-Stud Farm	GBRf 66	empty ballast boxes
-	05:35W	6M27	WO-Q	03:39 Hinksey VQ-Stud Farm	GBRf 66	empty ballast boxes
S05:40	-	6M09	FX	23:24 Dowlow-Walsall	EWS 66	loaded box wagons
-	05:45	4E01	SX	01:30 Millbrook-Leeds	F.Liner 66	Freightliner

Saturdays:

West	East	H'code	Runs	Train		Traction	Type of train
07:00	-	4O43		06:31 Birch Coppice-Eastleigh yard		EWS 66	Intermodal
S07:05W	-	4M07		02:47 Felixstowe-Burton on Trent		EWS 66	Intermodal
07:10W	-	4O14		07:37 Hams Hall-Southampton		F.Liner 66	Freightliner
-	08:10W	4M69		02:52 Southampton-Burton on Trent		EWS 66	Intermodal
08:50	-	4O54		05:27 Leeds-Southampton		F.Liner 66	Freightliner
09:20W	-	4M88		04:25 Felixstowe-Lawley Street		F.Liner 66	Freightliner
-	09:20W	4L90		08:30 Lawley Street-Felixstowe		F.Liner 66	Freightliner
-	09:45	6E89		05:00 Portbury-Doncaster Hexthorpe		GBRf 66	empty box wagons
-	S10:10W	4M07		02:27 Felixstowe-Burton on Trent		EWS 66	Intermodal
S11:50	-	4G76		11:21 Burton on Trent-Bescot yard		EWS 66	Intermodal
-	S12:45	6H64		12:07 Walsall-Dowlow		EWS 66	empty box wagons
19:40W	-	6V29	(Q)	16:35 Lincoln Terrace-Cardiff Tidal		EWS 66	scrap(in bogie boxes)
20:35	-	4V52	(Q)	09:31 Wakefield Europort-Didcot yard		EWS 66	Intermodal

Sundays:

West	East	H'code	Runs	Train		Traction	Type of train
-	19:45	6E47		13:45 Margam-Middlesbrough		EWS 66	loaded steel
-	22:30	6E30	(Q)	14:54 Margam-Hartlepool		EWS 66	loaded steel(coil)

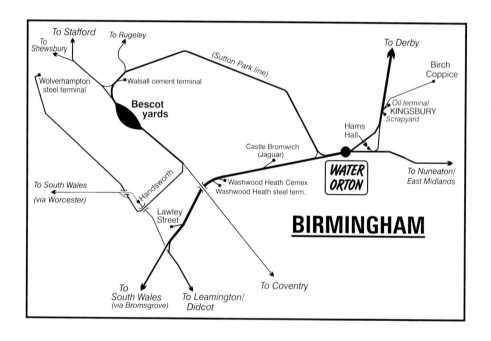

TAMWORTH
(High Level)

[06:00-21:00]

Mondays-Fridays:

South	North	H'code	Runs	Train	Traction	Type of train
-	07:25	4E01	MO	03:22 Southampton Maritime-Leeds	F.Liner 66	Freightliner
-	08:05	4M69	MX	02:35 Southampton-Burton on Trent	EWS 66	Intermodal
09:25	-	4O90		06:12 Leeds-Southampton	F.Liner 66/70	Freightliner
-	10:25	4E12	FO-Q	04:02 London Gateway-Rotherham S.T.	EWS 66	Intermodal
-	11:00	4M11	MWFO	10:00 Washwood Heath-Peak Forest	EWS 66	empty HTA hoppers
-	11:30	4M11	TThO	10:42 Washwood Heath-Peak Forest	EWS 66	empty HTA hoppers
12:00	-	4L07		11:38 Burton on Trent-Felixstowe	EWS 66	Intermodal
-	12:00	6E54		10:39 Kingsbury-Humber	EWS 60	empty bogie tanks
12:25	-	6M57		07:15 Lindsey-Kingsbury	EWS 60	loaded bogie tanks
-	12:25	6D44		11:09 Bescot-Toton	EWS 66	Departmental
-	12:35	4M07	MX	04:18 Felixstowe-Burton on Trent	EWS 66	Intermodal
-	12:35	4D76	MO	11:38 Bescot yard-Burton on Trent	EWS 66	Intermodal
-	12:50	6M96	FO-Q	05:51 Margam-Corby	EWS 66	loaded steel(coil)
13:20	-	6G65	(Q)	09:19 Earles-Walsall	F.Liner 66	loaded cement tanks
-	13:25	6M82	FX-Q	12:41 Walsall-Dowlow	EWS 66	empty box wagons
-	13:55	6Z34	TO-Q	09:46 Cardiff Tidal-Chaddesden(Derby)	DCR 66	empty box wagons
-	13:55	1Z20	FO-Q	10:09 Swansea-Derby RTC	HST	measurement train
13:55	-	6X01	TThO	10:17 Scunthorpe-Eastleigh	EWS 66	loaded rails
-	14:25	6E08	MThO	13:03 Wolverhampton S.T.-Immingham	EWS 60	empty steel
-	15:05	4Z69	MThO	09:32 Southampton-Rotherham S.T.	EWS 66	Intermodal
-	15:05	4E69	TFO	09:32 Southampton-Wakefield Europort	EWS 66	Intermodal
-	15:25	6E08	TWFO	13:03 Wolverhampton-Immingham	EWS 60	empty steel
-	15:30	6Z96	(Q)	14:40 Bescot VQ-Toton	DRS 66/68	Departmental
-	15:55	6E07		14:50 Washwood Heath-Boston	Colas 56	covered steel carriers
16:20	-	4O95	MX	12:12 Leeds-Southampton	F.Liner 66/70	Freightliner
-	16:30	6E79	W/ThO	15:02 Wolverhampton-Rotherham S.T.	EWS 66	empty steel
17:20	-	4O76		17:01 Burton on Trent-Southampton	EWS 66	Intermodal
17:25	-	4L10	FO-Q	15:18 Rotherham S.T.-London Gateway	EWS 66	Intermodal
18:20	-	6G45		16:53 Toton-Bescot	EWS 66	Departmental
18:25	-	6M35	FX-Q	11:10 Rylstone-Small Heath	GBRf 66	loaded bogie boxes
18:25	-	7X09	WO-Q	11:47 Old Dalby-West Ruislip	4 GBRf 20s	LUL tube stock
-	19:00	6E59		17:41 Kingsbury-Lindsey	EWS 60	empty bogie tanks
19:20	-	6M00		14:30 Humber-Kingsbury	EWS 60	loaded bogie tanks
20:00	-	6V80	FO-Q	14:08 Gascoigne Wood-Portbury	GBRf 66	gypsum(in box wagons)
20:25	-	6V35	MO-Q	17:44 Rotherham-Cardiff Tidal	EWS 66	empty steel
20:25	-	6V81	WFO	18:32 Rotherham-Cardiff Tidal	EWS 66	scrap(in bogie boxes)

Saturdays:

South	North	H'code	Runs	Train	Traction	Type of train
-	08:25	4M69		02:52 Southampton-Burton on Trent	EWS 66	Intermodal
08:40	-	4O54		05:27 Leeds-Southampton	F.Liner 66	Freightliner
-	09:55	6E89		05:00 Portbury-Doncaster Hexthorpe	GBRf 66	empty box wagons
-	10:55	4M07		02:27 Felixstowe-Burton on Trent	EWS 66	Intermodal
11:40	-	4O76		11:21 Burton on Trent-Bescot yard	EWS 66	Intermodal
-	12:05	6E54		10:40 Kingsbury-Humber	EWS 60	empty bogie tanks
12:20	-	6M57		07:15 Lindsey-Kingsbury	EWS 60	loaded bogie tanks
-	12:55	6H64		12:07 Walsall-Dowlow	EWS 66	empty box wagons
-	17:05	6E59		15:41 Kingsbury-Lindsey	EWS 60	empty bogie tanks
19:20	-	6M00		14:22 Humber-Kingsbury	EWS 60	loaded bogie tanks
19:25	-	6V29	(Q)	16:35 Lincoln Terrace-Cardiff Tidal	EWS 66	scrap(in bogie boxes)
20:20	-	4V52	(Q)	09:31 Wakefield Europort-Didcot yard	EWS 66	Intermodal

Saturdays:

South	North	H'code	Runs	Train	Traction	Type of train
-	11:35	6E68	(Q)	10:12 Kingsbury-Humber	EWS 60	empty bogie tanks
17:25	-	6M57	(Q)	11:06 Lindsey-Kingsbury	EWS 60	loaded bogie tanks
-	19:55	6E47		13:45 Margam-Middlesbrough	EWS 66	loaded steel

TAMWORTH
(Low Level)
[06:00-23:00]

Mondays-Fridays:

West	East	H'code	Runs	Train		Traction	Type of train
-	06:20	1M16		20:44	Inverness-Euston	class 90	Caledonian Sleeper
06:55	-	4S43		06:16	Daventry-Mossend	2 DRS 66s	'Tesco Express'
-	07:00	4L41	MX	06:04	Crewe Basford Hall-Felixstowe	F.Liner 66	Freightliner
07:20	-	4M83	WFO	02:59	London Gateway-Trafford Park	EWS 66	Intermodal
-	07:25	4Z55	MX	00:54	Coatbridge-Daventry	F.Liner 70	Intermodal
-	07:40	6Z15	WO-Q	01:01	Dowlow-Bow East	EWS 66	loaded box wagons
07:50	-	6S94	WO-Q	02:21	Dollands Moor-Irvine	2 EWS 90s	loaded china clay tanks
07:50	-	6X41	MO	03:30	Dagenham-Garston	GBRf 66	Ford cars
-	07:55	4O14	MX	05:36	Garston-Southampton	F.Liner 70	Freightliner
-	08:20	4L89	MO	07:18	Crewe-Felixstowe	F.Liner 70	Freightliner
08:55	-	4M45	MX	02:50	Felixstowe-Ditton	F.Liner 90	Freightliner
08:55	-	6M46	MO	04:54	Ripple Lane-Peak Forest	EWS 66	empty bogie boxes
09:20	-	6M44	MO	04:50	Southampton E.Docks-Halewood	EWS 66	empty car carriers
09:20	-	4M21	MX	03:10	Felixstowe-Trafford Park	GBRf 66	Intermodal
-	09:20	4L97	MX	05:01	Trafford Park-Felixstowe	F.Liner 70	Freightliner
-	09:55	6U76		08:59	Crewe Basford Hall-Mountsorrel	DRS 66/68	empty ballast boxes
-	10:30	4O49	MX	09:22	Crewe Basford Hall-Southampton	F.Liner 66/70	Freightliner
-	11:30	4O21		09:15	Trafford Park-Southampton	EWS 66	Intermodal
12:05	-	6M11	WO-Q	03:30	Theale-Dowlow	EWS 66	empty box wagons
12:50	-	4Z44		12:13	Daventry-Coatbridge	F.Liner 70	Intermodal
-	12:50	4Z27		05:25	Coatbridge-Daventry	F.Liner 70	Intermodal
13:05	-	6X43	TO	09:45	Dagenham-Garston	GBRf 92	Ford cars
-	13:30	4L90	MX	12:30	Crewe Basford Hall-Felixstowe	F.Liner 90	Freightliner
-	13:45	4M25		06:06	Mossend-Daventry	2 EWS 90s	Intermodal
13:50	-	4M81		08:01	Felixstowe-Crewe	F.Liner 66/70	Freightliner
-	14:00	6O42	(Q)	11:31	Halewood-Southampton E.Docks	EWS 66	loaded car carriers
-	14:35	4L90	MO	11:17	Trafford Park-Felixstowe	F.Liner 90	Freightliner
14:55	-	4M63		09:12	Felixstowe-Ditton	F.Liner 90	Freightliner
-	15:30	6Z11	MFO-Q	10:00	Dowlow-Southampton	EWS 66	loaded box wagons
-	15:30	6V11	TWO-Q	10:00	Dowlow-Theale	EWS 66	loaded box wagons
-	15:30	6Z11	ThO-Q	09:35	Dowlow-Bow East	EWS 66	loaded box wagons
-	15:55	4L56	MWFO	13:17	Trafford Park-London Gateway	EWS 66	Intermodal
-	16:30	4L92		14:03	Ditton-Felixstowe	F.Liner 70	Freightliner
-	16:35	4L18		14:18	Trafford Park-Felixstowe	GBRf 66	Intermodal
16:35	-	4M61		12:54	Southampton-Trafford Park	F.Liner 66/70	Freightliner
16:50	-	4M88		09:32	Felixstowe-Crewe Basford Hall	F.Liner 90	Freightliner
17:20	-	4M87		11:13	Felixstowe-Trafford Park	2 F.Liner 86s	Freightliner
-	18:00	4O29		15:18	Trafford Park-Southampton	F.Liner 66	Freightliner
18:10	-	1S96		16:22	Willesden PRDC-Shieldmuir	-	Mail(325 units)
-	18:20	1A91		17:00	Warrington RMT-Willesden PRDC	-	Mail(325 units)
-	18:35	6L48		15:49	Garston-Dagenham	GBRf 92	car carriers
18:50	-	4M68		13:53	Southampton-Garston	F.Liner 70	Freightliner
19:20	-	4Z45		18:39	Daventry-Coatbridge	F.Liner 70	Intermodal
-	19:25	4L86	FX	16:18	Trafford Park-Felixstowe	F.Liner 66	Freightliner
-	19:25	4L96	FO	16:18	Trafford Park-Felixstowe	F.Liner 66	Freightliner
19:50	-	4S47		19:13	Daventry-Mossend	2 EWS 90s	Intermodal
19:55	-	6M88	TThO	14:35	Middleton Towers-Ellesmere Port	EWS 66	sand(in box wagons)
-	20:45	1A97		19:18	Warrington RMT-Willesden PRDC	-	Mail(325 units)
20:45	-	4M99		16:57	Southampton-Trafford Park	F.Liner 70	Freightliner
-	21:30	4L71		18:41	Ditton-Felixstowe	F.Liner 90	Freightliner
-	21:55	4L60		19:46	Garston-Felixstowe	F.Liner 66	Freightliner
22:30	-	4S83		17:35	London Gateway-Coatbridge	F.Liner 70	Freightliner
22:40	-	4S49		21:58	Daventry-Grangemouth	EWS 66	Intermodal
22:50	-	1S25		21:15	Euston-Inverness	class 90	Caledonian Sleeper

Saturdays:

West	East	H'code	Runs	Train		Traction	Type of train
-	07:05	4Z55		00:55	Coatbridge-Daventry	F.Liner 70	Intermodal
-	07:25	4L97		04:57	Trafford Park-Felixstowe	F.Liner 70	Freightliner
07:25	-	4S43		06:40	Daventry-Mossend	2 DRS 66s	'Tesco Express'
08:55	-	4M45		02:57	Felixstowe-Ditton	F.Liner 90	Freightliner
09:25	-	4M21		03:15	Felixstowe-Trafford Park	GBRf 66	Intermodal
-	09:25	4L93		08:21	Crewe Basford Hall-Felixstowe	F.Liner 66	Freightliner
11:55	-	4S49		11:12	Daventry-Grangemouth	EWS 66	Intermodal
12:45	-	4Z44		12:05	Daventry-Coatbridge	F.Liner 70	Intermodal
-	12:50	4Z27		05:25	Coatbridge-Daventry	F.Liner 70	Intermodal
-	13:35	4L96		12:32	Crewe Basford Hall-Felixstowe	F.Liner 90	Freightliner
13:35	-	6M48		09:28	Southampton E.Docks-Halewood	EWS 66	empty car carriers
13:50	-	4M34		11:04	Acton yard-Peak Forest	EWS 66	empty bogie hoppers
14:50	-	4M87		09:46	Felixstowe-Crewe Basford Hall	F.Liner 90	Freightliner
15:20	-	4M93		08:46	Felixstowe-Crewe Basford Hall	F.Liner 70	Freightliner
15:35	-	6H50		12:18	Willesden-Tunstead	F.Liner 66	empty cement tanks
16:50	-	4M67		12:13	Felixstowe-Crewe	F.Liner 70	Freightliner
-	16:55	6L48		13:36	Garston-Dagenham	GBRf 66	car carriers
18:55	-	6M89		13:39	Middleton Towers-Warrington Arpley	EWS 66	sand(in box wagons)

Sundays:

West	East	H'code	Runs	Train		Traction	Type of train
-	10:50	6O38	(Q)	08:58	Halewood-Southampton E.Docks	EWS 66	loaded car carriers
19:20	-	4Z45		18:39	Daventry-Coatbridge	F.Liner 70	Intermodal
-	20:00	4Z55		14:05	Coatbridge-Daventry	F.Liner 70	Intermodal
-	20:45	4M48		14:43	Mossend-Daventry	2 DRS 66s	'Tesco Express'
21:55	-	4S49		21:16	Daventry-Grangemouth	EWS 66	Intermodal

SHREWSBURY

[06:00-midnight]

Mondays-Fridays:

North	South	H'code	Runs	Train		Traction	Type of train
-	X06:10	6V54	WFO	05:35	Chirk-Baglan Bay	Colas 70	empty timber carriers
06:25X	-	6M76		00:38	Margam-Dee Marsh	EWS 66	loaded steel(coil)
-	X08T10	1V91		05:33	Holyhead-Cardiff	class 67	Passenger
-	09:15T	6G51	ThO-Q	07:46	Warrington Arpley-Donnington	EWS 66	wagons for repair
-	X10:45	6V75		09:30	Dee Marsh-Margam	EWS 66	empty steel
T13:45	-	6F52	ThO-Q	13:15	Donnington-Warrington Arpley	EWS 66	wagons off repair
T15:45	-	6V09	T/ThO	10:51	Tinsley-Shrewsbury Coton Hill	GBRf 66	empty bogie hoppers
16:40X	-	6M86	WO-Q	10:29	Margam-Dee Marsh	EWS 66	loaded steel(coil)
19T09X	-	1W96		17:16	Cardiff-Holyhead	class 67	Passenger
-	20:00T	6Z35	T/ThO	19:56	Coton Hill-Tinsley	GBRf 66	loaded bogie hoppers
21:55	-	6M51	TThO	17:19	Baglan Bay-Chirk	Colas 70	loaded timber carriers
22:45	-	6X52	TThO	17:33	Portbury-Mossend	EWS 66	wagonload
-	X23:00T	6C37		22:25	Chirk-Carlisle yard	Colas 60	empty timber carriers
-	23:30	6V71	MWFO	18:26	Hardendale-Margam	EWS 66	containerised lime

Saturdays & Sundays: NO BOOKED TRAINS

'Route Knowledge':   (blank) = to/from Crewe;
                      X = to/from Wrexham;
                      T = to/from Telford

LEAMINGTON SPA

[06:00 - midnight]

Mondays-Fridays:

North	South	H'code	Runs	Train	Traction	Type of train
-	07T24	1H15		06:09 Kidderminster-London Marylebone	DRS 68	Passenger
-	07T44	1H17		06:38 Stourbridge Junc.-London Marylebone	DRS 68	Passenger
-	08T22	1H22		07:05 Kidderminster-London Marylebone	DRS 68	Passenger
08:05C	-	6M44	MO	04:50 Southampton E.Docks-Halewood	EWS 66	empty car carriers
-	08:30	4O43	MX	06:43 Birch Coppice-Southampton	EWS 66	Intermodal
08:35	-	6M66	MWFO	05:04 Southampton W.Docks-Garston	EWS 66	loaded car carriers
-	08:50	4O15	MX	07:43 Hams Hall-Southampton	F.Liner 66	Freightliner
-	C09:05	4O18	MO	07:24 Lawley Street-Southampton	F.Liner 66	Freightliner
-	C09:05	4O14	MX	05:36 Garston-Southampton	F.Liner 70	Freightliner
10T04	-	1R15		08:41 Marylebone-Birmingham(Moor Street)	DRS 68	Passenger
-	10:50	4O90		06:12 Leeds-Southampton	F.Liner 66/70	Freightliner
11:10	-	6M31	TO-Q	10:42 Banbury-Mountsorrel	EWS 66	empty box wagons
-	11T23	1H33		10:55 Birmingham(Moor Street)-Marylebone	DRS 68	Passenger
11T25	-	1R21		10:10 Marylebone-Birmingham(Moor Street)	DRS 68	Passenger
-	C11:30	4O49	MX	09:22 Crewe Basford Hall-Southampton	F.Liner 66/70	Freightliner
11:40	-	6M26	(Q)	08:50 Eastleigh VQ-Mountsorrel	GBRf 66	empty ballast wagons
11:50	-	4M55		08:55 Southampton-Lawley Street	F.Liner 66	Freightliner
-	12:25	4O48	MO	11:26 Hams Hall-Southampton	F.Liner 66	Freightliner
-	C12:50	4O21		09:15 Trafford Park-Southampton	EWS 66	Intermodal
13:10	-	4M28		09:32 Southampton-Ditton	F.Liner 66	Freightliner
-	13T23	1H45		12:55 Birmingham(Moor Street)-Marylebone	DRS 68	Passenger
13:35	-	4Z69	MThO	09:32 Southampton-Rotherham S.T.	EWS 66	Intermodal
13:35	-	4E69	TFO	09:32 Southampton-Wakefield Europort	EWS 66	Intermodal
13:45C	-	6M50	FX	07:55 Westbury VQ-Bescot VQ	Colas 70	Departmental
14:20C	-	4M18	MWFOQ	09:47 Fairwater yard-Washwood Heath	F.Liner 66	Departmental
14T27	-	1R33		13:10 Marylebone-Birmingham(Moor Street)	DRS 68	Passenger
14:40C	-	6M48		10:34 Southampton E.Docks-Halewood	EWS 66	empty car carriers
15:00	-	6M40		11:56 Westbury-Stud Farm	GBRf 66	empty ballast boxes
-	C15:15	6O42		11:31 Halewood-Southampton E.Docks	EWS 66	loaded car carriers
-	15:20	6V16	WO-Q	11:24 Stud Farm-Hinksey VQ	GBRf 66	loaded ballast boxes
15:40C	-	4M61		12:54 Southampton-Trafford Park	F.Liner 66/70	Freightliner
-	15:50	6X01	TThO	10:17 Scunthorpe-Eastleigh	EWS 66	loaded rails
-	16T22	1H62		15:55 Birmingham(Moor Street)-Marylebone	DRS 68	Passenger
17:10	-	4M52		11:32 Southampton E.Docks-Castle Bromwich	EWS 66	empty car carriers
17T26	-	1K45		16:15 London Marylebone-Kidderminster	DRS 68	Passenger
-	17:30	4O95	MX	12:12 Leeds-Southampton	F.Liner 66/70	Freightliner
17:35C	-	4M68		13:53 Southampton-Garston	F.Liner 70	Freightliner
-	C17:50	4O17		15:48 Lawley Street-Southampton	F.Liner 66	Freightliner
18T26	-	1K50		17:15 London Marylebone-Kidderminster	DRS 68	Passenger

'Route knowledge':   (blank) = to/from Birmigham (via Hatton and Tyseley;

C = to/from Coventry (via Kenilworth)

North South	H'code	Runs	Train	Traction	Type of train
- 19:20	4076		17:01 Burton on Trent-Southampton	EWS 66	Intermodal
- C19:25	4029		15:18 Trafford Park-Southampton	F.Liner 66	Freightliner
19T28 -	1K54		18:15 London Marylebone-Kidderminster	DRS 68	Passenger
19:40C -	4M99		16:57 Southampton-Trafford Park	F.Liner 70	Freightliner
19:55 -	6M28		18:16 Hinksey VQ-Bescot VQ	F.Liner 66	Departmental
20:35 -	4M66		16:40 Southampton-Birch Coppice	EWS 66	Intermodal
20:45C -	4M97		17:32 Southampton-Hams Hall	F.Liner 66	Freightliner
- 20:45	7X09	WO-Q	11:47 Old Dalby-West Ruislip	4 GBRf 20s	LUL tube stock
- 21:30	6V46	FX	19:00 Bescot VQ-Westbury VQ	Colas 70	Departmental
21:40C -	6X65		20:28 Didcot yard-Mossend	EWS 66	wagonload
22:05 -	4E76		19:01 Southampton-Leeds	F.Liner 66	Freightliner
23:20 -	6E03	WO	18:09 Appleford-Milford	EWS 66	empty flyash containers
- 23:20	4052	WO	18:27 Wakefield Europort-Southampton	EWS 66	Intermodal

Saturdays:

North South	H'code	Runs	Train	Traction	Type of train
- C07:05	4018		05:03 Lawley Street-Southampton	F.Liner 66	Freightliner
08:00 -	4M62		04:31 Southampton-Lawley Street	F.Liner 66	Freightliner
- 08:20	4043		06:31 Birch Coppice-Eastleigh yard	EWS 66	Intermodal
- 08T24	1H10		07:12 Kidderminster-London Marylebone	DRS 68	Passenger
- 08:55	4014		07:37 Hams Hall-Southampton	F.Liner 66	Freightliner
- 09:25	4027		05:21 Garston-Southampton	F.Liner 70	Freightliner
- 10:20	4054		05:27 Leeds-Southampton	F.Liner 66/70	Freightliner
- 10T24	1H17		09:10 Kidderminster-London Marylebone	DRS 68	Passenger
- 11:25	4029		08:20 Crewe Basford Hall-Southampton	F.Liner 66	Freightliner
12T27 -	1R25		11:10 Marylebone-Birmingham(Moor Street)	DRS 68	Passenger
12:40C -	6M48		09:28 Southampton E.Docks-Halewood	EWS 66	empty car carriers
- C13:50	4017		12:11 Lawley Street-Southampton	F.Liner 66	Freightliner
- 14T22	1H37		13:55 Birmingham(Moor Street)-Marylebone	DRS 68	Passenger
- C15:55	6042	(Q)	11:33 Halewood-Southampton	EWS 66	loaded car carriers
18T26 -	1G49		17:10 Marylebone-Birmingham(Snow Hill)	DRS 68	Passenger
19T26 -	1G53		18:10 Marylebone-Birmingham(Snow Hill)	DRS 68	Passenger

Sundays:

North South	H'code	Runs	Train	Traction	Type of train
- 12T20	1H27		11:55 Birmingham(Moor Street)-Marylebone	DRS 68	Passenger
19T25 -	1R53		18:10 Marylebone-Birmingham(Moor Street)	DRS 68	Passenger

STAFFORD

[24 hour]

Mondays-Fridays:

North	South	H'code	Runs	Train		Traction	Type of train
-	06:00	1M16		20:44	Inverness-Euston	F.Liner 90	Caledonian Sleeper
-	06:35	4L41	MX	06:04	Crewe Basford Hall-Felixstowe	F.Liner 66	Freightliner
-	06:45	4Z55	MX	00:54	Coatbridge-Daventry	F.Liner 70	Intermodal
-	07:05	6Z15	WO-Q	01:01	Dowlow-Bow East	EWS 66	loaded box wagons
07:20	-	4S43		06:16	Daventry-Mossend	2 DRS 66s	'Tesco Express'
-	07:30	4O14	MX	05:36	Garston-Southampton	F.Liner 70	Freightliner
07:40	-	6M13	MO	23:11(Sun)	Dollands Moor-Ditton	EWS 66	aluminium(cargowagons)
07:40	-	4M83	WFO	02:59	London Gateway-Trafford Park	EWS 66	Intermodal
-	07:55	4L89	MO	07:18	Crewe Basford Hall-Felixstowe	F.Liner 70	Freightliner
08:40	-	6X41	MO	03:30	Dagenham-Garston	GBRf 66	Ford cars
08:40	-	6S94	WO-Q	02:21	Dollands Moor-Irvine	2 EWS 90s	loaded china clay tanks
W08:40	-	6M90	TThO	05:06	Avonmouth-Clitheroe	EWS 66	empty cement tanks
-	08:55	4L97	MX	05:01	Trafford Park-Felixstowe	F.Liner 66	Freightliner
09:20	-	6M46	MO	04:54	Ripple Lane-Peak Forest	EWS 66	empty bogie boxes
09:20	-	4M45	MX	02:50	Felixstowe-Ditton	F.Liner 90	Freightliner
-	09:35	6U76		08:59	Crewe Basford Hall-Mountsorrel	DRS 66/68	empty ballast boxes
09:55	-	4M21	MX	03:10	Felixstowe-Trafford Park	GBRf 66	Intermodal
10:00	-	6M44	MO	04:50	Southampton E.Docks-Halewood	EWS 66	empty car carriers
-	10:00	4O49	MX	09:22	Crewe Basford Hall-Southampton	F.Liner 66/70	Freightliner
-	11:05	4O21		09:15	Trafford Park-Southampton	EWS 66	Intermodal
-	12:15	4Z27	(Q)	05:25	Coatbridge-Daventry	F.Liner 70	Intermodal
12:25	-	6M11	WO-Q	03:30	Theale-Dowlow	EWS 66	empty box wagons
-	13:00	6G94	MX-Q	12:21	Crewe VQ-Bescot E.S.	DRS 66/68	Departmental
-	13:05	4L90	MX	12:30	Crewe Basford Hall-Felixstowe	F.Liner 90	Freightliner
-	13:15	4M25		06:06	Mossend-Daventry	2 EWS 90s	Intermodal
13:25	-	4Z44		12:13	Daventry-Coatbridge	F.Liner 70	Intermodal
-	13:30	6O42		11:31	Halewood-Southampton E.Docks	EWS 66	loaded car carriers
-	13:35	4M33	MFX-Q	13:05	Crewe Basford Hall-Derby	F.Liner 66	EMU translator wagons
13:50	-	6X43	TO	09:45	Dagenham-Garston	GBRf 92	Ford cars
-	14:05	4L90	MO	11:17	Trafford Park-Felixstowe	F.Liner 90	Freightliner
14:25	-	4M81		08:01	Felixstowe-Crewe	F.Liner 66/70	Freightliner
-	14:55	6Z11	MFO-Q	10:00	Dowlow-Southampton	EWS 66	loaded box wagons
-	14:55	6V11	TWO-Q	10:00	Dowlow-Theale	EWS 66	loaded box wagons
-	14:55	6Z11	ThO-Q	09:35	Dowlow-Bow East	EWS 66	loaded box wagons
-	15:15	4L56	MWFO	13:17	Trafford Park-London Gateway	EWS 66	Intermodal
15:20	-	4M63		09:12	Felixstowe-Ditton	F.Liner 90	Freightliner
-	S15:35B	6G71	MO	15:08	Cliffe Vale(Stoke)-Bescot yard	EWS 66	empty china clay
15:35	-	6U77		13:42	Mountsorrel-Crewe VQ	DRS 66/68	loaded ballast boxes
W15:40	-	4M28		09:32	Southampton-Ditton	F.Liner 66	Freightliner
-	15:55	4L92		14:03	Ditton-Felixstowe	F.Liner 70	Freightliner
-	16:05	4L18		14:18	Trafford Park-Felixstowe	GBRf 66	Intermodal
B16:20	-	6M66	MWFO	05:04	Southampton W.Docks-Garston	EWS 66	loaded car carriers

'Route knowledge':

B=to/from Bescot;   **W**= via Walsall/Sutton Park line;   **X**= via Oxley chord/Wolverhampton
S=to/from Stoke-on-Trent (at Norton Bridge);   **(blank)** = WCML (Crewe - Strafford - Rugby)

North	South	H'code	Runs	Train	Traction	Type of train
-	16:20B	6G78	WO	14:13 Warrington Arpley-Bescot	EWS 66	wagonload
B16:40	-	6M48		10:34 Southampton E.Docks-Halewood	EWS 66	empty car carriers
17:10	-	6K50		15:13 Toton-Crewe VQ	GBRf 66	Departmental
17:15	-	4M61		12:54 Southampton-Trafford Park	F.Liner 66/70	Freightliner
W17:25	-	6M56	TO-Q	13:41 Berkeley-Crewe	2 DRS 37s	flasks
W17:25	-	6M63	WO-Q	11:58 Bridgwater-Crewe	2 DRS 37s	flasks
-	17:25	4029		15:18 Trafford Park-Southampton	F.Liner 66	Freightliner
17:35	-	4M88		09:32 Felixstowe-Crewe Basford Hall	F.Liner 90	Freightliner
17:50	-	4M87		11:13 Felixstowe-Trafford Park	2 F.Liner 86s	Freightliner
-	17:55	1A91		17:00 Warrington RMT-Willesden PRDC	-	Mail(325 units)
-	18:00	6L48		15:49 Garston-Dagenham	GBRf 92	car carriers
-	18:15B	6G74	ThO	17:39 Crewe IEMD-Bescot yard	EWS 90	wagons off repair
18:30	-	1S96		16:22 Willesden PRDC-Shieldmuir	-	Mail(325 units)
B18:45	-	6F80	WO	18:14 Bescot-Warrington Arpley	EWS 66	wagons for repair
-	18:55	4L86	FX	16:18 Trafford Park-Felixstowe	F.Liner 66	Freightliner
-	18:55	4L96	FO	16:18 Trafford Park-Felixstowe	F.Liner 66	Freightliner
19:30	-	4M68		13:53 Southampton-Garston	F.Liner 70	Freightliner
19:50	-	4Z45		18:39 Daventry-Coatbridge	F.Liner 70	Intermodal
-	20:05	6G06		19:30 Crewe VQ-Bescot E.S.	DRS 66	Departmental
20:20	-	4S47		19:13 Daventry-Mossend	2 EWS 90s	Intermodal
-	20:25	1A97		19:18 Warrington RMT-Willesden PRDC	-	Mail(325 units)
-	20:30	6D51		19:59 Crewe VQ-Toton	GBRf 66	Departmental
20:35	-	6M88	TThO	14:35 Middleton Towers-Ellesmere Port	EWS 66	sand(in box wagons)
-	20:55	4L71		18:41 Ditton-Felixstowe	F.Liner 90	Freightliner
B21:15	-	6F25	ThO	20:53 Bescot-Warrington Arpley	EWS 66	wagonload
21:20	-	4M99		16:57 Southampton-Trafford Park	F.Liner 70	Freightliner
-	21:20	4L60		19:46 Garston-Felixstowe	F.Liner 66	Freightliner
21:40	-	6K97	MX-Q	19:35 Crewe VQ	DRS 66/68	Departmental
23:05	-	4S83		17:35 London Gateway-Coatbridge	F.Liner 70	Freightliner
23:10	-	4S49		21:58 Daventry-Grangemouth	EWS 66	Intermodal
23:15	-	1S25		21:15 Euston-Inverness	F.Liner 90	Caledonian Sleeper
23:50	-	6M95	ThO-Q	21:15 Dungeness p.s.-Crewe	2 DRS 37s	flask(s)
23:55	-	6X65		20:28 Didcot yard-Mossend	EWS 66	wagonload
-	23:55B	6046		22:26 Halewood-Southampton Eastern Docks	EWS 66	loaded car carriers
-	00:05	4L82		21:30 Ditton-Felixstowe	F.Liner 66	Freightliner
00:05	-	4S88		16:13 Felixstowe-Coatbridge	F.Liner 90	Freightliner
X00:15	-	6C37		22:25 Chirk-Carlisle yard	Colas 60	empty timber carriers
-	00:20	4L80		21:53 Garston-Tilbury	2 F.Liner 86s	Freightliner
-	00:30	4M48		19:04 Mossend-Daventry	2 DRS 66s	'Tesco Express'
-	00:35B	6G35	WFO	18:55 Clitheroe-Bescot(-Avonmouth)	EWS 66	loaded cement tanks
-	00:40	6L47	WO	22:20(Tue) Garston-Dagenham	GBRf 92	empty car carriers
-	00:50	6066	TThO	23:31 Garston-Southampton Western Docks	EWS 66	empty car carriers
-	00:55B	4011		00:23 Crewe Basford Hall-Southampton	F.Liner 66	Freightliner
B00:55	-	4M40		19:59 Southampton-Trafford Park	F.Liner 70	Freightliner
W01:05	-	6F73	WO-Q	16:55(Tue) Saltley-Liverpool	EWS 66	scrap(in MBA box wagons)
01:15	-	4M89		14:33(14:46 Mon) Felixstowe-Ditton	F.Liner 70	Freightliner
-	01:15	6V56	WSO	21:30 Peak Forest-Acton yard	EWS 66	loaded Cemex hoppers
-	01:35	4L81		19:26 Coatbridge-London Gateway	F.Liner 70	Freightliner
01:40	-	4M60		20:42 Tilbury-Garston	F.Liner 70	Freightliner
-	02c05	6A50	SO	22:57 Tunstead-Willesden	EWS 66	loaded cement tanks
B02:05	-	6K02	SO	01:36 Bescot E.S.-Crewe	DRS 66	Departmental
02:15	-	1S26		23:50 Euston-Glasgow Central	F.Liner 90	Caledonian Sleeper
-	02:15	4L95		22:50 Ditton-Felixstowe	F.Liner 66	Freightliner
02:25	-	4M53		20:46 Felixstowe-Trafford Park	F.Liner 90	Freightliner
B02:35	-	6K02	SX	02:08 Bescot E.S.-Crewe	DRS 66	Departmental

Mondays-Fridays[cont.]:

North	South	H'code	Runs		Train	Traction	Type of train
-	02:35	6L85	TTh0	00:51	Warrington Arpley-Middleton Towers	EWS 66	empty box wagons
-	02:40W	6V74	WO-Q	02:00	Crewe-Bridgwater	2 DRS 37s	flask(s)
-	02:40	6062	Th0-Q	02:08	Crewe-Dungeness p.s.	2 DRS 37s	flask(s)
-	02:45X	6V15		17:27	Mossend-Didcot yard	EWS 66	wagonload
02:45	-	1F04		00:22	Willesden PRDC-Warrington RMT	-	Mail(325 units)
-	02:50	6B10	WFO	23:03	Peak Forest-Bletchley	EWS 66	loaded Cemex hoppers
-	03:00	4M30		19:10	Grangemouth-Daventry	EWS 66	Intermodal
W03:10	-	4M78		21:50	Southampton-Trafford Park	EWS 66	Intermodal
-	03:10	4L89	SO	22:01(Fri)	Coatbridge-Felixstowe	2 F.Liner 86s	Freightliner
-	03:25W	4022		01:47	Trafford Park-Southampton	F.Liner 70	Freightliner
03:35	-	4M73		21:41	Felixstowe-Ditton	F.Liner 66	Freightliner
03:45	-	4M59		21:31	Felixstowe-Ditton	F.Liner 66	Freightliner
-	03:45	4L91		02:10	Trafford Park-Felixstowe	F.Liner 90	Freightliner
-	04:00	6L85	SO	02:35	Warrington Arpley-Middleton Towers	EWS 66	empty box wagons
04:00	-	4M42		22:08	Felixstowe-Garston	F.Liner 70	Freightliner
B04c05	-	6M38		23:38	Southampton E.Docks-Halewood	EWS 66	empty car carriers
04:15	-	6X41		00:32	Dagenham-Garston	GBRf 92	Ford cars
-	04:15	4L89	SO	22:01(Fri)	Coatbridge-Felixstowe	F.Liner 70	Freightliner
-	04:25	1M11		23:40	Glasgow Central-Euston	F.Liner 90	Caledonian Sleeper
-	04:35	4L89	SX	22:01	Coatbridge-Felixstowe	2 F.Liner 86s	Freightliner
-	05:05W	6V73	TO-Q	04:33	Crewe-Berkeley	2 DRS 37s	flask(s)
-	05:15	6B10	SO	02:19	Peak Forest-Bletchley	EWS 66	loaded Cemex hoppers
05:15	-	6M14	WFO	00:12	Dollands Moor-Ditton	EWS 66	aluminium(cargowagons)
05:25	-	6Z12	ThFO	23:56	Bow East-Dowlow	EWS 66	empty box wagons
-	05:40	6M76	FO	21:46(Thurs)	Mossend-Wembley	2 EWS 90s	empty china clay tanks
B05:50S	-	6K72	MO	05:13	Bescot-Cliffe Vale(Stoke)	EWS 66	loaded china clay

Saturdays:

North	South	H'code	Runs	Train	Traction	Type of train
-	06:00	1M16		20:44(Fri) Inverness-Euston	F.Liner 90	Caledonian Sleeper
W06:25	-	4M46		02:13 Southampton-Garston	F.Liner 66	Freightliner
-	06:30	4Z55		00:55 Coatbridge-Daventry	F.Liner 70	Intermodal
-	06:50	4L97		04:57 Trafford Park-Felixstowe	F.Liner 70	Freightliner
-	07:25W	4O27		05:21 Garston-Southampton	F.Liner 70	Freightliner
08:05	-	4S43		06:40 Daventry-Mossend	2 DRS 66s	'Tesco Express'
08:25	-	4M45		02:54 Felixstowe-Ditton	F.Liner 70	Freightliner
W08:55	-	6M90		05:00 Avonmouth-Clitheroe	EWS 66	empty cement tanks
-	08:55W	4O29		08:20 Crewe Basford Hall-Southampton	F.Liner 66	Freightliner
-	09:00	4L93		08:21 Crewe Basford Hall-Felixstowe	F.Liner 66	Freightliner
09:20	-	4M45		02:57 Felixstowe-Ditton	F.Liner 70/66	Freightliner
09:45	-	4M21		03:15 Felixstowe-Trafford Park	GBRf 66	Intermodal
12:15	-	4S49		11:12 Daventry-Grangemouth	EWS 66	Intermodal
-	12:15	4Z27		05:25 Coatbridge-Daventry	F.Liner 70	Intermodal
-	13:05	4L96		12:32 Crewe Basford Hall-Felixstowe	F.Liner 90	Freightliner
13:15	-	4Z44		12:05 Daventry-Coatbridge	F.Liner 70	Intermodal
-	13:30B	6O42	(Q)	11:33 Halewood-Southampton	EWS 66	loaded car carriers
14:05	-	6M48		09:28 Southampton E.Docks-Halewood	EWS 66	empty car carriers
14:20	-	4M34		11:04 Acton yard-Peak Forest	EWS 66	empty bogie hoppers
15:20	-	4M87		09:46 Felixstowe-Crewe Basford Hall	F.Liner 90	Freightliner
15:45	-	4M93		08:46 Felixstowe-Crewe Basford Hall	F.Liner 70	Freightliner
16:05	-	6H50		12:18 Willesden-Tunstead	F.Liner 66	empty cement tanks
-	16:15	6L48		13:36 Garston-Dagenham	GBRf 66	car carriers
17:15	-	4M67		12:13 Felixstowe-Crewe	F.Liner 70	Freightliner
19:35	-	6M89		13:39 Middleton Towers-Warrington Arpley	EWS 66	sand(in box wagons)
20:20	-	4M41	(Q)	13:57 London Gateway-Crewe Basford Hall	F.Liner 70	Freightliner
-	22:15B	4M30		10:15 Grangemouth-Daventry	EWS 66	Intermodal
-	22:55B	6G35		19:05 Clitheroe-Bescot	EWS 66	loaded cement tanks

Sundays:

North	South	H'code	Runs	Train	Traction	Type of train
-	10:25	6O38	(Q)	08:58 Halewood-Southampton E.Docks	EWS 66	loaded car carriers
-	19:30	4Z55		14:05 Coatbridge-Daventry	F.Liner 70	Intermodal
20:00	-	4Z45		18:39 Daventry-Coatbridge	F.Liner 70	Intermodal
-	20:10	4M48		14:43 Mossend-Daventry	2 DRS 66s	'Tesco Express'
22:20	-	4S49		21:16 Daventry-Grangemouth	EWS 66	Intermodal
23:10	-	1S25		20:57 Euston-Inverness	F.Liner 90	Caledonian Sleeper

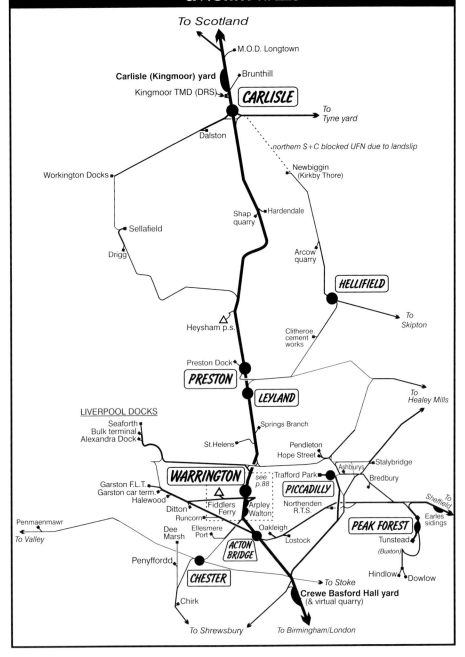

To Scotland

M.O.D. Longtown

Carlisle (Kingmoor) yard   Brunthill

Kingmoor TMD (DRS)   **CARLISLE**

To Tyne yard

Dalston

northern S+C blocked UFN due to landslip

Workington Docks

Newbiggin (Kirkby Thore)

Shap quarry   Hardendale

Sellafield

Drigg

Arcow quarry

HELLIFIELD

To Skipton

Heysham p.s.

Clitheroe cement works

Preston Dock

PRESTON

LEYLAND

To Healey Mills

LIVERPOOL DOCKS

Seaforth
Bulk terminal
Alexandra Dock

Springs Branch

St.Helens

Pendleton
Hope Street

Ashburys   Stalybridge

WARRINGTON

Garston F.L.T.
Garston car term.
Halewood

see p.88   Trafford Park   Bredbury

PICCADILLY

To Sheffield

Ditton   Fiddlers Ferry   Arpley Walton   Northenden R.T.S.

Earles sidings

Penmaenmawr

To Valley

Runcorn

Dee Marsh   Ellesmere Port   Oakleigh   Lostock

PEAK FOREST

Tunstead
(Buxton)

Penyffordd

ACTON BRIDGE

CHESTER

Hindlow   Dowlow

To Stoke

Crewe Basford Hall yard
(& virtual quarry)

Chirk

To Shrewsbury   To Birmingham/London

MANCHESTER PICCADILLY

[06:00-midnight]

Mondays-Fridays:

North	South	H'code	Runs	Train		Traction	Type of train
-	06:35	4K18	MX	06:22 Trafford Park-Crewe Basford Hall	F.Liner 90	Freightliner
06:35	-	4H60	MO	05:43 Basford Hall-Trafford Park	F.Liner 70	Freightliner
08:35	-	4H00	MO	07:27 Basford Hall-Trafford Park	F.Liner 70	Freightliner
-	08:51	1H82		07:38 Chester-Manchester Picc	class 67	Passenger
-	09:35	4O21		09:15 Trafford Park-Southampton	EWS 66	Intermodal
09:35	-	4H70	MO-Q	06:58 Warrington Arpley-Trafford Park	EWS 66	wagons off repair
09:35	-	4M83	WFO	02:59 London Gateway-Trafford Park	EWS 66	Intermodal
09:50	-	1D34		Manchester Picc-Llandudno	class 67	Passenger
-	10:20	4H21	MO-Q	10:09 Trafford Park-Longsight lathe	F.Liner 66	wagons for repair
11:30	-	4M21	MX	03:10 Felixstowe-Trafford Park	GBRf 66	Intermodal
11:30	-	4H23	MO	11:22 Longsight lathe-Trafford Park	F.Liner 66	wagons off repair
-	11:35	4L90	MO	11:17 Trafford Park-Felixstowe	2 F.Liner 86s	Freightliner
-	13:35	4L56	MWFO	13:17 Trafford Park-London Gateway	EWS 66	Intermodal
-	14:35	4L18		14:18 Trafford Park-Felixstowe	GBRf 66	Intermodal
-	15:30	4O29		15:18 Trafford Park-Southampton	F.Liner 66	Freightliner
-	15:51	1H89		13:01 Holyhead-Manchester Picc	class 67	Passenger
-	16:35	4L86	FX	16:18 Trafford Park-Felixstowe	F.Liner 66	Freightliner
-	16:35	4L96	FO	16:18 Trafford Park-Felixstowe	F.Liner 66	Freightliner
16:50	-	1D31		Manchester Picc-Llandudno	class 67	Passenger
17:30	-	4H81		16:31 Basford Hall-Trafford Park	F.Liner 66/70	Freightliner
19:30	-	4M61		12:54 Southampton-Trafford Park	F.Liner 66/70	Freightliner
20:30	-	4M87		11:13 Felixstowe-Trafford Park	2 F.Liner 86s	Freightliner
-	21:20	4K96		21:09 Trafford Park-Crewe	F.Liner 90	Freightliner
-	22:20	4K06		22:07 Trafford Park-Crewe	F.Liner 66/70	Freightliner
22:20	-	4H54		21:23 Basford Hall-Trafford Park	F.Liner 90	Freightliner
23:00	-	4M99		16:57 Southampton-Trafford Park	F.Liner 70	Freightliner

Saturdays:

North	South	H'code	Runs	Train		Traction	Type of train
-	06:20	4K89		06:09 Trafford Park-Crewe Basford Hall	F.Liner 90	Freightliner
11:30	-	4M21		03:15 Felixstowe-Trafford Park	GBRf 66	Intermodal
-	11:35	4K51		11:17 Trafford Park-Crewe Basford Hall	F.Liner 66	Freightliner

Sundays: NO BOOKED TRAINS

PEAK FOREST

[06:00-21:00]]

Mondays-Fridays:

Peak Forest	Great Rocks	code	Runs	Train		Traction	Type of train
08:45	08:55	6M28	ThO-Q	07:38	Guide Bridge-Tunstead	F.Liner 66	empty bogie hoppers
09c15	09:20	6Z12	ThFO	23:56	Bow East-Dowlow	EWS 66	empty box wagons
09c30	09:35	6H43		07:46	Pendleton-Tunstead	F.Liner 66	empty bogie hoppers
09:35	09:40	6M90	FO-Q	02:28	Brentford-Tunstead	F.Liner 66	empty bogie hoppers
10c25	-	6J46		09:54	Peak Forest-Hope Street	EWS 66	loaded bogie hoppers
10:30	10:35	6M88	MX-Q	03:48	West Thurrock-Tunstead	F.Liner 66	empty cement tanks
11c25	11:05	6Z11	MFO-Q	10:00	Dowlow-Southampton	EWS 66	loaded box wagons
11c25	11:05	6V11	TWO-Q	10:00	Dowlow-Theale	EWS 66	loaded box wagons
11c25	11:05	6Z11	ThO-Q	09:35	Dowlow-Bow East	EWS 66	loaded box wagons
-	11R35*	6H22		11:08	Tunstead-Hindlow{*arr.11R15}	F.Liner 66	loaded BLI hoppers
11:40	11:45	6M72	MO-Q	04:56	Westbury-Tunstead	F.Liner 66	empty cement tanks
12:05	12:00	6L89	(Q)	11:49	Tunstead-West Thurrock	F.Liner 66	loaded cement tanks
12:15	12:25	6M02	MO-Q	10:38	Barrow Hill-Tunstead	F.Liner 66	empty bogie hoppers
12c50	-	6E51	TThO	12:18	Peak Forest sidings-Selby	EWS 66	loaded bogie hoppers
12:55	13:05	6H81	MWO-Q	11:35	Guide Bridge-Tunstead	F.Liner 66	empty bogie hoppers
13c30	-	4M11	MWFO	10:00	Washwood Heath-Peak Forest	EWS 66	empty bogie hoppers
13:35	13:30	6V08	ThO-Q	13:27	Tunstead-Brentford	F.Liner 66	loaded bogie hoppers
13:50	13:55	6M03	Th/FO	12:06	Barrow Hill-Tunstead	F.Liner 66	empty bogie hoppers
13c55	-	6M46	MO	04:54	Ripple Lane-Peak Forest	EWS 66	empty bogie boxes
14:00	-	6F86	MO	13:54	Peak Forest-Warrington Arpley	EWS 66	wagons for repair
14c15	14:05	6H52		13:05	Dowlow-Ashburys	EWS 66	stone(in box wagons)
14:25	-	4M11	TThO	10:42	Washwood Heath-Peak Forest	EWS 66	empty HTA hoppers
14c55	-	6F07	MWO-Q	14:18	Peak Forest-Warrington Dallam	EWS 66	loaded box wagons
15c30	-	4H03	WFO	09:57	Bletchley-Peak Forest	EWS 66	empty bogie hoppers
15:55	16:00	6M22	MO-Q	11:20	Leeds Hunslet-Tunstead	F.Liner 66	empty cement tanks
16:05	16:00	6H41	FX-Q	15:51	Tunstead-Bredbury	F.Liner 66	loaded bogie hoppers
16c20	16:30	6M82	FX-Q	12:41	Walsall-Dowlow	EWS 66	empty box wagons
16c20	16:30	6M69	FO	13:52	Heck-Dowlow	EWS 66	empty box wagons
-	16R35*	6H23		15:50	Hindlow-Tunstead{*dep.16R55}	F.Liner 66	empty BLI hoppers
16c50	-	6H60		15:25	Hope Street-Peak Forest	EWS 66	empty bogie hoppers
17:30	17:25	6E04	MFX-Q	17:22	Tunstead-West Burton	F.Liner 66	loaded bogie hoppers
17c30	17:35	6M11	WO-Q	12:41	Theale-Dowlow	EWS 66	empty box wagons
18c35	18:40	6M69	TO-Q	13:52	Heck-Dowlow	EWS 66	empty box wagons
20c30	-	6E17	MWFO	19:52	Peak Forest-Leeds Stourton	EWS 66	loaded bogie hoppers

Saturdays:

09c45	-	6H43		07:52	Pendleton-Tunstead	F.Liner 66	empty bogie hoppers
10c15	-	6J46		09:10	Peak Forest-Hope Street	EWS 66	loaded bogie hoppers
11c20	10:25	6H52	(Q)	09:55	Dowlow-Ashburys	EWS 66	stone(in box wagons)
11:20	11:25	6M90		04:45	West Thurrock-Tunstead	F.Liner 66	empty cement tanks
-	13R10*	6H22	(Q)	12:47	Tunstead-Hindlow{*arr.12R50}	F.Liner 66	loaded BLI hoppers
16c35	16:45	6H64		12:07	Walsall-Dowlow	EWS 66	empty box wagons
-	17R10*	6H23	(Q)	15:57	Hindlow-Tunstead{*dep.17R30}	F.Liner 66	empty BLI hoppers
17:15	-	6J50		15:53	Hope Street-Peak Forest	EWS 66	empty bogie hoppers
17:20	-	4M34		11:04	Acton yard-Peak Forest	EWS 66	empty bogie hoppers
18:35	-	4H10		12:29	Bletchley-Peak Forest	EWS 66	empty bogie hoppers
19:15	19:20	6H50		12:18	Willesden-Tunstead	F.Liner 66	empty cement tanks

84

Mondays-Fridays:

Peak Forest	Great Rocks	code	Runs	Train	Traction	Type of train
-	09R50*	6H27		09:20 Tunstead-Hindlow{*arr.09R25}	F.Liner 66	loaded BLI hoppers
14:05	14:00	6V82		13:53 Tunstead-Westbury	F.Liner 66	loaded cement tanks
-	14R50*	6H29		13:45 Hindlow-Tunstead{*dep.15R15}	F.Liner 66	empty BLI hoppers
14c55	-	6M52		12:46 Attercliffe Road-Peak Forest	EWS 66	empty bogie boxes

CHESTER

[06:00-midnight]

Mondays-Fridays:

West	East	H'code	Runs	Train	Traction	Type of train
06:10	-	6D41	WFO-Q	05:41 Crewe-Valley	2 DRS 37s	flask(s)
X06:35W	-	6M18	WO-Q	16:08(Tue) Killoch-Penyffordd	EWS 66	coal(in MEA box wagons)
X07R15	07R10	1V91		05:33 Holyhead-Cardiff	class 67	Passenger
07R30	-	1D51		07:11 Crewe-Chester	class 67	Passenger
-	07R38	1H82		07:38 Chester-Manchester Picc	class 67	Passenger
11T00W	-	1D34		09:50 Manchester Picc-Holyhead	class 67	Passenger
-	14T46W	1H89		13:01 Holyhead-Manchester Picc	class 67	Passenger
-	16:00	6K41	WFO-Q	14:58 Valley-Crewe	2 DRS 37s	flask(s)
X18:35W	-	6J37		11:59 Carlisle yard-Chirk	Colas 60	loaded timber
18T00W	-	1D31		16:50 Manchester Picc-Llandudno	class 67	Passenger
20R06	20R01X	1W96		17:16 Cardiff-Holyhead	class 67	Passenger
-	20T46	1K96		19:34 Llandudno-Crewe	class 67	Passenger
-	X20:55W	6E41	WO	16:56 Penyffordd-Warrington Arpley	EWS 66	empty box wagons

Saturdays: NO BOOKED TRAINS

Sundays: NO BOOKED TRAINS

'Route Knowledge': **(blank)** = Crewe to/from North Wales Coast;
W = to/from Warrington via Helsby;
X = to/from Wrexham (at Saltney Junction)

ACTON BRIDGE

[06:00 -22:00]

Mondays-Fridays:

North	South	H'code	Runs	Train	Traction	Type of train
-	06:05	4014	MX	05:36 Garston-Southampton	F.Liner 70	Freightliner
06:10	-	6M38	MX	23:38 Southampton E.Docks-Halewood	EWS 66	empty car carriers
-	06:45	6F60	TFO	06:28 Warrington Arpley-Runcorn	EWS 66	chemicals
06:50	-	6C53	WThFO	06:30 Crewe-Sellafield	2 DRS 37s	flasks
06:55	-	6X41	MX	00:32 Dagenham-Garston	GBRf 92	Ford cars
-	07:10	4H70	MO	06:58 Warrington Arpley-Trafford Park	EWS 66	wagons off repair
07:25	-	6M14	WFO	00:12 Dollands Moor-Ditton	EWS 66	aluminium(cargowagons)
-	07:50	4K74	MX	06:50 Ditton-Crewe Basford Hall	F.Liner 66	Freightliner
07:50	-	6F60	TFO	06:28 Warrington Arpley-Runcorn	EWS 66	chemicals
08:25	-	4S43		06:16 Daventry-Mossend	2 DRS 66s	'Tesco Express'
-	08:40	4K44	MX	08:07 Garston-Crewe Basford Hall	F.Liner 70	Freightliner
08:50	-	4F45	MX	08:20 Crewe Basford Hall-Garston	F.Liner 90	Freightliner
09:25	-	6M13	MO	23:11(Sun) Dollands Moor-Ditton	EWS 66	aluminium(cargowagons)
09:40	-	6S94	WO-Q	02:21 Dollands Moor-Irvine	2 EWS 90s	loaded china clay tanks
-	09:55	6K32	WO	09:41 Warrington Arpley-Stoke Marcroft	EWS 66	wagons for repair
-	09:55	6H85	MO	09:40 Warrington Arpley-Peak Forest	EWS 66	wagons off repair
10:00	-	6X41	MO	03:30 Dagenham-Garston	GBRf 66	Ford cars
10:00	-	6M90	TThO	05:06 Avonmouth-Clitheroe	EWS 66	empty cement tanks
-	10:05	4Z27		05:25 Coatbridge-Daventry	F.Liner 70	Intermodal
11:00	-	4M45	MX	02:50 Felixstowe-Ditton	F.Liner 66	Freightliner
11:00	-	6M44	MO	04:50 Southampton E.Docks-Halewood	EWS 66	empty car carriers
-	11:20	6J34		10:58(10:52 Mon) Runcorn-Pendleton RTS	F.Liner 66	empty GMC 'binliner'
-	11:25	6K32	WFO-Q	11:07 Warrington Arpley-Stoke Marcroft	EWS 66	wagons for repair
11:35	-	6M44	MWX-Q	05:36 Southampton E.Docks-Halewood	EWS 66	empty car carriers
-	11:40	6F62	TFO	11:12 Runcorn Folly Lane-Warrington Arpley	EWS 66	chemicals
-	11:50	6042		11:31 Halewood-Southampton E.Docks	EWS 66	loaded car carriers
12:00	-	6F33		09:16 Bredbury R.T.S.-Runcorn	F.Liner 66	loaded GMC 'binliner'
-	12:15	4M25		06:06 Mossend-Daventry	2 EWS 90s	Intermodal
-	12:20	4K64		11:46 Garston-Crewe Basford Hall	F.Liner 90	Freightliner
12:30	-	6F62	TFO	11:12 Runcorn Folly Lane-Warrington Arpley	EWS 66	chemicals
-	13:15	6E10		08:20 Liverpool biomass term.-Drax p.s.	GBRf 66	loaded biomass hoppers
-	13:40	6K74	TThO	13:31 Warrington Arpley-Crewe IEMD	EWS 66	wagons for repair
-	13:55	6H35		13:30 Runcorn-Northenden R.T.S.	F.Liner 66	empty GMC 'binliner'
-	14:25	6678	WO	14:13 Warrington Arpley-Bescot	EWS 66	wagonload
14:30	-	4Z44		12:13 Daventry-Coatbridge	F.Liner 70	Intermodal
14:35	-	5J00	(Q)	14:01 Crewe IEMD-Warrington RMT	-	325 unit
-	14:50	4L92		14:03 Ditton-Felixstowe	F.Liner 70	Freightliner
15:05	-	6F52	ThO-Q	13:15 Donnington-Warrington Arpley	EWS 66	wagonload
15:05	-	6F31	FO	14:04 Stoke Marcroft-Warrington Arpley	EWS 66	wagons off repair
15:40	-	6F86	MO-Q	13:54 Peak Forest-Warrington Arpley	EWS 66	wagons for repair
15:50	-	6X43	TO	09:45 Dagenham-Garston	GBRf 92	Ford cars
16:30	-	4M63		09:12 Felixstowe-Ditton	F.Liner 90	Freightliner
16:35	-	4M51		10:00 Drax p.s.-Liverpool	GBRf 66	empty biomass hoppers
16:40	-	6F07	MWO-Q	14:18 Peak Forest-Warrington Dallam	EWS 66	loaded box wagons
-	16:45	6L48		15:49 Garston-Dagenham	GBRf 92	car carriers
17:10	-	6S96	ThO-Q	13:17 Sinfin-Grangemouth	Colas 60	empty tanks
-	17:15	1A91		17:00 Warrington RMT-Willesden PRDC	-	Mail(325 units)
-	17:20	6K05		10:43 Carlisle yard-Crewe Basford Hall	DRS 66	Departmental

North	South	H'code	Runs	Train		Traction	Type of train
17:10	–	6S96	ThO-Q	13:17	Sinfin-Grangemouth	Colas 60	empty tanks
17:35	–	4F71	MX	17:03	Crewe Basford Hall-Garston	F.Liner 70	Freightliner
17:40	–	6M66	MWFO	05:04	Southampton W.Docks-Garston	EWS 66	loaded car carriers
17:50	–	6M48		10:34	Southampton E.Docks-Halewood	EWS 66	empty car carriers
18:00	–	4F71	MO	17:27	Crewe Basford Hall-Garston	F.Liner 90	Freightliner
19:00	–	4M28		09:32	Southampton-Ditton	F.Liner 66	Freightliner
–	19:20	4L71		18:41	Ditton-Felixstowe	F.Liner 90	Freightliner
19:20	–	1S96		16:22	Willesden PRDC-Shieldmuir	–	Mail(325 units)
19:25	–	6F94	TO	18:36	Crewe IEMD-Warrington Arpley	EWS 90	wagons off repair
19:40	–	6F80	WO	18:14	Bescot-Warrington Arpley	EWS 66	wagons for repair
–	19:45	1A97		19:18	Warrington RMT-Willesden PRDC	–	Mail(325 units)
19:55	–	6F35		18:57	Northenden R.T.S.-Runcorn	F.Liner 66	loaded GMC 'binliner'
–	20:05	6K27	MWFO	14:43	Carlisle yard-Crewe Basford Hall	DRS 66	Departmental
–	20:20	4L60		19:46	Garston-Felixstowe	F.Liner 70	Freightliner
–	20:50	6K73	FX	17:18	Sellafield-Crewe	2 DRS 37s	flasks
21:00	–	4Z45		18:39	Daventry-Coatbridge	F.Liner 70	Intermodal
21:20	–	4S56		20:50	Crewe Basford Hall-Coatbridge	2 F.Liner 86s	Freightliner
–	21:25	6G35	TThO	18:55	Clitheroe-Bescot(-Avonmouth)	EWS 66	loaded cement tanks
–	21:25	6H37	FO	20:54	Runcorn-Bredbury R.T.S.	F.Liner 66	empty GMC 'binliner'
21:25	–	4M68		13:53	Southampton-Garston	F.Liner 70	Freightliner
21:35	–	4S47		19:13	Daventry-Mossend	2 EWS 90s	Intermodal
–	21:35	6H39	FX	21:13	Runcorn-Bredbury R.T.S.	F.Liner 66	empty GMC 'binliner'
–	21:40	6016	MWFO	20:21	Ditton-Dollands Moor	EWS 66	empty cargowagons
–	21:55	6V71	MWFO	18:26	Hardendale-Margam	EWS 66	containerised lime
21:55	–	6M88	TThO	14:35	Middleton Towers-Ellesmere Port	EWS 66	sand(in box wagons)

Saturdays:

06:50	–	6C53	(Q)	06:30	Crewe-Sellafield	2 DRS 37s	flasks
–	07:20	4K74		06:30	Ditton-Crewe Basford Hall	F.Liner 66	Freightliner
07:20	–	6X41		00:29	Dagenham-Garston	GBRf 92	Ford cars
09:00	–	4M46		02:13	Southampton-Garston	F.Liner 66	Freightliner
09:25	–	4S43		06:40	Daventry-Mossend	2 DRS 66s	'Tesco Express'
–	09:40	4K64		09:16	Garston-Crewe Basford Hall	F.Liner 90	Freightliner
–	10:10	4Z27		05:25	Coatbridge-Daventry	F.Liner 70	Intermodal
11:00	–	4M45		02:54	Felixstowe-Ditton	F.Liner 66	Freightliner
11:25	–	6M90		05:00	Avonmouth-Clitheroe	EWS 66	empty cement tanks
–	11:50	6042	(Q)	11:33	Halewood-Southampton	EWS 66	loaded car carriers
13:30	–	4S49		11:12	Daventry-Grangemouth	EWS 66	Intermodal
–	14:20	4K45		12:52	Ditton-Crewe Basford Hall	F.Liner 66	Freightliner
–	14:25	6L48		13:36	Garston-Dagenham	GBRf 66	car carriers
14:30	–	4Z44		12:05	Daventry-Coatbridge	F.Liner 70	Intermodal
15:15	–	6M48		09:28	Southampton E.Docks-Halewood	EWS 66	empty car carriers
–	20:20	4M30		10:15	Grangemouth-Daventry	EWS 66	Intermodal
20:50	–	6M89		13:39	Middleton Towers-Warrington Arpley	EWS 66	sand(in box wagons)
–	21:45	6G35		19:05	Clitheroe-Bescot	EWS 66	loaded cement tanks

Sundays:

20:25	–	4S45		18:25	Daventry-Coatbridge	DRS 66	Intermodal
–	20:40	4M48		14:43	Mossend-Daventry	2 DRS 66s	'Tesco Express'
–	21:40	4M82		16:04	Coatbridge-Daventry	DRS 66	Intermodal
–	22:05	6E27		20:59	Tuebrook(Edge Hill)-Drax p.s.	GBRf 66	loaded biomass hoppers
23:35	–	4S49		21:28	Daventry-Grangemouth	EWS 66	Intermodal

87

WARRINGTON *(Bank Quay station)*

[24-hour]

Mondays-Fridays:

North	South	H'code	Runs	Train	Traction	Type of train
07:00	–	6C53	WThFO 06:30	Crewe-Sellafield	2 DRS 37s	flasks
–	07c55	4F36	MFX-Q 04:02	Newbiggin-Fiddlers Ferry	GBRf 66	empty gypsum containers
08T09	–	1H82	07:38	Chester-Manchester Picc	class 67	Passenger
08:40	–	4S43	06:16	Daventry-Mossend	2 DRS 66s	'Tesco Express'
–	09:45	4Z27	(Q) 05:25	Coatbridge-Daventry	F.Liner 70	Intermodal
09c50	–	6S94	WO-Q 02:21	Dollands Moor-Irvine	2 EWS 90s	loaded china clay tanks
10:05	–	6F50	WO-Q 10:00	Arpley yard-Wigan WRD	EWS 67	wagons for repair
–	10T27	1D34	09:50	Manchester Picc-Holyhead	class 67	Passenger
10:50	–	6M90	TThO 05:06	Avonmouth-Clitheroe	EWS 66	empty cement tanks
–	12:05	4M25	06:06	Mossend-Daventry	2 EWS 90s	Intermodal
–	12:10	6F47	WO-Q 11:54	Wigan WRD-Arpley yard	EWS 67	wagons off repair
–	12:55	6E10	08:20	Liverpool biomass term.-Drax p.s.	GBRf 66	loaded biomass hoppers
14:35	–	4Z44	12:13	Daventry-Coatbridge	F.Liner 70	Intermodal
14:40	–	5J00	(Q) 14:01	Crewe IEMD-Warrington RMT	–	325 unit
15T18	–	1H89	13:01	Holyhead-Manchester Picc	class 67	Passenger
16:40	–	4M51	10:00	Drax p.s.-Liverpool	GBRf 66	empty biomass hoppers
16:55	–	6F07	MWO-Q 14:18	Peak Forest-Warrington Dallam	EWS 66	loaded box wagons
–	17:00	6K05	10:43	Carlisle yard-Crewe Basford Hall	DRS 66	Departmental
–	17:05	1A91	17:00	Warrington RMT-Willesden PRDC	–	Mail(325 units)
17:20	–	6S96	ThO-Q 13:17	Sinfin-Grangemouth	Colas 60	empty tanks
–	17T28	1D31	16:50	Manchester Picc-Llandudno	class 67	Passenger
–	17c55	6J37	11:59	Carlisle yard-Chirk	Colas 60	loaded timber
18c50	–	4C38	MFX-Q 16:23	Fiddlers Ferry-Newbiggin	GBRf 66	containerised gypsum
–	19:05	6Z82	MO-Q 17:57	St.Helens-Arpley yard	EWS 66	empty box wagons
–	19:50	6K27	MWFO 14:43	Carlisle yard-Crewe Basford Hall	DRS 66/68	Departmental
–	20:35	6K73	FX 17:18	Sellafield-Crewe	2 DRS 37s	flasks
–	20c55	6G35	TThO 18:55	Clitheroe-Bescot(-Avonmouth)	EWS 66	loaded cement tanks
–	21:05	6M30	WFO 16:45	Doncaster Railport-Arpley yard	EWS 66	wagonload
–	21c10	6V71	MWFO 18:26	Hardendale-Margam	EWS 66	containerised lime
21:10	–	4Z45	18:39	Daventry-Coatbridge	F.Liner 70	Intermodal
21:35	–	4S56	20:50	Crewe Basford Hall-Coatbridge	2 F.Liner 86s	Freightliner
21:40	–	4S47	19:13	Daventry-Mossend	2 EWS 90s	Intermodal
–	21:55	6E27	FX 19:37	Liverpool biomass term.-Drax p.s.	GBRf 66	loaded biomass hoppers
–	22:20	4M11	17:34	Coatbridge-Crewe Basford Hall	2 F.Liner 86s	Freightliner
–	22:45	4M48	19:04	Mossend-Daventry	2 DRS 66s	'Tesco Express'
–	23:40	4L81	19:26	Coatbridge-London Gateway	2 F.Liner 86s	Freightliner

North	South	H'code	Runs	Train	Traction	Type of train
00c10	–	4S49		21:58 Daventry-Grangemouth	EWS 66	Intermodal
00:15	–	1S25		21:15 Euston-Inverness	class 90	Caledonian Sleeper
00:35	–	4S83		17:35 London Gateway-Coatbridge	2 F.Liner 86s	Freightliner
00:40	–	6X52	WFO	17:33 Portbury-Mossend	EWS 90	wagonload
–	00:55	6V15		17:27 Mossend-Didcot yard	2 EWS 90s	wagonload
–	01c05	6V16	TO-Q	17:02(Mon) Mossend-Cardiff Tidal	EWS 66	empty steel
–	01c25	4M30		19:10 Grangemouth-Daventry	EWS 66	Intermodal
01c40	–	6C37		22:25 Chirk-Carlisle yard	Colas 60	empty timber carriers
–	01:50	4L89		22:01 Coatbridge-Felixstowe	2 F.Liner 86s	Freightliner
02:05	–	6F69	ThO-Q	01:18 Crewe Basford Hall-Liverpool EMR	F.Liner 66	Departmental
02:05	–	6S16	FO-Q	20:28(Thurs) Cardiff Tidal-Mossend	EWS 66	loaded steel
02:15	–	6X65		20:28 Didcot yard-Mossend	EWS 66	wagonload
02:25	–	4S88		16:13 Felixstowe-Coatbridge	2 F.Liner 86s	Freightliner
02:35	–	6C50	TO	02:00 Crewe-Sellafield	2 DRS 37s	flasks
02:35	–	6M75	MWFO	20:28 Margam-Carlisle yard	EWS 66	wagonload
–	02:50	6M76	TThFO	21:46 Mossend-Arpley(Wembley FO)	2 EWS 90s	wagonload
03:00	–	1S26		23:50 Euston-Glasgow Central	F.Liner 90	Caledonian Sleeper
–	03:35	6E37		02:10 Liverpool biomass term.-Drax p.s.	GBRf 66	loaded biomass hoppers
–	03:40	1M11		23:40 Glasgow Central-Euston	F.Liner 90	Caledonian Sleeper
03:40	–	1F04		00:22 Willesden PRDC-Warrington RMT	–	Mail(325 units)
–	04:05	6M18	WO-Q	16:08(Tue) Killoch-Penyffordd	EWS 66	coal(in MEA box wagons)
05:00	–	6C02		04:22 Crewe-Carlisle yard	DRS 66	Departmental
–	05:00	6M65	ThO-Q	21:15(Wed) Grangemouth-Sinfin	Colas 60	loaded tanks
–	05:05	1M16		20:44 Inverness-Euston	F.Liner 90	Caledonian Sleeper
–	05:20	4Z55		00:54 Coatbridge-Daventry	F.Liner 70	Intermodal
–	05:35	6F16	FO-Q	04:30 Liverpool EMR-Crewe Basford Hall	F.Liner 66	Departmental

Saturdays:

North	South	H'code	Runs	Train	Traction	Type of train
07:00	–	6C53	(Q)	06:30 Crewe-Sellafield	2 DRS 37s	flasks
09:35	–	4S43		06:40 Daventry-Mossend	2 DRS 66s	'Tesco Express'
–	09:45	4Z27		05:25 Coatbridge-Daventry	F.Liner 70	Intermodal
11c40	–	6M90		05:00 Avonmouth-Clitheroe	EWS 66	empty cement tanks
13c40	–	4S49		11:12 Daventry-Grangemouth	EWS 66	Intermodal
14:40	–	4Z44		12:05 Daventry-Coatbridge	F.Liner 70	Intermodal
–	20c05	4M30		10:15 Grangemouth-Daventry	EWS 66	Intermodal
–	21c05	6G35		19:05 Clitheroe-Bescot	EWS 66	loaded cement tanks

Sundays:

North	South	H'code	Runs	Train	Traction	Type of train
–	18c25	4Z55		14:05 Coatbridge-Daventry	F.Liner 70	Intermodal
–	19:05	4M48		14:43 Mossend-Daventry	2 DRS 66s	'Tesco Express'
21:25	–	4Z45		18:39 Daventry-Coatbridge	F.Liner 70	Intermodal
–	21:40	6E27		18:54 Liverpool biomass term.-Drax p.s.	GBRf 66	loaded biomass hoppers
23c35	–	4S49		21:16 Daventry-Grangemouth	EWS 66	Intermodal

Other trains in the Warrington area:

- For trains on the 'low level' line under the station, please see overleaf.

- For trains running south of Arpley or Walton yards, please refer to the Acton Bridge/Helsby tables.

WARRINGTON *(Low Level)*

[06:00-21:00]

Mondays-Fridays:

West	East	H'code	Runs	Train	Traction	Type of train
06:40	–	6F42	WO-Q	06:20 Arpley yard-Garston	EWS 66	car carriers
07:25	–	6F68	M/FO	04:13 Tunstead-Fiddlers Ferry	F.Liner 66	loaded bogie hoppers
10:55	–	4F36	MFX-Q	04:02 Newbiggin-Fiddlers Ferry	GBRf 66	empty gypsum containers
–	11:30	6F49	WO-Q	11:10 Halewood-Arpley yard	EWS 66	car carriers
–	13:10	6H48	M/FO	12:54 Fiddlers Ferry-Guide Bridge	F.Liner 66	empty FHH hoppers
–	16:40	4C38	MFX-Q	16:23 Fiddlers Ferry-Newbiggin	GBRf 66	containerised gypsum
–	17:30	6F55	(Q)	17:04 Garston-Arpley yard	EWS 66	car carriers

Saturdays & Sundays: NO BOOKED TRAINS

90

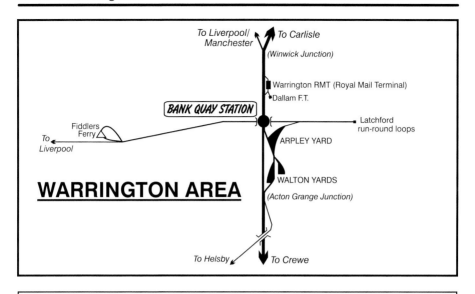

WARRINGTON AREA

(Acton Grange Junction)

[06:00-21:00]

Mondays-Fridays:

West	East	H'code	Runs	Train	Traction	Type of train
-	E06:05	6F92	WFO	05:35 Ellesmere Port-Warrington Arpley	EWS 66	empty box wagons
06:15	-	6M18	WO-Q	16:08(Tue) Killoch-Penyffordd	EWS 66	coal(in MEA box wagons)
-	07T48	1H82		07:38 Chester-Manchester Picc	class 67	Passenger
10T45	-	1D34		09:50 Manchester Picc-Holyhead	class 67	Passenger
-	14T55	1H89		13:01 Holyhead-Manchester Picc	class 67	Passenger
17T48	-	1D31		16:50 Manchester Picc-Llandudno	class 67	Passenger
18:20	-	6J37		11:59 Carlisle yard-Chirk	Colas 60	loaded timber

Saturdays: NO BOOKED TRAINS

Sundays: NO BOOKED TRAINS

'Route Knowledge': **(blank)** = to/from Chester;
E = to/from Ellesmere Port

PRESTON *and* LEYLAND

[06:00-midnight]

Mondays-Fridays:

Preston	Leyland	code	Runs	Train		Traction	Type of train
07:35	07:25	6C53	WThFO	06:30	Crewe-Sellafield	2 DRS 37s	flasks
07:45	-	6M32	FX-Q	03:18	Lindsey-Preston Docks	Colas 60	loaded bogie tanks
09:05	-	6E32	FX-Q	08:40	Preston Docks-Lindsey	Colas 60	empty bogie tanks
09:10	09:00	4S43		06:16	Daventry-Mossend	2 DRS 66s	'Tesco Express'
09:15	09:25	4Z27		05:25	Coatbridge-Daventry	F.Liner 70	Intermodal
09:35	-	2C32		05:15	Carlisle-Preston	DRS 37	Passenger(loco on rear)
10:04	-	2C47			Preston-Barrow	DRS 37	Passenger
10:25	10:20	6S94	WO-Q	02:21	Dollands Moor-Irvine	2 EWS 90s	loaded china clay tanks
10:55	-	4M00	MWFO	07:02	Mossend-Clitheroe	EWS 66	empty cement tanks
11:30	11:40	4M25		06:06	Mossend-Daventry	2 EWS 90s	Intermodal
-	11:40	6M90	TThO	05:06	Avonmouth-Clitheroe	EWS 66	empty cement tanks
15:05	15:00	4Z44		12:13	Daventry-Coatbridge	F.Liner 70	Intermodal
16:20	16:35	6K05		10:43	Carlisle yard-Crewe	DRS 66	Departmental
16:45	16:50	6J37		11:59	Carlisle yard-Chirk	Colas 60	loaded timber
18:10	-	6S00	MWFO	17:05	Clitheroe-Mossend	EWS 66	loaded cement tanks
18:10	18:05	6S96	ThO-Q	13:17	Sinfin-Grangemouth	Colas 60	empty tanks
18:30	18:35	1M44		16:17	Shieldmuir-Warrington RMT	-	Mail(325 units)
18:40	19:10	6K27	MWFO	14:43	Carlisle yard-Crewe Basford Hall	DRS 66	Departmental
-	19:30	4C38	MFX-Q	16:23	Fiddlers Ferry-Newbiggin	GBRf 66	containerised gypsum
19:40	19:45	6K73	FX	17:18	Sellafield-Crewe	2 DRS 37s	flasks
-	20:05	6G35	TThO	18:55	Clitheroe-Bescot(-Avonmouth)	EWS 66	loaded cement tanks
20c00	20:05	1M03		17:49	Shieldmuir-Warrington RMT	-	Mail(325 units)
20:25	20:20	1S96		16:22	Willesden PRDC-Shieldmuir	-	Mail(325 units)
20:30	20:40	6V71	MWFO	18:26	Hardendale-Margam	EWS 66	containerised lime
21:40	21:35	4Z45		18:39	Daventry-Coatbridge	F.Liner 70	Intermodal
21:55	21:50	4S56		20:50	Crewe Basford Hall-Coatbridge	2 F.Liner 86s	Freightliner
21:55	22:05	4M11		17:34	Coatbridge-Crewe Basford Hall	2 F.Liner 86s	Freightliner
22:10	22:05	4S47		19:13	Daventry-Mossend	2 EWS 90s	Intermodal
22:20	22:30	4M48		19:04	Mossend-Daventry	2 DRS 66s	'Tesco Express'
23:15	23:20	4L81		19:26	Coatbridge-London Gateway	2 F.Liner 86s	Freightliner

Saturdays:

07:25	07:15	6C53	(Q)	06:30	Crewe-Sellafield	2 DRS 37s	flasks
09:15	09:25	4Z27		05:25	Coatbridge-Daventry	F.Liner 70	Intermodal
10:10	10:00	4S43		06:40	Daventry-Mossend	2 DRS 66s	'Tesco Express'
-	12:15	6M90		05:00	Avonmouth-Clitheroe	EWS 66	empty cement tanks
14:20	14:15	4S49		11:12	Daventry-Grangemouth	EWS 66	Intermodal
15:10	15:05	4Z44		12:05	Daventry-Coatbridge	F.Liner 70	Intermodal
19:35	19:40	4M30		10:15	Grangemouth-Daventry	EWS 66	Intermodal
-	20:25	6G35		19:05	Clitheroe-Bescot	EWS 66	loaded cement tanks

Sundays:

17:45	17:50	4Z55		14:05	Coatbridge-Daventry	F.Liner 70	Intermodal
18:35	18:40	4M48		14:43	Mossend-Daventry	2 DRS 66s	'Tesco Express'
22c05	21:55	4Z45		18:39	Daventry-Coatbridge	F.Liner 70	Intermodal

[06:00-21:00]

Mondays-Fridays:

North	South	H'code	Runs	Train		Traction	Type of train
06:40	-	6M69	T/ThO 03:22	Ferryhill-Arcow quarry		GBRf 66	empty bogie hoppers
06:40	-	6M67	WO-Q 02:53	Pendleton-Arcow quarry		GBRf 66	empty bogie hoppers
-	13:55	6E69	ThO-Q 12:12	Arcow quarry-Leeds Hunslet		GBRf 66	loaded bogie hoppers
-	13:55	6M33	TO-Q 12:12	Arcow quarry-Pendleton		GBRf 66	loaded bogie hoppers
-	13:55	6M34	WO-Q 12:12	Arcow quarry-Bredbury		GBRf 66	loaded bogie hoppers

Saturdays: NO BOOKED TRAINS

Sundays: NO BOOKED TRAINS

'Route Knowledge': **(blank)** = to/from Skipton;
C = to/from Clitheroe

CARLISLE *(station)*

[24-hour]

Mondays-Fridays:

North	South	H'code	Runs	Train	Traction	Type of train
-	06:25W	6C17	ThO	06:14 Carlisle yard-Workington	EWS 66	wagonload
06:25	-	6C18	WFO	03:03 Crewe Basford Hall-Carlisle	DRS 66/68	Departmental
06:50	-	6C34	MX	06:22 Dalston-Carlisle yard	Colas 60	empty bogie tanks
-	07:00W	6C22	FO-Q	06:56 Carlisle Kingmoor-Sellafield	2 DRS 37s	flasks
X07c05	-	4S04	(Q)	04:57 Tyne Dock-Hunterston	GBRf 66	empty GBRf coal hoppers
07:25	-	6C02	MX	04:22 Crewe-Carlisle yard	DRS 66	Departmental
-	07:45	4Z27		05:25 Coatbridge-Daventry	F.Liner 70	Intermodal
-	07:50X	6E44	TO-Q	07:41 Carlisle Kingmoor-Seaton	2 DRS 37s	flasks
-	08:00W	6C35	MX	07:45 Carlisle yard-Dalston	Colas 60	loaded bogie tanks
W08:33	-	2C33		05:46 Barrow-Carlisle	DRS 37	Passenger(diagram 2)
X08c40	-	4S84	(Q)	04:18 Doncaster Decoy-Greenburn	GBRf 66	empty GBRf coal hoppers
-	08:42	2C40		Carlisle-Barrow	DRS 37	Passenger(diagram 2)
08:55	-	6S13	TO-Q	03:56 Doncaster Belmont-Killoch	EWS 66	empty box wagons
-	09c10	4M00	MWFO	07:02 Mossend-Clitheroe	EWS 66	empty cement tanks
W09c20	-	6S36	MX	08:32 Dalston-Grangemouth	Colas 60	empty bogie tanks
-	09:20	4M25		06:06 Mossend-Daventry	2 EWS 90s	Intermodal
-	10:00	6C27	MX-Q	09:42 Carlisle VQ-Shap quarry	DRS 66	empty ballast
X10:20	-	4S62	MX-Q	05:53 Milford-Hunterston	EWS 66	empty EWS coal hoppers
10:35	-	4S43		06:16 Daventry-Mossend	2 DRS 66s	'Tesco Express'
-	11:00	6K05		10:43 Carlisle yard-Crewe Basford Hall	DRS 66	Departmental
12:10	-	6C25	FO-Q	11:25 Shap Quarry-Carlisle yard	EWS 66	loaded bogie hoppers
12:20	-	6S94	WO-Q	02:21 Dollands Moor-Irvine	2 EWS 90s	loaded china clay tanks
W12:20	-	6C48	ThO	11:12 Workington Docks-Carlisle yard	EWS 66	wagonload
-	12:20	6J37		11:59 Carlisle yard-Chirk	Colas 60	loaded timber
-	13:55X	6E50	(Q)	13:48 Carlisle yard-Tyne yard	EWS 66	Departmental
W14:25	-	2C49		11:38 Barrow-Carlisle	DRS 37	Passenger(diagram 2)
-	14:35W	2C34		Carlisle-Barrow	DRS 37	Passenger(diagram 2)
-	14:50	6K27	MWFO	14:43 Carlisle yard-Crewe Basford Hall	DRS 66/68	Departmental
15:35	-	6C28	MX-Q	14:50 Shap Quarry-Carlisle VQ	DRS 66	loaded ballast
-	16:55X	6H97	(Q)	12:35 Hunterston-Drax p.s.	GBRf 66	loaded GBRf coal hoppers
X17c15	-	4S15	(Q)	15:01 Tyne Dock-Hunterston	GBRf 66	empty GBRf coal hoppers
-	17:25	1M44		16:17 Shieldmuir-Warrington RMT	-	Mail(325 units)
W17:28	-	2C41		14:37 Barrow-Carlisle	DRS 37	Passenger(diagram 1)
17c30	-	4Z44		12:13 Daventry-Coatbridge	F.Liner 70	Intermodal
-	17:37W	2C42		Carlisle-Barrow	DRS 37	Passenger(diagram 1)
-	18:25W	6M22	WO-Q	12:17 Hunterston-Sellafield	2 DRS 37s	flasks
-	18:50	1M03		17:49 Shieldmuir-Warrington RMT	-	Mail(325 units)

'Route Knowledge': **(blank)** = WCML via Shap
S = to/from Settle & Carlisle
X = to/from Hexham Line
W = to/from Workington line

North	South	H'code	Runs		Train	Traction	Type of train
-	20:00X	6B70	(Q)	15:25	Greenburn-West Burton p.s.	GBRf 66	loaded GBRf coal hoppers
W20:31	-	2C47		17:31	Barrow-Carlisle	DRS 37	Passenger(diagram 2)
-	20c35	4M11		17:34	Coatbridge-Crewe Basford Hall	2 F.Liner 86s	Freightliner
-	20c45	4M48		19:04	Mossend-Daventry	2 DRS 66s	'Tesco Express'
-	20c50	6M18	ThO-Q	15:10	Killoch-Ketton	EWS 66	coal(in MEA box wagons)
20c50	-	6S96	ThO-Q	13:17	Sinfin-Grangemouth	Colas 60	empty tanks
W21:10	-	6C46	FX-Q	19:31	Sellafield-Kingmoor Depot	2 DRS 37s	flasks
21:15	-	6S00	MWFOQ	17:05	Clitheroe-Mossend	EWS 66	loaded cement tanks
21:35	-	1S96		16:22	Willesden PRDC-Shieldmuir	-	Mail(325 units)
-	21:45	4L81		19:26	Coatbridge-London Gateway	2 F.Liner 86s	Freightliner
-	21:55X	6M59	MX-Q	17:05	Hunterston-Ratcliffe p.s.	EWS 66	loaded EWS coal hoppers
-	22:00	6V16	MO-Q	17:02	Mossend-Cardiff Tidal	EWS 66	empty steel
-	22:10	6V15		17:27	Mossend-Didcot yard	2 EWS 90s	wagonload
-	23c00	4M30		19:10	Grangemouth-Daventry	EWS 66	Intermodal
23c15	-	4Z45		18:39	Daventry-Coatbridge	F.Liner 70	Intermodal
23c20	-	4S56		20:50	Crewe Basford Hall-Coatbridge	2 F.Liner 86s	Freightliner
-	23c50	4L89		22:01	Coatbridge-Felixstowe	2 F.Liner 86s	Freightliner
23c55	-	4S47		19:13	Daventry-Mossend	2 EWS 90s	Intermodal
-	03:55	6Z23	FO-Q	23:47	Carlisle yard-Washwood Heath	EWS 66	loaded bogie hoppers
-	00c20	6M65	ThO-Q	21:15(Wed)	Grangemouth-Sinfin	Colas 60	loaded tanks
-	00c50	6M76	TThO	21:46(MWO)	Mossend-Warrington Arpley	2 EWS 90s	wagonload
-	00c50	6M76	FO	21:46(Thurs)	Mossend-Wembley	2 EWS 90s	empty china clay tanks
-	00:55	6M18	WO-Q	16:08(Tue)	Killoch-Penyffordd	EWS 66	coal(in MEA box wagons)
00:55	-	1S55		23:30	Warrington RMT-Shieldmuir	-	Mail(325 units)
-	01T40	1M11		23:40	Glasgow Central-Euston	F.Liner 90	Caledonian Sleeper
02c15	-	1S25		21:15	Euston-Inverness	F.Liner 90	Caledonian Sleeper
02:25	-	4S83		17:35	London Gateway-Coatbridge	2 F.Liner 86s	Freightliner
02:35	-	6Z33	ThO-Q	23:34(Wed)	Warrington Arpley-Killoch	EWS 66	empty MEA box wagons
-	02:50W	6M34		21:26	Grangemouth-Dalston	Colas 60	loaded bogie tanks
-	02c55	4Z55		00:54	Coatbridge-Daventry	F.Liner 70	Intermodal
-	03c00	1M16		20:44	Inverness-Euston	F.Liner 90	Caledonian Sleeper
03c15	-	6X52	WFO	17:33	Portbury-Mossend	EWS 66	wagonload
03c25	-	4S49		21:58	Daventry-Grangemouth	EWS 66	Intermodal
03:50	-	6C37		22:25	Chirk-Carlisle yard	Colas 60	empty timber carriers
W04:20	-	6C32		03:38	Dalston-Carlisle yard	Colas 60	empty bogie tanks
04:35	-	4S88		16:13	Felixstowe-Coatbridge	2 F.Liner 86s	Freightliner
04c55	-	6S16	FO-Q	20:28(Thurs)	Cardiff Tidal-Mossend	EWS 66	loaded steel
05T05	-	1S26		23:50	Euston-Glasgow Central	F.Liner 90	Caledonian Sleeper
05:15	-	6X65		20:28	Didcot yard-Mossend	2 EWS 90s	wagonload
-	05:15W	2C32		05:15	Carlisle-Barrow	DRS 37	Passenger(diagram 1)
-	05:30W	6C33		05:19	Carlisle yard-Dalston	Colas 60	loaded bogie tanks
-	05:45X	6E94		23:53	Hunterston-Drax p.s.	GBRf 66	loaded GBRf coal hoppers

95

Saturdays:

North	South	H'code	Runs	Train	Traction	Type of train
W06:55	-	6C34		06:22 Dalston-Carlisle yard	Colas 60	empty bogie tanks
07:25	-	6C02		04:22 Crewe-Carlisle yard	DRS 66	Departmental
-	07:50	4Z27		05:25 Coatbridge-Daventry	F.Liner 70	Intermodal
-	08:00W	6C35		07:45 Carlisle yard-Dalston	Colas 60	loaded bogie tanks
W08:33	-	2C33		05:46 Barrow-Carlisle	DRS 37	Passenger(diagram 2)
-	08:42W	2C40		Carlisle-Barrow	DRS 37	Passenger(diagram 2)
W09:45	-	6S36		08:32 Dalston-Grangemouth	Colas 60	empty bogie tanks
W11:35	-	2C41		08:45 Barrow-Carlisle	DRS 37	Passenger(diagram 1)
11:35	-	4S43		06:40 Daventry-Mossend	2 DRS 66s	'Tesco Express'
-	11:56W	2C48		Carlisle-Lancaster	DRS 37	Passenger(diagram 1)
W14:24	-	2C45		11:38 Barrow-Carlisle	DRS 37	Passenger(diagram 2)
-	14:33W	2C34		Carlisle-Barrow	DRS 37	Passenger(diagram 2)
16c35	-	4S49		11:12 Daventry-Grangemouth	EWS 66	Intermodal
-	17c10	4M30		10:15 Grangemouth-Daventry	EWS 66	Intermodal
17c35	-	4Z44		12:05 Daventry-Coatbridge	F.Liner 70	Intermodal
W20:29	-	2C47		17:32 Barrow-Carlisle	DRS 37	Passenger(diagram 2)

Sundays:

-	16:15	4Z55		14:05 Coatbridge-Daventry	F.Liner 70	Intermodal
-	16:55	4M48		14:43 Mossend-Daventry	2 DRS 66s	'Tesco Express'
23c45	-	4Z45		18:39 Daventry-Coatbridge	F.Liner 70	Intermodal

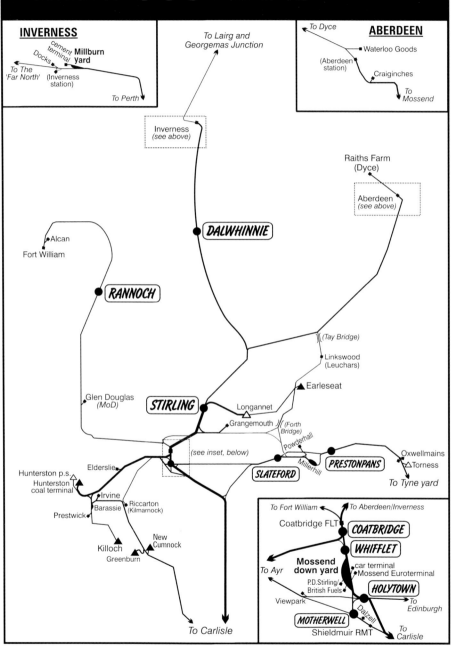

INVERNESS

cement
terminal **Millburn**
Docks **Yard**
To The
'Far North' (Inverness
station)
(Inverness
station)
To Perth

To Lairg and
Georgemas Junction

ABERDEEN

To Dyce
Waterloo Goods
(Aberdeen
station)
Craiginches
To
Mossend

Inverness
(see above)

Raiths Farm
(Dyce)

Aberdeen
(see above)

DALWHINNIE

Alcan
Fort William

RANNOCH

(Tay Bridge)
Linkswood
(Leuchars)

Earleseat

Glen Douglas
(MoD)

STIRLING

Longannet

Grangemouth (Forth
Bridge)

Powderhall

Millerhill

Oxwellmains
Torness

To Tyne yard

(see inset, below)

Eldersie

PRESTONPANS

SLATEFORD

Hunterston p.s.
Hunterston
coal terminal

Irvine
Barassie Riccarton
(Kilmarnock)

Prestwick

New
Cumnock

Killoch
Greenburn

To Carlisle

To Fort William
Coatbridge FLT

To Aberdeen/Inverness

COATBRIDGE

WHIFFLET

car terminal
Mossend Euroterminal

**Mossend
down yard**

To Ayr

P.D.Stirling/
British Fuels

HOLYTOWN

Viewpark

To
Edinburgh

Dalzell

MOTHERWELL

Shieldmuir RMT

To
Carlisle

97

HOLYTOWN and MOTHERWELL

[06:00-midnight]

Mondays-Fridays:

Motherwell	Holytown	code	Runs	Train	Traction	Type of train
-	06:15	4M25		06:06 Mossend-Daventry	2 EWS 90s	Intermodal
06:25	-	6S54	WO-Q	04:42 Carlisle Kingmoor-Hunterston	2 DRS 37s	flasks
07D00	-	1S26		23:50 Euston-Glasgow Central	F.Liner 90	Caledonian Sleeper
-	07:10	4M00	MWFO	07:02 Mossend-Clitheroe	EWS 66	empty cement tanks
-	08:30	6M49		08:22 Mossend-Carlisle yard	GBRf 92	Departmental
-	08:40	6X65	MX	20:28 Didcot yard-Mossend	2 EWS 90s	wagonload
09:15	-	5B26		08:18 Edinburgh-Polmadie	GBRf 92	empty sleeper stock
-	09c25	6S62	TO-Q	01:35 Tunstead-Viewpark(Uddingston)	F.Liner 66	loaded cement tanks
-	10:00S	6D62	W/ThO	07:47 Oxwellmains-Viewpark(Uddingston)	Colas 60	loaded cement tanks
-	10:40S	5G02		09:00 Edinburgh-Motherwell TMD	DRS 68	empty stock
-	11:00	4S99		04:22 Tees Dock-Mossend Euroterminal	EWS 66	Intermodal
-	12:15	6S36	MX	08:32 Dalston-Grangemouth	Colas 60	empty bogie tanks
-	13c15S	6S45	TThO	06:25 North Blyth-Fort William	GBRf 66	loaded alumina tanks
-	13:45	4S43		06:16 Daventry-Mossend	2 DRS 66s	'Tesco Express'
-	14:05	6M22	WO-Q	12:17 Hunterston-Sellafield	2 DRS 37s	flasks
-	15:05S	5G13		14:54 Motherwell TMD-Edinburgh	DRS 68	empty stock
-	15:05	6S51		12:16 Carlisle yard-Mossend	GBRf 92	Departmental
-	15:15	4E99		15:11 Mossend Euroterminal-Tees Dock	EWS 66	Intermodal
-	15c25S	6E45	MWFO	08:07 Fort William-North Blyth	GBRf 66	empty alumina tanks
-	16:10S	5L69		16:04 Motherwell TMD-Edinburgh	DRS 68	empty stock
16:10	-	6S94	WO-Q	02:21 Dollands Moor-Irvine	2 EWS 90s	loaded china clay tanks
-	16:30S	6B34	W/ThO	16:21 Viewpark-Oxwellmains	Colas 60	empty cement tanks
17:00	-	5M03		16:54 Mossend yard-Shieldmuir RMT	-	empty 325 units
-	17:10S	6S48	MX	10:11 Tyne yard-Mossend	GBRf 66	Departmental
-	17:35	6V15		17:27 Mossend-Didcot yard	2 EWS 90s	wagonload
-	18:00S	6E34	TO-Q	17:50 Viewpark(Uddingston)-Tunstead	F.Liner 66	empty cement tanks
-	18:55	4M11		17:34 Coatbridge-Crewe Basford Hall	2 F.Liner 86s	Freightliner
-	19:10	4M48		19:04 Mossend-Daventry	2 DRS 66s	'Tesco Express'
-	19:45	4L81		19:26 Coatbridge-London Gateway	2 F.Liner 86s	Freightliner
-	19:55	4Z44		12:13 Daventry-Coatbridge	F.Liner 70	Intermodal
-	20:00S	6E49	FX	19:55 Mossend-Tyne yard	GBRf 66	Departmental
-	20:45S	5K14		19:47 Edinburgh-Mossend yard	DRS 68	empty stock
21:00	-	5C11		20:43 Polmadie-Edinburgh	GBRf 92	empty sleeper stock
-	20:55	4M30		19:10 Grangemouth-Daventry	EWS 66	Intermodal
-	21:55	6M76	MWThO	21:46 Mossend-Arpley MWO/Wembley ThO	2 EWS 90s	wagonload
22:25	-	4L89		22:01 Coatbridge-Felixstowe	2 F.Liner 86s	Freightliner
22:30	-	6M65	WO-Q	21:15 Grangemouth-Sinfin	Colas 60	loaded tanks
-	23:10	6M34		21:26 Grangemouth-Dalston	Colas 60	loaded bogie tanks
23:30	-	5S96		23:24 Shieldmuir RMT-Mossend yard	-	empty 325 units
23U55	-	1M11		23:41 Glasgow Central-Euston	class 90	Caledonian Sleeper

'**Route Knowledge**': (**blank**) = to/from Law Junction;
      S = to/from Shotts; **H** = to/from Hamilton;

Saturdays:

Motherwell	Holytown	code	Runs	Train		Traction	Type of train
07D00	–	1S26		23:50(Fri)	Euston-Glasgow Central	class 90	Caledonian Sleeper
–	08:20	6X65		20:28(Fri)	Didcot yard-Mossend	2 EWS 90s	wagonload
–	08:40	4D01	(Q)	07:20	Millerhill-Mossend	EWS 66	wagons off repair
09:10	–	5B26		08:23	Edinburgh-Polmadie	GBRf 92	empty sleeper stock
–	12:15	4M30		10:15	Grangemouth-Daventry	EWS 66	Intermodal
–	12:50	6S36		08:32	Dalston-Grangemouth	Colas 60	empty bogie tanks
–	13:45	4B01	(Q)	13:38	Mossend-Millerhill	EWS 66	wagons for repair
–	13:50	4S43		06:40	Daventry-Mossend	2 DRS 66s	'Tesco Express'
–	14c15	6S45		09:25	North Blyth-Fort William	GBRf 66	loaded alumina tanks
–	19:55	4Z44		12:05	Daventry-Coatbridge	F.Liner 70	Intermodal
–	20:55	4S49		11:12	Daventry-Grangemouth	EWS 66	Intermodal

Sundays:

14:20	–	4Z55		14:05	Coatbridge-Daventry	F.Liner 70	Intermodal
15:00	–	4M48		14:43	Mossend-Daventry	2 DRS 66s	'Tesco Express'
–	21:05	5C11		20:47	Polmadie-Edinburgh	class 92	empty sleeper stock

DALWHINNIE

[06:00-midnight]

Mondays-Fridays:

North	South	H'code	Runs	Train		Traction	Type of train
06:20	–	6H44	FO-Q	03:43	Mossend-Lairg	EWS 66	loaded oil tanks
07D00	–	1S25		21:20	London Kings Cross-Inverness	DB 67	Caledonian Sleeper
08:05	–	4H47	ThX-Q	05:04	Mossend-Inverness	DRS 66	Intermodal
08:05	–	6H51	T/ThO	03:00	Oxwellmains-Inverness	Colas 60	loaded cement tanks
08:25	–	4H47	ThO-Q	05:04	Mossend-Inverness	DRS 66	Intermodal
–	08:55	1E13		07:55	Inverness-London Kings Cross	–	Passenger(HST)
–	15:00	4D47		13:19	Inverness-Mossend	DRS 66	Intermodal
19:00	–	1S16		12:00	London Kings Cross-Inverness	–	Passenger(HST)
–	19:35	6B31	T/ThO	17:59	Inverness-Oxwellmains	Colas 60	empty cement tanks
–	22U05	1M16		20:44	Inverness-London Kings Cross	DB 67	Caledonian Sleeper

Saturdays:

07D00	–	1S25		21:20	London Kings Cross-Inverness	DB 67	Caledonian Sleeper
07:45	–	4H47		05:04	Mossend-Inverness	DRS 66	Intermodal
–	08:55	1E13		07:55	Inverness-London Kings Cross	–	Passenger(HST)
–	13:35	6H66	(Q)	08:11	Lairg-Mossend	EWS 66	empty oil tanks
–	15:05	4D47		13:19	Inverness-Mossend	DRS 66	Intermodal
19:00	–	1S15		12:00	London Kings Cross-Inverness	–	Passenger(HST)

Sundays:

–	21U50	1M16		20:25	Inverness-London Kings Cross	DB 67	Caledonian Sleeper

99

COATBRIDGE and WHIFFLET

[06:00-midnight]

Mondays-Fridays:

Coatbridge	Whifflet	code	Runs	Train	Traction	Type of train
06:10	06:05	6A32	WO	05:52 Mossend-Aberdeen Waterloo	EWS 66	bogie clay tanks
07:15	07:10	6A32	FO	07:07 Mossend-Aberdeen Waterloo	EWS 66	bogie clay tanks
07:20C	–	6R46	TFO-Q	06:41 Grangemouth-Prestwick	Colas 60	loaded 4-wheel tanks
–	C07:35	6R52	MO	07:20 Mossend-Irvine	EWS 66	loaded china clay tanks
07:55C	–	6B01	MO-Q	06:56 Grangemouth-Riccarton	Colas 60	empty 4-wheel tanks
08:35	08:30	6Y15	TO-Q	08:23 Mossend-Fort William	EWS 66	loaded 4-wheel tanks
11:05	11:10	5K19		08:47 Edinburgh-Motherwell TMD	DRS 66	empty stock
12:10	12:05	4D51		11:00 Grangemouth-Mossend yard	EWS 66	Intermodal
13:05C	–	6D61	MO-Q	10:28 Riccarton-Grangemouth	Colas 60	empty 4-wheel tanks
13:20	13:15	6S45	TThO	06:25 North Blyth-Fort William	GBRf 66	loaded alumina tanks
13:55	13:50	6S36	MX	08:32 Dalston-Grangemouth	Colas 60	empty bogie tanks
14:20	14:15	4N30		14:08 Mossend yard-Grangemouth	EWS 66	Intermodal
15:00	15:05	6E45	MWFO	08:07 Fort William-North Blyth	GBRf 66	empty alumina tanks
17:35	17:40	4M11		17:34 Coatbridge-Crewe Basford Hall	2 F.Liner 86s	Freightliner
17:50	17:55	4D47		13:19 Inverness-Mossend	DRS 66	Intermodal
18:00	18:05	6D17	M/ThO	17:20 Grangemouth-Mossend	EWS 66	loaded bogie tanks
–	C18:05	6D79	ThO	15:42 Irvine-Mossend	EWS 66	empty china clay tanks
–	C18:45	6S94	WO-Q	02:21 Dollands Moor-Irvine	EWS 66	loaded china clay tanks
19:05C	–	6N47	TFO-Q	16:56 Prestwick-Grangemouth	Colas 60	empty 4 wheel tanks
19:10	19:15	6D84	WO	13:45 Aberdeen Waterloo-Mossend	EWS 66	bogie clay tanks
19:30	19:35	4L81		19:26 Coatbridge-London Gateway	2 F.Liner 86s	Freightliner
20:05	20:10	6D16	WO-Q	13:29 Fort William-Mossend	EWS 66	empty 4-wheel tanks
20:15	20:10	4Z44		12:13 Daventry-Coatbridge	F.Liner 70	Intermodal
20:40	20:45	4M30		19:10 Grangemouth-Daventry	EWS 66	Intermodal
20:45	20:50	5L70		18:24 Cardenden-Mossend yard	DRS 68	empty stock
22:00	22:05	6M65	WO-Q	21:15 Grangemouth-Sinfin	Colas 56	loaded tanks
22:05	22:10	4L89		22:01 Coatbridge-Felixstowe	2 F.Liner 86s	Freightliner
22:25	22:45	6M34		21:26 Grangemouth-Dalston	Colas 60	loaded bogie tanks

Saturdays:

11:15	11:20	4M30		10:15 Grangemouth-Daventry	EWS 66	Intermodal
12:55	12:50	6S36		08:32 Dalston-Grangemouth	Colas 60	empty bogie tanks
14:35	14:30	6S45		09:25 North Blyth-Fort William	GBRf 66	loaded alumina tanks
16:10	16:15	6H66	(Q)	08:11 Lairg-Mossend	EWS 66	empty oil tanks
17:45	17:50	4D47		13:19 Inverness-Mossend	DRS 66	Intermodal
19:45	20:40	4S55		09:54 Daventry-Coatbridge	DRS 66	Intermodal
20:15	20:10	4Z44		12:05 Daventry-Coatbridge	F.Liner 70	Intermodal
21:15	21:10	4S49		11:12 Daventry-Grangemouth	EWS 66	Intermodal
23:05	23:10	6D84		18:00 Aberdeen Waterloo-Mossend	EWS 66	bogie clay tanks

Sundays:

14:10	14:15	4Z55		14:05 Coatbridge-Daventry	F.Liner 70	Intermodal
23:25	23:30	4M30		22:33 Grangemouth-Daventry	EWS 66	Intermodal

'Route Knowledge': C = to/from Carmyle; S = to/from Sunnyside Junction

RANNOCH

[06:00-midnight]

Mondays-Fridays:

North	South	H'code	Runs	Train	Traction	Type of train
08T43	-	1Y11		04:50 Edinburgh-Fort William	DB 67	Caledonian Sleeper
-	10:00	6E45	MWFO	08:07 Fort William-North Blyth	GBRf 66	empty alumina tanks
12:40	-	6Y15	TO-Q	08:23 Mossend-Fort William	EWS 66	loaded 4-wheel tanks
-	14:25	6D16	WO-Q	13:29 Fort William-Mossend	EWS 66	empty 4-wheel tanks
18:40	-	6S45	TThO	06:25 North Blyth-Fort William	GBRf 66	loaded alumina tanks
-	21T05	1B01		19:50 Fort William-Edinburgh	DB 67	Caledonian Sleeper

Saturdays:

North	South	H'code	Runs	Train	Traction	Type of train
08T43	-	1Y11		04:50 Edinburgh-Fort William	DB 67	Caledonian Sleeper
20:10	-	6S45		09:25 North Blyth-Fort William	GBRf 66	loaded alumina tanks

Sundays:

North	South	H'code	Runs	Train	Traction	Type of train
-	20T15	1B01		19:00 Fort William-Edinburgh	DB 67	Caledonian Sleeper

SLATEFORD *(Edinburgh West)*

[06:00-midnight]

Mondays-Fridays:

West	East	H'code	Runs	Train		Traction	Type of train
-	07:10	1B26		06:34	Carstairs-Edinburgh	GBRf 92	Caledonian Sleeper
08:25	-	5B26		08:18	Edinburgh-Polmadie	GBRf 92	empty sleeper stock
-	08:55	6S43	ThO-Q	06:23	Carlisle Kingmoor-Torness	2 DRS 37s	flasks
09:10	-	6D62	ThO-Q	07:47	Oxwellmains-Viewpark(Uddingston)	Colas 60	loaded cement tanks
09:25	-	4S99		04:22	Tees Dock-Mossend Euroterminal	EWS 66	Intermodal
09:45	-	5G02		09:00	Edinburgh-Motherwell TMD	DRS 68	empty stock
12:25	-	6S45	TThO	06:25	North Blyth-Fort William	GBRf 66	loaded alumina tanks
-	15:45	5G13		14:54	Motherwell TMD-Edinburgh	DRS 68	empty stock
16:25	-	6S48	MX	10:11	Tyne yard-Mossend	GBRf 66	Departmental
-	16:25	6E45	MWFO	08:07	Fort William-North Blyth	GBRf 66	empty alumina tanks
-	16:40	4E99		15:11	Mossend Euroterminal-Tees Dock	EWS 66	Intermodal
-	16:50	5L69		16:04	Motherwell TMD-Edinburgh	DRS 68	empty stock
-	17:15	6B34	ThO-Q	16:21	Viewpark-Oxwellmains	Colas 60	empty cement tanks
17:25	-	6M50	ThO-Q	15:12	Torness-Carlisle Kingmoor	2 DRS 37s	flasks
20:10	-	5K14		19:47	Edinburgh-Mossend yard	DRS 68	empty stock

Saturdays:

West	East	H'code	Runs	Train		Traction	Type of train
-	07:10	1B26		06:34	Carstairs-Edinburgh	GBRf 92	Caledonian Sleeper
07:50	-	4D01	(Q)	07:20	Millerhill-Mossend	EWS 66	wagons off repair
08:30	-	5B26		08:23	Edinburgh-Polmadie	GBRf 92	empty sleeper stock
13:30	-	6S45	(Q)	09:25	North Blyth-Fort William	GBRf 66	loaded alumina tanks
-	14:40	4B01	(Q)	13:38	Mossend-Millerhill	EWS 66	wagons for repair

Sundays: NO BOOKED TRAINS

PRESTONPANS *(Edinburgh East)*

[06:00-22:00]

Mondays-Fridays:

West	East	H'code	Runs	Train	Traction	Type of train
06:35	–	6A65	MWO	06:07(05:55 Mon) Oxwellmains-Aberdeen	Colas 60	loaded cement
08:20	–	6D62	ThO-Q	07:47 Oxwellmains-Viewpark(Uddingston)	Colas 60	loaded cement tanks
08:35	–	4S99		04:22 Tees Dock-Mossend Euroterminal	EWS 66	Intermodal
–	09:45	6S43	ThO-Q	06:23 Carlisle Kingmoor-Torness	2 DRS 37s	flasks
–	10:45	6B45	(Q)	10:25 Powderhall-Oxwellmains	EWS 67	loaded 'binliner'
10:55	–	6S45	TThO	06:25 North Blyth-Fort William	GBRf 66	loaded alumina tanks
13:45	–	6B46	(Q)	13:26 Oxwellmains-Powderhall	EWS 67	empty 'binliner'
14:20	–	6S48	MX	10:11 Tyne yard-Mossend	GBRf 66	Departmental
15:35	–	6M50	ThO-Q	15:12 Torness-Carlisle Kingmoor	2 DRS 37s	flasks
–	17:45	6E45	MWFO	08:07 Fort William-North Blyth	GBRf 66	empty alumina tanks
–	17:55	6B34	ThO-Q	16:21 Viewpark-Oxwellmains	Colas 60	empty cement tanks
–	18:50	4E99		15:11 Mossend Euroterminal-Tees Dock	EWS 66	Intermodal

Saturdays:

West	East	H'code	Runs	Train	Traction	Type of train
12:40	–	6S45	(Q)	09:25 North Blyth-Fort William	GBRf 66	loaded alumina tanks

Sundays: NO BOOKED TRAINS

103

[06:00-midnight]

Mondays-Fridays:

North	South	H'code	Runs	Train		Traction	Type of train
06:45	–	6A32	WO	05:54	Mossend-Aberdeen Waterloo	EWS 66	bogie clay tanks
08:15	–	6A32	FO	07:07	Mossend-Aberdeen Waterloo	EWS 66	bogie clay tanks
08:40	–	6A65	MWFOQ	06:07(05:55 Mon)	Oxwellmains-Aberdeen	Colas 60	loaded cement
13:20	–	4A13		12:23	Grangemouth-Aberdeen	DRS 68	Intermodal
–	17:15	4D47		13:19	Inverness-Mossend	DRS 66	Intermodal
–	18c25	6D84	WO	13:45	Aberdeen Waterloo-Mossend	EWS 66	bogie clay tanks
–	21:30	4N83		18:20	Aberdeen-Grangemouth	DRS 68	Intermodal
–	22:15	6B31	T/ThO	17:59	Inverness-Oxwellmains	Colas 60	empty cement tanks

Saturdays:

North	South	H'code	Runs	Train		Traction	Type of train
13:20	–	4A13		12:23	Grangemouth-Aberdeen	DRS 68	Intermodal
–	15:30	6H66	(Q)	08:11	Lairg-Mossend	EWS 66	empty oil tanks
–	17:10	4D47		13:19	Inverness-Mossend	DRS 66	Intermodal
–	22:30	6D84		18:00	Aberdeen Waterloo-Mossend	EWS 66	bogie clay tanks
–	22:40	4N83		19:31	Aberdeen-Grangemouth	DRS 68	Intermodal

Sundays:

North	South	H'code	Runs	Train		Traction	Type of train
12:40	–	4A13		11:45	Grangemouth-Aberdeen	DRS 68	Intermodal
–	20:30	4N83		18:09	Aberdeen-Grangemouth	DRS 68	Intermodal

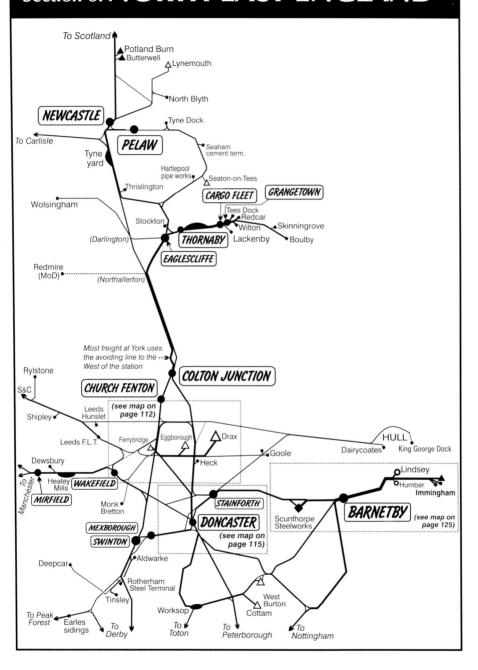

TYNESIDE
(Newcastle *and* Pelaw)

[06:00-21:00]

Mondays-Fridays:

Newcastle	Pelaw	code	Runs		Train	Traction	Type of train
06:30	-	4S99		04:22	Tees Dock-Mossend Euroterminal	EWS 66	Intermodal
06:35	-	6E92	T/ThO	03:42	Oxwellmains-Seaham Harbour	Colas 60	loaded cement tanks
-	06:35	4N34		02:38	Drax p.s.-Tyne Dock	GBRf 66	empty biomass hoppers
-	07:00	4N24	MX	03:35	Doncaster Decoy-Tyne Dock	GBRf 66	empty GBRf coal hoppers
07:25	07:00	4N67		06:40	Tyne Dock-North Blyth	GBRf 66	empty GBRf coal hoppers
-	07:55	6E92	T/ThO	03:42	Oxwellmains-Seaham Harbour	Colas 60	loaded cement tanks
-	07:55	6E92	T/ThO	02:29	Tunstead-Seaham Harbour	F.Liner 66	loaded cement tanks
09c25	-	4N44	MTX-Q	06:43	Doncaster Decoy-North Blyth	GBRf 66	empty GBRf coal hoppers
-	10:05	6E44	TO-Q	07:41	Carlisle-Seaton-on-Tees	2 DRS 37s	flasks
10:25	-	6S48	MX	10:11	Tyne yard-Mossend	GBRf 66	Departmental
11:25	-	4N04	WO-Q	09:34	Ferryhill-North Blyth	F.Liner 66	empty FHH coal hoppers
12:45	13:05	6B89		11:48	North Blyth-West Burton p.s.	GBRf 66	loaded GBRf coal hoppers
-	14:25	6M60	TO-Q	13:23	Seaton-on-Tees-Sellafield	2 DRS 37s	flasks
14:50	-	6B39	MTX-Q	13:53	North Blyth-West Burton p.s.	GBRf 66	loaded GBRf coal hoppers
14:50	-	6M07	WO-Q	13:53	North Blyth-Ratcliffe p.s.	F.Liner 66	loaded FHH coal hoppers
15c25	15:05	6N49	FX-Q	07:05	Ferrybridge p.s.-North Blyth	GBRf 66	coal(in box wagons)
-	15:25	4S15	(Q)	15:01	Tyne Dock-Hunterston	GBRf 66	empty GBRf coal hoppers
15:50	15:30	6S26	T/WO	14:47	Seaham Harbour-Oxwellmains	Colas 60	empty cement tanks
-	16:35	6M26	T/ThO	16:04	Seaham Harbour-Tunstead	F.Liner 66	empty cement tanks
-	18:35	4N30		15:29	Drax p.s.-Tyne Dock	GBRf 66	empty biomass hoppers
-	19:05	6H97	(Q)	12:35	Hunterston-Drax p.s.	GBRf 66	loaded GBRf coal hoppers

Saturdays:

-	06:10	4N34		02:50	Drax p.s.-Tyne Dock	GBRf 66	empty biomass hoppers
-	14:10	4N80		11:34	Doncaster Decoy-Tyne Dock	GBRf 66	empty GBRf coal hoppers
-	16:00	6H98		15:38	Tyne Dock-Drax p.s.	GBRf 66	loaded biomass hoppers

Sundays:

-	12:20	4N99		09:25	Drax p.s.-Tyne Dock	GBRf 66	empty biomass hoppers
-	12:30	6H94		12:09	Tyne Dock-Drax p.s.	GBRf 66	loaded biomass hoppers
-	16:20	4N30	(Q)	13:30	Drax p.s.-Tyne Dock	GBRf 66	empty biomass hoppers
-	16:30	6H98		16:10	Tyne Dock-Drax p.s.	GBRf 66	loaded biomass hoppers

TEESSIDE EAST
(Cargo Fleet *and* Grangetown)

[06:00-21:00]

Mondays-Fridays:

Cargo Fleet	Grangetown	code	Runs	Train	Traction	Type of train
-	07R35	6F31	MX-Q	07:10 Tees Dock-Boulby	F.Liner 66	empty hoppers
-	07R55	6F34		06:57 Boulby-Tees Dock	F.Liner 66	loaded hoppers(Potash)
10:40	10:30	6F32		09:34 Boulby-Middlesbrough Goods	F.Liner 66	loaded hoppers(rock salt)
12:00	11:55	6N55	MX-Q	11:15 Skiningrove-Tees yard	EWS 66	empty steel
12:10	-	6N31		07:41 Scunthorpe-Lackenby	EWS 66	loaded steel
12:40	12:45	4N01	TWThO	10:27 Leeds FLT-Tees Dock	F.Liner 66	Freightliner
-	13R15	6F33		12:49 Tees Dock-Boulby	F.Liner 66	empty hoppers
-	13R25	6F24	FX-Q	12:28 Boulby-Tees Dock	F.Liner 66	loaded hoppers(Potash)
13:40	-	6D11		13:29 Lackenby-Scunthorpe	EWS 66	empty steel
13:40	13:45	6N40	WFX-Q	13:26 Tees yard-Skiningrove	EWS 66	loaded steel
15:05	14:55	4D07	TWThO	14:48 Tees Dock-Leeds FLT	F.Liner 66	Freightliner
16:10	16:05	4L79		15:55 Tees Dock-Felixstowe	F.Liner 66	Freightliner
-	16R25	6F34	(Q)	15:23 Boulby-Tees Dock	F.Liner 66	loaded hoppers(Potash)
-	18R45	6F35	FX-Q	18:10 Tees Dock-Boulby	F.Liner 66	empty hoppers
19:10	19:15	6F35	(Q)	18:30 Middlesbrough Goods-Boulby	F.Liner 66	empty hoppers
-	19R25	6F26	(Q)	18:22 Boulby-Tees Dock	F.Liner 66	loaded hoppers(Potash)

Saturdays:

12:55	-	6D05		12:42 Lackenby-Scunthorpe	EWS 66	empty steel

Sundays:

10:30	-	6D37	(Q)	10:15 Lackenby-Scunthorpe	EWS 66	empty steel

107

TEESSIDE WEST
(Eaglescliffe _and_ Thornaby)

[06:00-21:00]

Mondays-Fridays:

Eaglescliffe	Thornaby	code	Runs	Train		Traction	Type of train
07:50	-	6H12		06:25 Tyne Dock-Drax p.s.		GBRf 66	loaded biomass hoppers
08:15	-	4N23		06:14 Doncaster Decoy-Tyne Dock		GBRf 66	empty GBRf coal hoppers
-	09:20	6N90	WX	09:17 Tees yard-Thrislington		EWS 66	empty containers
10:15	-	4N47		08:24 Drax p.s.-Tyne Dock		GBRf 66	empty biomass hoppers
10:30	10:40	6N31		07:41 Scunthorpe-Lackenby		EWS 66	loaded steel
11:15	-	6H30		09:49 Tyne Dock-Drax p.s.		GBRf 66	loaded biomass hoppers
12:15	12:25	4N01	TWThO	10:27 Leeds FLT-Tees Dock	F.Liner 66		Freightliner
13:15	-	6N49	MFX-Q	07:05 Ferrybridge p.s.-North Blyth		GBRf 66	coal(in box wagons)
-	13:55	6N91	WX	13:07 Thrislington-Tees yard		EWS 66	containerised limestone
-	14:05	6N27	(Q)	14:05|Hartlepool-Tees yard		EWS 66	empty coil carriers
14:15	-	6B64	MX-Q	12:49 Tyne Dock-West Burton p.s.		GBRf 66	loaded GBRf coal hoppers
14:20	-	6B89		11:48 North Blyth-West Burton p.s.		GBRf 66	loaded GBRf coal hoppers
14:50	-	4N61		12:45 Drax p.s.-Tyne Dock		GBRf 66	empty biomass hoppers
15:00	14:50	6D11	MX	13:23 Lackenby-Scunthorpe		EWS 66	empty steel
15:15	-	4N35	MX-Q	13:28 Drax p.s.-Tyne Dock		GBRf 66	empty GBRf coal hoppers
15:20	15:10	4D07	TWThO	14:48 Tees Dock-Leeds FLT	F.Liner 66		Freightliner
15:50	15:40	6D11	MO	13:23 Lackenby-Scunthorpe		EWS 66	empty steel
15:55	-	6H55		14:37 Tyne Dock-Drax p.s.		GBRf 66	loaded biomass hoppers
16:50	16:40	4L79		15:55 Tees Dock-Felixstowe	F.Liner 66		Freightliner
17:25	-	6Z35	ThO-Q	17:01 Stockton-Cardiff Tidal		DCR 56	scrap(in box wagons)
18:45	-	6Z34	WO-Q	14:25 Chaddesden(Derby)-Stockton		DCR 56	empty box wagons
18:50	18:40	6V02		18:37 Tees yard-Margam		EWS 66	empty steel/lime
19:20	-	6H98		18:00 Tyne Dock-Drax p.s.		GBRf 66	loaded biomass hoppers
19:50	-	6V00	TO-Q	19:30 Port Clarence-Cardiff Docks		GBRf 66	loaded bogie tanks
19:50	19:35	6V49	MWFO	19:34 Tees yard-Margam		EWS 66	empty steel

Saturdays:

Eaglescliffe	Thornaby	code	Runs	Train	Traction	Type of train
08:35	–	6H85		07:11 Tyne Dock-Drax p.s.	GBRf 66	loaded biomass hoppers
10:15	–	6H30		08:56 Tyne Dock-Drax p.s.	GBRf 66	loaded biomass hoppers
11:15	–	6D30	(Q)	09:49 Tyne Dock-Doncaster Decoy	GBRf 66	loaded GBRf coal hoppers
11:15	–	4N96		09:18 Drax p.s.-Tyne Dock	GBRf 66	empty biomass hoppers
13:50	13:40	6D05		12:42 Lackenby-Scunthorpe	EWS 66	empty steel
14:50	–	4N62		12:44 Drax p.s.-Tyne Dock	GBRf 66	empty biomass hoppers
16:35	–	4N30		14:27 Drax p.s.-Tyne Dock	GBRf 66	empty biomass hoppers

Sundays:

09:50	–	6H30		08:31 Tyne Dock-Drax p.s.	GBRf 66	loaded biomass hoppers
11:40	11:30	6D37	(Q)	10:15 Lackenby-Scunthorpe	EWS 66	empty steel

YORK SOUTH
(Colton Junction _and_ Church Fenton)

[06:00-21:00]

Mondays-Fridays:

Colton Junction	Church Fenton	code	Runs	Train		Faction	Type of train
06:55	–	4N23		06:14	Doncaster Decoy-Tyne Dock	GBRf 66	empty GBRf coal hoppers
09:10	–	6N31		07:41	Scunthorpe-Lackenby	EWS 66	loaded steel
09:15	09:05	4N47		08:24	Drax p.s.-Tyne Dock	GBRf 66	empty biomass hoppers
09:35	09:20	6N49	MFX-Q	07:05	Ferrybridge p.s.-North Blyth	GBRf 66	coal(in box wagons)
09:30	09:40	6H12		06:25	Tyne Dock-Drax p.s.	GBRf 66	loaded biomass hoppers
10:10	10:00	4S62	(Q)	09:39	Milford-Hunterston	EWS 66	empty EWS coal hoppers
11:00	10:55	4N01	TWThO	10:27	Leeds FLT-Tees Dock	F.Liner 66	Freightliner
11:00	11:10	6E94	MX-Q	23:53	Hunterston-Drax p.s.	GBRf 66	loaded GBRf coal hoppers
12:40	12:30	6E88	MWFO	09:45	Mountsorrel-Tyne yard	F.Liner 66	loaded ballast
12:40	12:50	6H30		09:49	Tyne Dock-Drax p.s.	GBRf 66	loaded biomass hoppers
13:45	13:40	4N61		12:45	Drax p.s.-Tyne Dock	GBRf 66	empty biomass hoppers
14:05	–	6N70		13:30	Doncaster-Tyne yard	EWS 66	Departmental
14:15	14:05	4N35	MX-Q	13:28	Drax p.s.-Tyne Dock	GBRf 66	empty GBRf coal hoppers
15:40	15:50	6B64	MX-Q	12:49	Tyne Dock-West Burton p.s.	GBRf 66	loaded GBRf coal hoppers
16:20	16:30	6D11	MX	13:23	Lackenby-Scunthorpe	EWS 66	empty steel
16:40	16:35	4N30		15:29	Drax p.s.-Tyne Dock	GBRf 66	empty biomass hoppers
16:40	16:50	6B89		11:48	North Blyth-West Burton p.s.	GBRf 66	loaded GBRf coal hoppers
16:55	17:00	4D07	TWThO	14:48	Tees Dock-Leeds FLT	F.Liner 66	Freightliner
17:15	–	6D11	MO	13:23	Lackenby-Scunthorpe	EWS 66	empty steel
17:35	17:25	6Z34	WO-Q	14:25	Chaddesden(Derby)-Stockton	DCR 56	empty box wagons
17:35	17:45	6H55		14:37	Tyne Dock-Drax p.s.	GBRf 66	loaded biomass hoppers
18:15	–	4L79		15:55	Tees Dock-Felixstowe	F.Liner 66	Freightliner
18:20	18:30	6B39	MWX-Q	13:53	North Blyth-West Burton p.s.	GBRf 66	loaded GBRf coal hoppers
18:20	18:30	6M07	WO-Q	13:53	North Blyth-Ratcliffe p.s.	F.Liner 66	loaded FHH coal hoppers
20:30	20:35	6V02		18:37	Tees yard-Margam	EWS 66	empty steel/lime
20:40	20:50	6H98		18:00	Tyne Dock-Drax p.s.	GBRf 66	loaded biomass hoppers
21:00	21:10	6V49	MWFO	19:34	Tees yard-Margam	EWS 66	empty steel
21:10	–	6N73		19:47	Scunthorpe-Lackenby	EWS 66	loaded steel

Saturdays:

Colton Junction	Church Fenton	code	Runs	Train	Traction	Type of train
06:05	06:15	6H45		03:27 Tyne Dock-Drax p.s.	GBRf 66	loaded biomass hoppers
10:00	10:10	6H85		07:11 Tyne Dock-Drax p.s.	GBRf 66	loaded biomass hoppers
10:15	10:15	4N96		09:18 Drax p.s.-Tyne Dock	GBRf 66	empty biomass hoppers
11:00	11:10	6E94		23:47(Fri) Hunterston-Drax p.s.	GBRf 66	loaded GBRf coal hoppers
11:35	11:20	4N99	(Q)	10:55 Milford-Tyne yard	EWS 66	empty EWS coal hoppers
11:40	11:50	6H30		08:56 Tyne Dock-Drax p.s.	GBRf 66	loaded biomass hoppers
12:05	–	4N80		11:34 Doncaster Decoy-Tyne Dock	GBRf 66	empty GBRf coal hoppers
12:35	12:45	6D30	(Q)	09:49 Tyne Dock-Doncaster Decoy	GBRf 66	loaded GBRf coal hoppers
13:45	13:35	4N62		12:44 Drax p.s.-Tyne Dock	GBRf 66	empty biomass hoppers
15:25	15:15	4N30		14:27 Drax p.s.-Tyne Dock	GBRf 66	empty biomass hoppers
15:40	15:50	6D05		12:42 Lackenby-Scunthorpe	EWS 66	empty steel
18:55	19:05	6H98		15:38 Tyne Dock-Drax p.s.	GBRf 66	loaded biomass hoppers
20:35	20:20	6N80		18:45 Scunthorpe-Tees yard	EWS 66	loaded steel

Sundays:

Colton Junction	Church Fenton	code	Runs	Train	Traction	Type of train
10:35	10:25	4N99		09:25 Drax p.s.-Tyne Dock	GBRf 66	empty biomass hoppers
11:10	11:20	6H30		08:31 Tyne Dock-Drax p.s.	GBRf 66	loaded biomass hoppers
13:10	–	6D37	(Q)	10:15 Lackenby-Scunthorpe	EWS 66	empty steel
14:35	14:20	4N30	(Q)	13:30 Drax p.s.-Tyne Dock	GBRf 66	empty biomass hoppers
16:20	16:30	6H94		12:09 Tyne Dock-Drax p.s.	GBRf 66	loaded biomass hoppers
17:55	–	4N64	(Q)	17:25 Doncaster RMT-Tyne Dock	GBRf 66	empty GBRf coal hoppers
19:15	19:25	6H98		16:10 Tyne Dock-Drax p.s.	GBRf 66	loaded biomass hoppers
20:35	20:25	4N94		19:05 Drax p.s.-Tyne Dock	GBRf 66	empty biomass hoppers

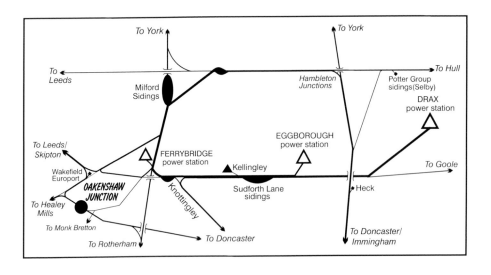

112

WAKEFIELD (Oakenshaw Junction)

[06:00-21:00]

Mondays-Fridays:

West	East	H'code	Runs	Train	Traction	Type of train
06:25	–	4E48	MX	23:01 Southampton Maritime-Leeds	F.Liner 66	Freightliner
–	06:40	4090		06:12 Leeds FLT-Southampton	F.Liner 66/70	Freightliner
–	07:05	6E33	WFO	03:57 Warrington-Doncaster Railport	EWS 66	wagonload
–	07:20	6E37		02:10 Liverpool-Drax p.s.	GBRf 66	loaded biomass hoppers
08:45	–	4E01	MX	01:30 Southampton Millbrook-Leeds	F.Liner 66	Freightliner
–	09:15	4L87	MX	08:47 Leeds FLT-Felixstowe	F.Liner 66	Freightliner
09:45	–	4E01	MO	03:22 Southampton Maritime-Leeds	F.Liner 66	Freightliner
–	09:50	4L45		09:36 Wakefield Europort-Felixstowe	EWS 66	Intermodal
–	10:15	6M89	(Q)	09:50 Dewsbury-Earles	F.Liner 66	empty cement tanks
10:30	–	4E08	TThO	03:41 London Gateway-Wakefield Europort	EWS 66	Intermodal
10:40	–	4M51		10:00 Drax p.s.-Liverpool	GBRf 66	empty biomass hoppers
11:30	–	6D79	WO	08:34 Lindsey-Neville Hill	EWS 66/60	fuel oil tanks
–	11:45	6E32	FX-Q	08:40 Preston Docks-Lindsey	Colas 60	empty bogie tanks
–	12:40	4095	MX	12:12 Leeds FLT-Southampton	F.Liner 66/70	Freightliner
13:45	–	4E22	MX	05:50 Felixstowe-Leeds	F.Liner 66	Freightliner
–	14:40	6M35	FX-Q	11:10 Rylstone-Small Heath	GBRf 66	loaded bogie boxes
–	14:55	6D80	WO	14:05 Neville Hill-Lindsey	EWS 66/60	fuel oil tanks
–	15:45	4L08	TThO	15:28 Wakefield Europort-London Gateway	EWS 66	Intermodal
18:25	–	6M30	WFO	16:45 Doncaster Railport-Warrington	EWS 66	wagonload
–	18:25	6E10		08:20 Liverpool-Drax p.s.	GBRf 66	loaded biomass hoppers
–	18:40	4052	WO	18:27 Wakefield Europort-Southampton	EWS 66	Intermodal
19:10	–	4E69	TFO	09:32 Southampton-Wakefield Europort	EWS 66	Intermodal
–	20:40	4007		20:18 Leeds FLT-Southampton Millbrook	F.Liner 66	Freightliner

Saturdays:

West	East	H'code	Runs	Train	Traction	Type of train
–	09:45	4V52	(Q)	09:31 Wakefield Europort-Didcot yard	EWS 66	Intermodal
–	10:20	6M68		09:55 Dewsbury-Earles	F.Liner 66	empty cement tanks
–	11:45	4L85		11:23 Leeds-Ipswich yard	F.Liner 66	Freightliner
13:40	–	4E22		06:14 Felixstowe-Leeds FLT	F.Liner 66	Freightliner

Sundays: NO BOOKED TRAINS

DONCASTER *(Station)*

[24-hour]

Monday-Fridays:

North	South	H'code	Runs	Train	Traction	Type of train
06:20	-	4N23		06:14 Decoy(down) yard-Tyne Dock	GBRf 66	empty GBRf coal hoppers
-	H06:45R	6D33	TThO	05:18 Goole Glassworks-Roberts Road	GBRf 66	empty 4-wheel hoppers
07:00H	-	6D74		06:54 Decoy(up) yard-Scunthorpe	EWS 66	Departmental
07:15	-	4Z78	MX	01:58 Felixstowe-Selby	GBRf 66	Intermodal
07:50H	-	6G80	T/ThO	07:41 Belmont yard-Immingham	EWS 66	empty MEA box wagons
-	W07:55	6E33	WFO	03:57 Warrington-Doncaster Railport	EWS 66	wagonload
R08:40	-	6E56	ThO	06:22 Tunstead-Drax p.s.	EWS 66	loaded bogie hoppers
09:15W	-	4E08	TThO	03:42 London Gateway-Wakefield Europort	EWS 66	Intermodal
-	H09:35	6D75		08:45 Scunthorpe-Decoy(up) yard	EWS 66	Departmental(rails)
-	W09:45	4L87	MX	08:47 Leeds FLT-Felixstowe	F.Liner 66	Freightliner
-	W10:30	4L45		09:36 Wakefield Europort-Felixstowe	EWS 66	Intermodal
-	W11:15	4D67	MO-Q	10:47 Wrenthorpe-Decoy yard	GBRf 66	empty GBRf coal hoppers
-	12:40	4Z79		12:00 Selby-Felixstowe	GBRf 66	Intermodal
12:55W	-	4E22	MX	05:50 Felixstowe-Leeds FLT	F.Liner 66	Freightliner
13:35	-	6N70		13:30 Decoy(up) yard-Tyne yard	EWS 66	Departmental
-	14c10R	6M69	TFO-Q	13:52 Heck-Dowlow	EWS 66	empty box wagons
14:25W	-	6D27	MTX-Q	13:29 Rossington-Roxby	EWS 66	loaded spoil
R14:50	-	6E51	TThO	12:18 Peak Forest-Selby	EWS 66	loaded bogie hoppers
14:55	-	6E84	MFX-Q	08:20 Middleton Towers-Monk Bretton	GBRf 66	4-wheel sand hoppers
14:55H	-	6E84	MFO	08:20 Middleton Towers-Barnby Dun	GBRf 66	4-wheel sand hoppers
15:15W	-	4E26		08:13 Dollands Moor-Scunthorpe	EWS 66	empty steel
-	H15c15	6D88	(Q)	14:36 Goole Docks-Scunthorpe	EWS 66	empty steel
-	W15:20R	6M35	FX-Q	11:10 Rylstone-Small Heath	GBRf 66	loaded bogie boxes
-	W16:15	4L08	TThO	15:28 Wakefield Europort-London Gateway	EWS 66	Intermodal
16:50	-	6G64	MWO-Q	16:47 Hexthorpe yard-Gascoigne Wood	GBRf 66	gypsum(in box wagons)
16:55H	-	6D88	(Q)	14:36 Goole Docks-Scunthorpe	EWS 66	empty steel
-	17:15	6B64	MX-Q	12:49 Tyne Dock-West Burton p.s.	GBRf 66	loaded GBRf coal hoppers
17:45W	-	6M30	WFO	16:45 Doncaster Railport-Warrington	EWS 66	wagonload
17:50	-	4N14	FO-Q	17:45 Decoy(down)yard-Tyne Dock	GBRf 66	empty GBRf coal hoppers
-	18:45	4L79		15:55 Tees Dock-Felixstowe	F.Liner 66	Freightliner
-	19:10	6B89		11:48 North Blyth-West Burton p.s.	GBRf 66	loaded GBRf coal hoppers
-	H19c15	6L49	TO	17:49 Lindsey-Ipswich yard	F.Liner 66	fuel oil tanks
19:20	-	4E25		11:25 Bow/14:36 Biggleswade-Heck	EWS 66	empty PLASMOR wagons
-	19:50	6B39	MWX-Q	13:53 North Blyth-West Burton p.s.	GBRf 66	loaded GBRf coal hoppers
20:00H	-	6E88	MWFO	12:39 Middleton Towers-Goole Glassworks	GBRf 66	loaded sand hoppers
20:05	-	4N41		19:59 Decoy(down) yard-Tyne Dock	GBRf 66	empty GBRf coal hoppers
-	H20:05	6V04		18:59 Scunthorpe-Southall yard	EWS 66	empty 'binliner'
-	20:30R	6D10	WFX-Q	19:52 Ferrybridge-Hexthorpe yard	GBRf 66	empty box wagons
-	20:40R	6M43	TThO	19:54 Selby-Peak Forest	EWS 66	empty bogie hoppers
-	21:30R	6D22	MFX-Q	20:17 Monk Bretton-Roberts Road	GBRf 66	empty 4-wheel hoppers
-	H21c30R	6D66	MFO	21:10 Barnby Dun-Roberts Road	GBRf 66	empty 4-wheel hoppers
21:30	-	4H91	FX-Q	21:20 Decoy(down)yard-Drax p.s.	GBRf 66	empty gypsum containers
21:40H	-	4R77		21:33 Decoy(down) yard-Immingham	GBRf 66	empty GBRf coal hoppers

'Route Knowledge' The trains in the table are routed E.C.M.L. through the station apart from:

W=Wakefield direction.   **R**=Rotherham direction.   **H** = Hull direction.

North	South	H'code	Runs	Train		Traction	Type of train
-	21:55	6L70	FX	21:39	Heck-Bow	EWS 66	Blocks[PLASMOR]
-	21:55	6H93	FO	21:39	Heck-Biggleswade	EWS 66	Blocks[PLASMOR]
22:15	-	4N37		22:08	Decoy(down)yard-Tyne Dock	GBRf 66	empty GBRf coal hoppers
-	W22:30	6D29	MTX-Q	20:33	Roxby-Belmont yard	EWS 66	spoil empties
-	22:35	6D67		18:45	Tyne yard-Belmont yard	EWS 66	Departmental
22:45W	-	4E50		17:45	Felixstowe-Leeds FLT	F.Liner 66	Freightliner
-	23c10	1M80		21:43	Low Fell RMT-Willesden PRDC	-	Mail(325 unit)
-	23:20R	6B81	MX-Q	22:00	Gascoigne Wood-Hexthorpe yard	GBRf 66	empty box wagons
-	23:35	4O28		22:40	Scunthorpe-Dollands Moor	EWS 66	loaded steel(to Ebange)
00:05	-	4E60		18:21	Felixstowe-Tees Dock	F.Liner 66	Freightliner
-	W00:35	4L88		23:49	Leeds FLT-London Gateway	F.liner 66	Freightliner
01c10	-	1E06		22:45	Willesden PRDC-Low Fell RMT	-	Mail(325 unit)
02:45W	-	4E66		21:13	London Gateway-Leeds	F.Liner 66	Freightliner
-	W03c05	4L83		01:42	Leeds FLT-Felixstowe	F.liner 66	Freightliner
04:25W	-	4E45		22:49	Felixstowe-Wakefield Europort	EWS 66	Intermodal
04c45H	-	6E02		22:58	Brentford-Scunthorpe	EWS 66	loaded 'binliner'

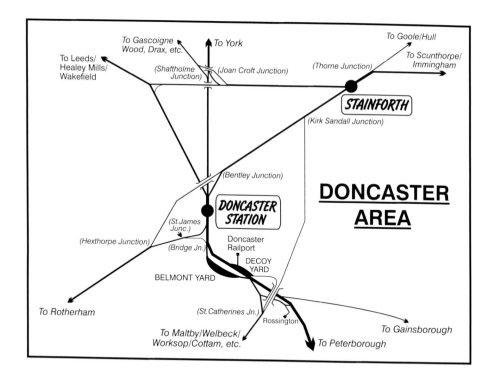

Saturdays:

North	South	H'code	Runs	Train		Traction	Type of train
-	H06:45	6D33		05:58	Goole-Decoy yard	GBRf 66	empty 4-wheel hoppers
06:55	-	4Z78		01:54	Felixstowe-Selby	GBRf 66	Intermodal
08:55W	-	4D67		08:50	Decoy yard-Wrenthorpe	GBRf 66	empty GBRf coal hoppers
11:40	-	4N80		11:34	Decoy(down)yard-Tyne Dock	GBRf 66	empty GBRf coal hoppers
-	W12:15	4L85		11:23	Leeds-Ipswich yard	F.Liner 66	Freightliner
12:55W	-	4E22		06:14	Felixstowe-Leeds FLT	F.Liner 66	Freightliner
-	13:50	6D30	(Q)	09:49	Tyne Dock-Decoy(down) yard	GBRf 66	loaded GBRf coal hoppers
14:25	-	4D56		11:32	Biggleswade-Heck	EWS 66	empty PLASMOR wagons
17:05W	-	4E26		09:14	Dollands Moor-Scunthorpe	EWS 66	empty steel(ex Ebange)
-	18:35	6H86		18:12	Heck-Peterborough yard	EWS 66	Plasmor breeze blocks

Sundays:

North	South	H'code	Runs	Train		Traction	Type of train
-	H13:30R	6M57	(Q)	11:06	Lindsey-Kingsbury	EWS 60	loaded bogie tanks
17:30	-	4N64	(Q)	17:25	Doncaster RMT-Tyne Dock	GBRf 66	empty GBRf coal hoppers
19:20H	-	4E32		12:05	Dollands Moor-Scunthorpe	EWS 66	empty steel(ex Ebange)
-	H21:05	6007		20:15	Scunthorpe-Dollands Moor	EWS 66	loaded steel(to Ebange)

[06:00-midnight]

Mondays-Fridays:

West	East	H'code	Runs	Train		Traction	Type of train
-	06:05	6E33	WFO	03:57	Warrington-Doncaster Railport	EWS 66	wagonload
-	H07:00	6E37		02:10	Liverpool-Drax p.s.	GBRf 66	loaded biomass hoppers
-	C11:25	6E32	FX-Q	08:40	Preston Docks-Lindsey	Colas 60	empty bogie tanks
12:55H	-	4M51		10:00	Drax p.s.-Liverpool	GBRf 66	empty biomass hoppers
13:35	-	6M22	MO-Q	11:20	Leeds Hunslet-Tunstead	F.Liner 66	empty cement tanks
-	H18:00	6E10		08:20	Liverpool-Drax p.s.	GBRf 66	loaded biomass hoppers
18:55	-	6M30	WFO	16:45	Doncaster Railport-Warrington	EWS 66	wagonload
19:35	-	6M33	TO-Q	12:12	Arcow quarry-Pendleton	GBRf 66	loaded bogie hoppers
19:35	-	6M34	WO-Q	12:12	Arcow quarry-Bredbury	GBRf 66	loaded bogie hoppers
21:30	-	4M90		20:39	Drax p.s.-Liverpool	GBRf 66	empty biomass hoppers

Saturdays & Sundays: NO BOOKED TRAINS

'Route Knowledge':   **(blank)** = to/from Manchester via Huddersfield & Diggle

H = to/from Manchester via Hebden Bridge & Rochdale

C = to/from Blackburn via Hebden Bridge & Copy Pit

SWINTON
(& Mexborough)

[06:00-21:00]

Mondays-Fridays:

Swinton	Mexboro'	code	Runs	Train	Traction	Type of train
#	06:00	6J03	TThO	03:56 Immingham-Tinsley	EWS 60	steel empties
07:05	-	4090		06:12 Leeds-Southampton	F.Liner 66/70	Freightliner
07:05	07:10	6E20	TO	23:08(Mon) Llanwern-Immingham	EWS 66	loaded/empty steel
07:20	-	6M59	MX	22:15 Hunterston-Ratcliffe p.s.	EWS 66	loaded FHH coal hoppers
08:10	-	4E01	MX	01:30 Southampton Millbrook-Leeds	F.Liner 66	Freightliner
08:20	08:25	6E56	ThO	06:22 Tunstead-Drax p.s.	EWS 66	loaded bogie hoppers
#	08:25	6M18	FO-Q	07:23 Doncaster Decoy-Toton	DRS 66	Departmental
09:10	-	4E01	MO	03:22 Southampton Maritime-Leeds	F.Liner 66	Freightliner
11:05	11:10	6Z46	MWFOQ	07:15 Stud Farm-Doncaster Decoy	GBRf 66	loaded ballast
11:10	-	6M89	(Q)	09:50 Dewsbury-Earles	F.Liner 66	empty cement tanks
#	11:20	6X01	TThO	10:17 Scunthorpe-Eastleigh	EWS 66	loaded rails
#	11:45	6M73		10:52 Doncaster Decoy-Toton	GBRf 66	Departmental
11:45	-	6E88	MWFO	09:45 Mountsorrel-Tyne yard	F.Liner 66	loaded ballast
13:10	-	4095	MX	12:12 Leeds-Southampton	F.Liner 66/70	Freightliner
13:40	-	4E54	MX-Q	11:46 Ratcliffe p.s.-Milford	EWS 66	empty EWS coal hoppers
#	14:05	6M23	MX-Q	12:57 Doncaster Decoy-Mountsorrel	GBRf 66	empty ballast wagons
#	14:10	6E20	FO-Q	12:27 Toton-Doncaster Decoy	DRS 66	Departmental
#	14:30	6E51	TThO	12:18 Peak Forest-Selby	EWS 66	loaded bogie hoppers
#	14:30	6M69	TFO-Q	13:52 Heck-Dowlow	EWS 66	empty box wagons
14:50	14:45	6J94	TX-Q	12:25 Hull steel terminal-Rotherham	EWS 66	empty steel
15:05	15:10	6E53	TO	10:27 Ipswich yard-Lindsey	F.Liner 66	empty TTA tanks
15:25	15:25	6J94	TO	12:25 Hull steel terminal-Rotherham	EWS 66	empty steel
15:25	15:20	6Z94	WO	13:08 Hull steel terminal-Rotherham	EWS 66	loaded steel
#	15:40	6M35	FX-Q	11:10 Rylstone-Small Heath	GBRf 66	loaded bogie boxes
#	15:40	6V80	FO-Q	14:08 Gascoigne Wood-Portbury	GBRf 66	gypsum(in box wagons)
#	16:05	6Z49	TO-Q	15:14 Rotherham-Doncaster Belmont	EWS 66	empty box wagons
16:40	-	6Z34	WO-Q	14:25 Chaddesden(Derby)-Stockton	DCR 56	empty box wagons
17:40	17:45	4E83	MX-Q	13:15 Hotchley Hill-Doncaster Decoy	GBRf 66	containerised gypsum
18:05	-	4E69	TFO	09:32 Southampton-Wakefield Europort	EWS 66	Intermodal
#	18:30	6D95	ThO-Q	18:00 Rotherham-Goole Docks	EWS 66	empty steel
18:45	18:50	6E08	FX	13:03 Wolverhampton-Immingham	EWS 60	empty steel
19:20	-	6M07	WO-Q	13:53 North Blyth-Ratcliffe p.s.	F.Liner 66	loaded FHH coal hoppers
19:25	-	4052	WO	18:27 Wakefield Europort-Southampton	EWS 66	Intermodal
20:15	20:20	6D03	MWO	19:49 Tinsley-Immingham	EWS 60	loaded steel
#	20:30	6V19	ThFO	17:22 Immingham-Llanwern	EWS 66	steel/empties

= these trains are booked to avoid Swinton by taking the 'Great Central' line between Mexborough and Rotherham (visible from Swinton station footbridge)

118

Saturdays:

Swinton	Mexboro'	code	Runs	Train	Traction	Type of train
06:20	–	4O54		05:27 Leeds-Southampton	F.Liner 66	Freightliner
07:35	07:40	6E20		23:08(Fri) Llanwern-Immingham	EWS 66	empty steel
10:25	–	4V52	(Q)	09:31 Wakefield Europort-Didcot yard	EWS 66	Intermodal
11:05	–	6M68		09:55 Dewsbury-Earles	F.Liner 66	empty cement tanks
14:10	14:15	6D03	(Q)	13:45 Tinsley-Immingham	EWS 60	loaded steel

Sundays:

14:10	14:05	6M57	(Q)	11:06 Lindsey-Kingsbury	EWS 60	loaded bogie tanks
14:10	14:15	6E68	(Q)	10:12 Kingsbury-Humber	EWS 60	empty bogie tanks
16:55	–	6V85	(Q)	16:05 Milford-Appleford	EWS 66	containerised flyash
17:30	17:25	4M48	(Q)	09:04 Mossend-Daventry	2 DRS 66s	'Tesco Express'

119

STAINFORTH

[06:00-21:00]

Mondays-Fridays:

North	South	H'code	Runs	Train	Traction	Type of train
G06:15D	-	6D33	TThO 05:18	Goole Glassworks-Roberts Road	GBRf 66	empty 4-wheel hoppers
-	D06:30G	6D94	(Q) 05:36	Rotherham-Hull steel terminal	EWS 66	loaded steel
06:45	-	6D73	FO-Q 05:35	Lindsey-Drax p.s.	EWS 60	fuel oil tanks
-	D07:10	6D74	06:54	Doncaster up Decoy-Scunthorpe	EWS 66	Departmental
-	D07:30	6E20	TO 23:08(Mon)	Llanwern-Immingham	EWS 66	loaded/empty steel
-	D08:05G	6D94	WO-Q 06:57	Rotherham-Goole Docks	EWS 66	loaded steel
-	D08:10	6G80	ThO-Q 07:41	Doncaster Belmont-Immingham	EWS 66	empty MEA box wagons
08:10	-	6H61	06:42	Immingham-Drax p.s.	EWS 66	loaded biomass hoppers
08:20	-	6N31	07:41	Scunthorpe-Lackenby	EWS 66	loaded steel
-	08:25	4R49	07:00	Drax p.s.-Immingham	EWS 66	empty biomass hoppers
09:10D	-	6D75	08:45	Scunthorpe-Doncaster up Decoy	EWS 66	Departmental(rails)
09:55	-	6D79	WO 08:34	Lindsey-Neville Hill	EWS 66/60	fuel oil tanks
10:15	-	6H62	MX 08:51	Immingham-Drax p.s.	EWS 66	loaded biomass hoppers
10:50D	-	6X01	TThO 10:17	Scunthorpe-Eastleigh	EWS 66	loaded rails
-	10:50	4R50	(Q) 05:35	Drax/10:01 Milford-Immingham	EWS 66	empty biomass hoppers
-	12:50	6E32	FX-Q 08:40	Preston Docks-Lindsey	Colas 60	empty bogie tanks
-	13:20	4R51	11:45	Drax p.s.-Immingham	EWS 66	empty biomass hoppers
-	13:50	4R17	(Q) 07:30/12:15	Drax p.s.-Immingham	EWS 66	empty EWS coal hoppers
G14:00D	-	6J94	(Q) 12:25	Hull steel terminal-Rotherham	EWS 66	empty steel
14:05	-	6H63	12:15	Immingham-Drax p.s.	EWS 66	loaded biomass hoppers
-	14:45	6D27	MTX-Q 13:29	Rossington-Roxby	EWS 66	loaded spoil
G14:55D	-	6Z94	WO 13:08	Hull steel terminal-Rotherham	EWS 66	loaded steel
G15:00D	-	6D88	(Q) 14:36	Goole Docks-Scunthorpe	EWS 66	empty steel
-	15:00	4R53	MFX-Q 10:45	Drax p.s.-Immingham	EWS 66	empty biomass hoppers
-	D15:35	6E53	TO 10:27	Ipswich yard-Lindsey	F.Liner 66	empty TTA tanks
-	15:55	4E26	08:13	Dollands Moor-Scunthorpe	EWS 66	empty steel(ex Ebange)
-	16:00	6D80	WO 14:05	Neville Hill-Lindsey	EWS 66/60	fuel oil tanks
16:20	-	6H75	(Q) 14:08	Immingham-Drax p.s.	EWS 66	loaded biomass hoppers
-	D17:10	6D88	(Q) 14:36	Goole Docks-Scunthorpe	EWS 66	empty steel
-	17:20	4R54	16:22	Drax p.s.-Immingham	EWS 66	empty biomass hoppers
17:50	-	6H77	16:30	Immingham-Drax p.s.	EWS 66	loaded biomass hoppers
-	17:50	6D11	13:23	Lackenby-Scunthorpe	EWS 66	empty steel
-	18:20	4R55	FX 17:15	Drax p.s.-Immingham	EWS 66	empty biomass hoppers
18:20	-	6H17	(Q) 16:45	Immingham-Drax p.s.	EWS 66	loaded EWS coal hoppers
18:55D	-	6L49	TO 17:49	Lindsey-Ipswich yard	F.Liner 66	fuel oil tanks
-	D19:05	6E08	FX 13:03	Wolverhampton-Immingham	EWS 60	empty steel
-	19:20	4R23	FO 17:20	Drax p.s.-Immingham	EWS 66	empty biomass hoppers
19:50	-	6H79	MX 18:10	Immingham-Drax p.s.	EWS 66	loaded biomass hoppers
19:55D	-	6V04	18:59	Scunthorpe-Southall yard	EWS 66	empty 'binliner'
20:00D	-	6V19	ThFO 17:22	Immingham-Llanwern	EWS 66	steel/empties
-	D20:15	6E88	MWFO 12:39	Middleton Towers-Goole Glassworks	GBRf 66	loaded sand hoppers
20:25	-	6N73	19:47	Scunthorpe-Lackenby	EWS 66	loaded steel

120

Saturdays:

North	South	H'code	Runs	Train	Traction	Type of train
G06:20D	-	6D33		05:58 Goole-Doncaster Decoy	GBRf 66	empty bogie hoppers
-	D07:55	6E20		23:08(Fri) Llanwern-Immingham	EWS 66	loaded/empty stee
08:00	-	6H06		06:45 Immingham-Drax p.s.	EWS 66	loaded biomass hoppers
-	08:40	4R49		06:25 Drax p.s.-Immingham	EWS 66	empty biomass hoppers
11:00	-	6H62		09:37 Immingham-Drax p.s.	EWS 66	loaded biomass hoppers
13:25	-	6H63		12:02 Immingham-Drax p.s.	EWS 66	loaded biomass hoppers
-	D14:40	6D03	(Q)	13:45 Tinsley-Immingham	EWS 60	loaded steel
-	16:40	6D05		12:42 Lackenby-Scunthorpe	EWS 66	empty steel
-	17:40	4E26		09:14 Dollands Moor-Scunthorpe	EWS 66	empty steel(ex Ebange)
19:20	-	6N80		18:45 Scunthorpe-Tees yard	EWS 66	loaded steel

Sundays:

[coal and biomass trains to/from Immingham may also run on Sundays, depending on demand/engineering work]

'Route Knowledge':   **(blank)** = Scunthorpe to/from Applehurst Junction;

D = to/from Doncaster;   **G** = to/from Goole (at Thorne Junction)

[06:00-midnight]

Mondays-Fridays:

West	East	H'code	Runs	Train	Traction	Type of train
-	06:30	4R48	MX	03:41 Drax p.s.-Immingham	EWS 66	empty biomass hoppers
-	06:50	6K20		06:32 Santon-Immingham	F.liner 66	empty iron ore tipplers
07:00	-	6T21		06:35 Immingham-Santon	F.liner 66	loaded iron ore
07:15	-	6H61		06:42 Immingham-Drax p.s.	EWS 66	loaded biomass hoppers
07:45L	-	6M57		07:15 Lindsey-Kingsbury	EWS 60	loaded bogie tanks
-	08:10	4C71	(Q)	07:44 Scunthorpe-Immingham	F.liner 66	empty EWS coal hoppers
-	08:30	6K21		08:11 Santon-Immingham	F.liner 66	empty iron ore tipplers
08:35	-	6T22		08:02 Immingham-Santon	F.liner 66	loaded iron ore
09:00	-	6D79	WO	08:34 Lindsey-Neville Hill	EWS 66/60	fuel oil tanks
-	09c10	6G80	T/ThO	07:41 Doncaster Belmont-Immingham	EWS 66	empty MEA box wagons
09:15	-	6H62	MX	08:51 Immingham-Drax p.s.	EWS 66	loaded biomass hoppers
-	L09:25	6E46	MX	04:37 Kingsbury-Lindsey	EWS 60	empty bogie tanks
-	09:40	6E20	TO	23:08(Mon) Llanwern-Immingham	EWS 66	loaded/empty steel
-	09:45	4R49		07:00 Drax p.s.-Immingham	EWS 66	empty biomass hoppers
10:05L	-	6D31	TFX-Q	09:40 Lindsey-West Burton p.s.	EWS 66/60	fuel oil tanks
-	10:05	6K22		09:42 Santon-Immingham	F.liner 66	empty iron ore tipplers
10:25	-	6T23		09:55 Immingham-Santon	F.liner 66	loaded iron ore
11:00	-	6C75	(Q)	10:33 Immingham-Scunthorpe	F.liner 66	loaded coal hoppers
-	11:45	4R50	(Q)	05:35 Drax/10:01 Milford-Immingham	EWS 66	empty biomass hoppers
-	12:00	6K23		11:42 Santon-Immingham	F.liner 66	empty iron ore tipplers
12:10	-	6T24		11:38 Immingham-Santon	F.liner 66	loaded iron ore
12:40	-	6H63		12:15 Immingham-Drax p.s.	EWS 66	loaded biomass hoppers
13:25L	-	6M88	T/ThO	12:56 Immingham-Ketton	EWS 66	coal(in MEA box wagons)
-	13:35	6K24		13:16 Santon-Immingham	F.liner 66	empty iron ore tipplers
-	13:45	6E32	FX-Q	08:40 Preston Docks-Lindsey	Colas 60	empty bogie tanks
14:00	-	6T25		13:34 Immingham-Santon	F.liner 66	loaded iron ore
-	14:00	4C75	(Q)	13:35 Scunthorpe-Immingham	F.liner 66	empty coal hoppers
-	14:10	4R51		11:45 Drax p.s.-Immingham	EWS 66	empty biomass hoppers
-	14:30	4R17	(Q)	07:30/12:15 Drax p.s.-Immingham	EWS 66	empty EWS coal hoppers
14:35	-	6H75	(Q)	14:08 Immingham-Drax p.s.	EWS 66	loaded biomass hoppers
-	L14:50	6E54		10:39 Kingsbury-Humber	EWS 60	empty bogie tanks
15:00L	-	6M00		14:30 Humber-Kingsbury	EWS 60	loaded bogie tanks
-	15:35	6K25		15:17 Santon-Immingham	F.liner 66	empty iron ore tipplers
15:40	-	6T26		15:04 Immingham-Santon	F.liner 66	loaded iron ore
-	15:40	4R53	MFX-Q	10:45 Drax p.s.-Immingham	EWS 66	empty biomass hoppers
-	L15:50	6E82	MWX-Q	12:16 Rectory Junction-Lindsey	Colas 60	empty bogie tanks
-	16:45	6E53	TO	10:27 Ipswich yard-Lindsey	F.liner 66	empty fuel oil tanks
-	16:45	6D80	WO	14:05 Neville Hill-Lindsey	EWS 66/60	fuel oil tanks
-	B16:45	6D34	TFX-Q	16:00 West Burton p.s.-Lindsey	EWS 66/60	fuel oil tanks
-	17:00	6K26		16:42 Santon-Immingham	F.liner 66	empty iron ore tipplers

'Route Knowledge':

(blank) =to from Scunthorpe line;   **L**=to/from Lincoln line;   **B**=to/from Brigg line

West	East	H'code	Runs		Train	Traction	Type of train
17:00	–	6H77		16:30	Immingham-Drax p.s.	EWS 66	loaded biomass hoppers
17:05	–	6C79	(Q)	16:39	Immingham-Scunthorpe	F.liner 66	loaded coal hoppers
17:20	–	6H17	(Q)	16:45	Immingham-Drax p.s.	EWS 66	loaded EWS coal hoppers
17:30	–	6T27		16:58	Immingham-Santon	F.liner 66	loaded iron ore
17:40L	–	6M24		17:13	Lindsey-Kingsbury	EWS 60	loaded bogie tanks
17:45	–	6V19	ThFO	17:22	Immingham-Llanwern	EWS 66	steel/empties
–	18:00	4R54		16:22	Drax p.s.-Immingham	EWS 66	empty biomass hoppers
18:10	–	6L49	TO	17:49	Lindsey-Ipswich yard	F.Liner 66	fuel oil tanks
18:40	–	6H79	MX	18:10	Immingham-Drax p.s.	EWS 66	loaded biomass hoppers
–	18:55	6K27		18:42	Santon-Immingham	F.liner 66	empty iron ore tipplers
19:05	–	6T28		18:39	Immingham-Santon	F.liner 66	loaded iron ore
–	19:15	4R55	FX	17:15	Drax p.s.-Immingham	EWS 66	empty biomass hoppers
–	19:45	6E08	FX	13:03	Wolverhampton-Immingham	EWS 60	empty steel
20:15	–	6H83		19:47	Immingham-Drax p.s.	EWS 66	loaded biomass hoppers
20:35	–	6T29		20:11	Immingham-Santon	F.liner 66	loaded iron ore
–	20:35	6K28		20:19	Santon-Immingham	F.liner 66	empty iron ore tipplers
–	20:40	6D13	FO-Q	18:42	Drax p.s.-Lindsey	EWS 66	fuel oil tanks
–	20:45	4R23	FO	17:15	Drax p.s.-Immingham	EWS 66	empty biomass hoppers
–	21:15	4C79	(Q)	20:58	Scunthorpe-Immingham	F.liner 66	empty coal hoppers
21:15	–	6M99		20:53	Immingham-Wolverhampton	EWS 66	loaded steel
–	L21:35	6E38	MWFO	13:54	Colnbrook-Lindsey	Colas 60	empty bogie tanks
–	21:45	6D03	MWO	19:49	Tinsley-Immingham	EWS 60	loaded steel
–	22:10	6K29		21:53	Santon-Immingham	F.liner 66	empty iron ore tipplers
22:15	–	6T30		21:52	Immingham-Santon	F.liner 66	loaded iron ore
–	L22:35	6E59		17:41	Kingsbury-Lindsey	EWS 60	empty bogie tanks
22:50L	–	6V70	TThO	22:26	Lindsey-Colnbrook	Colas 60	loaded bogie tanks
–	23:45	6K30		23:26	Santon-Immingham	F.liner 66	empty iron ore tipplers
23:05	–	6H41	FO	22:45	Immingham-Drax p.s.	EWS 66	loaded biomass hoppers

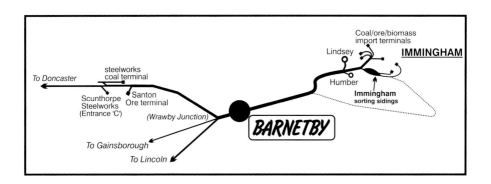

Saturdays:

West	East	H'code	Runs	Train	Traction	Type of train
-	06:35	6K20		06:18 Santon-Immingham	F.liner 66	empty iron ore tipplers
07:00	-	6T21		06:36 Immingham-Santon	F.liner 66	loaded iron ore
-	07:00	4R48		05:06 Drax p.s.-Immingham	EWS 66	empty biomass hoppers
07:20	-	6H06		06:45 Immingham-Drax p.s.	EWS 66	loaded biomass hoppers
07:45L	-	6M57		07:15 Lindsey-Kingsbury	EWS 60	loaded bogie tanks
08:25	-	6T22		07:55 Immingham-Santon	F.liner 66	loaded iron ore
-	08:35	6K21		08:20 Santon-Immingham	F.liner 66	empty iron ore tipplers
-	L09:05	6E46		04:25 Kingsbury-Lindsey	EWS 60	empty bogie tanks
-	09:40	4R49		06:25 Drax p.s.-Immingham	EWS 66	empty biomass hoppers
-	10:00	6K22		09:43 Santon-Immingham	F.liner 66	empty iron ore tipplers
10:05	-	6H62		09:37 Immingham-Drax p.s.	EWS 66	loaded biomass hoppers
10:25	-	6T23		09:59 Immingham-Santon	F.liner 66	loaded iron ore
-	10:35	6E20		23:08(Fri) Llanwern-Immingham	EWS 66	empty steel
-	11:50	6K23		11:33 Santon-Immingham	F.liner 66	empty iron ore tipplers
12:00	-	6T24	(Q)	11:35 Immingham-Santon	F.liner 66	loaded iron ore
12:25	-	6H63		12:02 Immingham-Drax p.s.	EWS 66	loaded biomass hoppers
-	13:40	6K24	(Q)	13:25 Santon-Immingham	F.liner 66	empty iron ore tipplers
14:00	-	6T25		13:32 Immingham-Santon	F.liner 66	loaded iron ore
14:45L	-	6M00		14:22 Humber-Kingsbury	EWS 60	loaded bogie tanks
-	L14:50	6E54		10:40 Kingsbury-Humber	EWS 60	empty bogie tanks
-	15:30	6K25		15:15 Santon-Immingham	F.liner 66	empty iron ore tipplers
15:35	-	6T26		15:03 Immingham-Santon	F.liner 66	loaded iron ore
-	15:45	6D03	(Q)	13:45 Tinsley-Immingham	EWS 60	loaded steel
-	16:55	6K26		16:36 Santon-Immingham	F.liner 66	empty iron ore tipplers
17:30	-	6T27	(Q)	17:02 Immingham-Santon	F.liner 66	loaded iron ore
19:10	-	6T28	(Q)	18:40 Immingham-Santon	F.liner 66	loaded iron ore
-	19:10	6K27	(Q)	18:52 Santon-Immingham	F.liner 66	empty iron ore tipplers
-	L20:25	6E59		15:41 Kingsbury-Lindsey	EWS 60	empty bogie tanks
-	20:35	6K28	(Q)	20:19 Santon-Immingham	F.liner 66	empty iron ore tipplers

Sundays:

West	East	H'code	Runs	Train		Traction	Type of train
11:30	–	6M57	(Q)	11:06	Lindsey-Kingsbury	EWS 60	loaded bogie tanks
14:05	–	6T25	(Q)	13:37	Immingham-Santon	F.liner 66	loaded iron ore
–	14:05	4R17	(Q)	12:36	Milford-Immingham	EWS 66	empty biomass hoppers
–	15:15	6E68	(Q)	10:12	Kingsbury-Humber	EWS 60	empty bogie tanks
15:25	–	6T26	(Q)	14:55	Immingham-Santon	F.liner 66	loaded iron ore
–	15:35	6K25	(Q)	15:16	Santon-Immingham	F.liner 66	empty iron ore tipplers
–	16:30	4R54		14:35	Milford-Immingham	EWS 66	empty biomass hoppers
–	16:45	6K26	(Q)	16:23	Santon-Immingham	F.liner 66	empty iron ore tipplers
17:10	–	6H17		16:45	Immingham-Drax p.s.	EWS 66	loaded biomass hoppers
17:30	–	6T27	(Q)	17:02	Immingham-Santon	F.liner 66	loaded iron ore
–	18:55	4R55		17:19	Milford-Immingham	EWS 66	empty biomass hoppers
19:15	–	6T28	(Q)	18:49	Immingham-Santon	F.liner 66	loaded iron ore
19:20	–	6H79		18:55	Immingham-Drax p.s.	EWS 66	loaded biomass hoppers
–	19:30	6K27	(Q)	19:15	Santon-Immingham	F.liner 66	empty iron ore tipplers
–	20:40	6K28	(Q)	20:27	Santon-Immingham	F.liner 66	empty iron ore tipplers
–	21:30	4R56		19:23	Drax p.s.-Immingham	EWS 66	empty biomass hoppers
21:35L	–	6V70	(Q)	21:09	Lindsey-Colnbrook	Colas 60	loaded bogie tanks
21:40	–	6H83		21:13	Immingham-Drax p.s.	EWS 66	loaded biomass hoppers

FREIGHTMASTER ONLINE

Do you want to keep up to date with the latest changes to Freight services?

If so, you should seriously consider taking out an <u>online</u> subscription!

FREIGHTMASTER ONLINE

While this book gives an excellent <u>overview</u> of freight traffic in this country, train timings/headcodes change on a weekly basis, so despite being published four times a year, *Freightmaster* only provides a 'snapshot' of the traffic flows at the time of going to press...

Because of this, we also offer an 'online' version of Freightmaster, featuring:

* over 100 timetables updated <u>at least 52 times a year</u> , so details of new/amended freight services are available up to three months <u>before</u> they appear in the printed version of Freightmaster!

* trains in the online timetables are **colour coded by FOC**

* the online timetables can be 'filtered' by day of the week
      (e.g. only show trains booked to run on a Tuesday)

* details of short term diversions and temporary workings such as water cannon trains.

* exclusive 'interactive' forum with railfreight news, loco lists, etc.

NEW FEATURE : **Freightmaster realtime maps!**
FMonline now features dozens of 'live' maps which show all passenger and freight movements around the timetable hotspots at a signal to signal level - invaluable out at the lineside, but also addictive to follow from your armchair at home...

...altogether, FMonline is an indispensable tool for all serious rail enthusiasts!

EXTRA TIMETABLES!

In addition to all the locations in this book, *Freightmaster Online* also features many 'exclusive' tables, such as Reading, Taunton, Uffington, Princes Risborough, Dagenham, Barking, Trimley, Leicester, Nottingham, Derby, Walsall, Worcester, Bletchley, Kirkby Stephen, Leeds, Selby, Hexham, Aviemore and many more!

For instant access to Freightmaster Online, you can pay online by debit or credit card - for the latest prices/special offers, please see **www.freightmaster.net/offers**

FREIGHTMASTER GLOSSARY

The following is a list of the railway terminology & abbreviations used throughout this book.

Types of Train

Binliner	- containerised domestic waste.
'blue train'	- Transfesa/Ford intermodal service between Dagenham and Silla(Spain)
Departmental	- infrastucture service (i.e. ballast, spoil, sleepers, rails, etc.)
wagonload	- DBS mixed-traffic service (anything from a single wagon upwards!)
Freightliner	- Brand name for deep sea intermodal rail network
Intermodal	- containers, etc. which use both rail and road 'modes' during their journey
MBAs	- DBS bogie box wagon, mainly used for aggregate services
MEAs	- four wheel EWS box wagon, converted from redundant HEA hoppers
MGR	- Merry Go Round coal train to/from power stations, steelworks and cement works, formed of 4-wheel HAA/HDA, etc. hoppers.

Abbreviations

A.D.J.	- Alexandra Dock Junction, west of Newport
arr.	- arrives
B.H.	- Basford Hall yard, Crewe
BLI	- Buxton Lime Industries, operator of Tunstead quarry, Peak Forest
BM	- Brunner Mond, operator of the chemical plants at Northwich.
dep.	- departs
DRS	- Direct Rail Services
EWS	- English, Welsh & Scottish Railway (now DBS, but most wagons and locos still carry EWS branding)
FHH	- Freightliner Heavy Haul
F.Y.	- Foster Yeoman (as in Acton F.Y.)
Jn. or Junc.	- Junction (e.g. Hoo Jn.)
l/e	- light engine
l.i.p.	- loco inspection point
MoD	- Ministry of Defence
p.s.	- power station
RMC	- Ready Mixed Concrete, operator of Dove Holes quarry, Peak Forest
RMT	- Royal Mail Terminal (e.g. Warrington RMT)
R.T.S.	- Refuse Transfer Station (e.g. Bredbury R.T.S.)
s.d.t	- self discharge train, as used by Redland Lefarge aggregates.
S.T.	- Steel Terminal (e.g. Rotherham/Wolverhampton)
S+C	- the Settle & Carlisle line
TMD	- Traction Maintenance Depot
TPO	- Travelling Post Office (also known as a 'Postal')
VQ	- Virtual Quarry (e.g. Bescot VQ)
WRD	- Wagon Repair Depot
yd.	- yard

This is not an exhaustive list, but covers the most commonly used terms.

BESSACARR JUNCTION

[8am - 8pm]

Mondays-Fridays:

West	East	code	Runs	Train	Traction	Type of train
06:55	-	4Z78	MX	01:58 Felixstowe-Selby	GBRf 66	Intermodal
08:05	-	4Z33	MWFOQ	05:20 Whitemoor-Doncaster Wood yard	F.Liner 66	Departmental
08:55	-	4E08	TThO	03:41 London Gateway-Wakefield Europort	EWS 66	Intermodal
10:40	-	4E62	MX	05:38 Felixstowe-Doncaster Railport	F.Liner 66	Freightliner
-	10:40	4L45		09:36 Wakefield Europort-Felixstowe	EWS 66	Intermodal
-	12:25	4L85		12:13 Doncaster Railport-Felixstowe	F.Liner 66	Freightliner
-	12:40	4Z79		12:00 Selby-Felixstowe	GBRf 66	Intermodal
-	16:30	4L55		16:20 Doncaster Railport-Felixstowe	F.Liner 66	Freightliner
-	16:55	4L08	TThO	15:28 Wakefield Europort-London Gateway	EWS 66	Intermodal
17:05	-	4Z33		11:22 Felixstowe-Doncaster Railport	GBRf 66	Intermodal
17:15	-	4E25		11:25 Bow/14:36 Biggleswade-Heck	EWS 66	empty PLASMOR wagons
17:55	-	6E88	MWFO	12:39 Middleton Towers-Goole	GBRf 66	loaded sand hoppers
-	19:00	6V09	TO	13:00 West Burton p.s.-Acton yard	EWS 66	flyash(in box wagons)
-	19:50	6L49	TO	17:49 Lindsey-Ipswich yard	F.Liner 66	fuel oil tanks

Saturdays:

West	East	code		Train	Traction	Type of train
06:35	-	4Z78		01:54 Felixstowe-Selby	GBRf 66	Intermodal
10:25	-	4E62		05:15 Felixstowe-Doncaster Railport	F.Liner 66	Freightliner

Sundays: NO BOOKED TRAINS

128

'On Location'

DONCASTER
and
HATFIELD & STAINFORTH

Compiled By
Martin Buck

Hexthorpe (Doncaster)

Steel : Class 60 No.60059 'Swinden Dalesman' (above) 60059 pulls out from the Doncaster Station avoiding line and onto the Doncaster - Swinton main line at Hexthorpe Junction on 29th June 2015 with a rake of 'BYAs' loaded with imported steel, running as 6J94, the 13:09 Hull - Rotherham.

Departmental : GBRf Class 66/7 No.66721 'Harry Beck' (above) passes Hexthorpe on 27th January 2014 with 6M73, the 10:52 Doncaster Decoy - Toton departmental; a service once the preserve of DBS. Hexthorpe Junction is where the lines from Bentley Junction, Doncaster Station and Bridge junction (ECML) meet.

Gypsum : In 2014, a flow of gypsum started from Drax power station to Portbury Dock, Bristol, followed by a flow from West Burton power station, both operated by GBRf using bogie box wagons. On 5th February 2016, GBRf Class 66/7 No.66757 'West Somerset Railway' (below) heads west at Hexthorpe with 6V80, the 14:08 Gascoigne Wood - Portbury. In the background are the CE Plant Depot and Roberts Road loco Depot.

Kirk Sandall

Steel : DBS Class 60 No.60071 'Ribblehead Viaduct' (above) crosses the River Don Navigation on 27th April 2011 with 6D88, the 14:36 Goole - Scunthorpe steel empties. This service has to run to Doncaster Decoy to run round as there is no direct access to Scunthorpe form Goole.

Ebange Steel : Although 'booked' for a DBS Class 66/0 loco between Scunthorpe and Doncaster, Class 60s can turn up from time to time, like on 11th February 2013. DBS liveried 'tug' No.60040 'The Territorial Army Centenary' (below) passes Kirk Sandall Junction with 6O26, the 14:22 Scunthorpe - Dollands Moor loaded steel bound for Ebange, Northern France. The consist is modified 'FIA' wagons and the Class 60 will hand over to Class 92 No.92030 'Ashford' at Doncaster, from where the train will proceed under a 4O26 reporting code.

Industrial Sand : On 2nd July 2015, GBRf Class 66/7 No.66711 (above) heads over the River Don bridge at Kirk Sandall with loaded 'PAA' 2-axle sand hoppers, which form 6E84, the 08:20 Middleton Towers - Barnby Dun, The livery of Turquoise, Grey and Blue Stripes with GB Railfreight and Aggregate Industries Logos marks GBRf's new Bardon Hill aggregates contract. Exactly one month later, No.66711 is named 'Sence' by GB Railfreight MD John Smith & Aggregate Industries Director Phillippe Frenay at Bardon Hill Quarry.

Fuel Oil : More trackside clearance is in evidence here, as FHH Class 66 No.66416 (below) approaches Kirk Sandall on 27th October 2015 hauling 6E53, the 08:50, (TO) Ipswich - Lindsey empty fuel oil tanks, formed of 'TTA' 2-axle tank wagons. This flow previously emanated from Fawley, operated by DBS.

South Yorkshire Joint Line

The South Yorkshire Joint Line links Kirk Sandall Junction - St. Catherines Junction - Shireoaks for just over 21 miles, taking freight traffic away from the congested Doncaster station and ECML.

99% of traffic is coal to Cottam and West Burton power stations.

Coal : EWS-liveried Class 66/0 No.66128 (above) leaves the Doncaster - Scunthorpe main line on 2nd October 2014, heading towards the SYJ line at Kirk Sandall with 6F10, Immingham - Cottam loaded 'HTAs'

Coal : There are occasional flows of imported coal through Hull Docks, like in 2013 when GBRf operated a flow to West Burton ps.

On 31st January 2013, the aptly named GBRf Class 66/7 No.66703 'Doncaster PSB 1981-2002' (middle) is seen on the single track in Cantley, Doncaster, carrying coal in open boxes, forming 6B70, the 05:00 Hull Docks - West Burton.

Coal : DBS Class 66/0 No.66185 (left) heads down the rather drab SYJ line at Sandall Beat, Cantley, on 17th March 2014 with 4D37, the 10:15 Cottam ps - Hull coal empties.

Stainforth Junction

Steel : The 'freight only' line from Adwick Junction joins the main line from Doncaster at Stainforth Junction, which can be seen curving in behind the rear wagons of 6D03, 13:37 Tinsley - Immingham loaded steel. This train of 'BVA' steel carriers is hauled by DBS Class 60 No.60065 'Spirit of Jaguar' (above), a pretty solid 'tug- diagram.

Bitumen : The trees are starting to become quite colourful as autumn draws near. Colas 'tug' No.60021 (below) passes under Station Road bridge into Hatfield & Stainforth station on 5th October 2015 with 6E32, the 08:55 Preston Docks - Lindsey empty bitumen bogie tanks. Colas took over this flow, along with two other petrochemical flows from Lindsey to Colnbrook and Rectory Junction, in January 2015 from DBS.

vii

Hatfield & Stainforth

Coal : Hatfield & Stainforth is another popular freight 'hotspot', only 7 miles east of Doncaster, easily accessible by both rail and road. Viewed from Station Road bridge, two FHH Class 66/5 locos draw up alongside each other at Hatfield & Stainforth on 16th January 2012 with loaded coal hoppers, hauled by No.66545 and No.66953, respectively. Without any 'gen', it is almost impossible to identify the respective workings.

Steel : On 5th March 2014, DBS Class 60 No.60054 (below) enters the station with a rake of empty steel carriers, forming 6J94, the 12:25 Hull Steel terminal - Rotherham Masborough steel terminal. In the background is the familiar sight of the now closed Hatfield coal mine.

Biomass : This is the new order for power station consumption; imported biomass, which is gradually replacing coal. The majority of biomass consumed by Drax power station arrives in the UK via Immingham and there are several loaded trains running each day. Here, on 28th January 2015, DBS liveried Class 66/0 No.66097 (above) passes through Hatfield & Stainforth with 6H60, the 10:45 Immingham - Drax biomass.

Domestic Waste : Following the loss of the Trans-Pennine GMC 'Binliners' to Roxby, the vacuum was filled by the Greater London 'Binliner' switching from the Calvert landfill site to Scunthorpe. Here, the brightly coloured containers forming 6V04, the 18:59 Scunthorpe - Southall empty 'binliner' approach Stainforth Junction on 13th July 2014, hauled by DBS Class 66/0 No.66081 (below), in some nice evening light.

DONCASTER

It seemed ironic that GBRf and DRS rushed through their new locos to beat EU directives on emissions when they could still run heritage locos that are hardly 'clean', not that enthusiasts complained, mind you! GBRf hired-in from Riviera Trains Class 47s to work timetabled gypsum and industrial sand trains to destinations in Yorkshire.

Gypsum : On 9th September 2014, Class 47s No.D1916 (47812) + No.47843 'Vulcan' (above) put on the power as the signal clears with 4D19, the 14:29 (TThO) Drax - Doncaster Down Decoy containerised gypsum.

Industrial Sand : It's a busy day for No.47843 'Vulcan' (below), as it runs through Doncaster on 9th July 2014 with 6E88, the 12:39 (MWFO) Middleton Towers - Goole, having previously worked 4D95 loaded gypsum from Hull.

Wagonload : On 5th June 2013, Class 66/0 No.66095 (right) enters the station with 6E33, the 03:57 (WFO) Warrington - Doncaster 'Wagonload', comprising imported vehicles which arrived in the UK at Portbury Docks.

Coal : GBRf Class 66/7 No.66721 (bottom) passes Bridge Junction, Doncaster, with empty 'HYA' coal hoppers from Ferrybridge power station destined for Doncaster Decoy.

No.66721 is decorated on one side with a representation of the 1933 London Underground map and a 2013 version on the other side. This celebrates the 150th Anniversary of the London Underground.

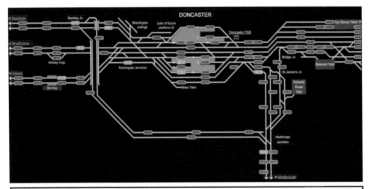

DONCASTER PSB PANEL
This illustration will be familiar to FM OnLine subscribers, who can access these for many locations listed in Freightmaster. It shows in *"Real Time"* the passage of trains, signal by signal, as seen on a power signal box panel - in this case, Doncaster.

Doncaster Decoy

'Up' : *Freightliner* : Class 66/5 No.66517 (above) heads past the 'Up' Decoy Yard with 4L87, the 08:47 Leeds - Felixstowe freightliner. The train will run ECML to Peterborough, where it then heads into East Anglia via March. In the yard is a rake of 'JNA' *(Falcon)* ballast wagons, 'PAA' 2-axle sand hoppers and some Autoballasters.

'Down' : *Coal* : 2015 saw a massive decline in the movement of coal, due in no small part to higher running costs, carbon taxes and the closure of several coal mines, like Hatfield, Kellingley and Thoresby. The 'Down' Decoy Yard acts as a staging point for coal trains and on 10th May 2011 there was a healthy line up of GBRf operated coal trains, albeit empty, which are headed by (from left to right, below) Nos.66721, 66707, 66579 and 66714. Note, also, the redundant Royal Mail terminal on the right of the yard.

Bessacarr

Bessacarr is in the South West of Doncaster and Bessacarr Junction marks the start of the non-electrified line to Gainsborough and Lincoln.

Coal : DBS Class 66/0 loco No.66213 (above) approaches the junction on 25th March 2013 with the diverted 4D08, empty 'HTAs' from Drax back to Immingham Bulk Import Terminal. This train was diverted via Lincoln due to the Hatfield landslip in February 2013.

Rails : Another diversion and DBS-liveried 'tug' No.60059 'Swinden Dalesman' (middle) crosses the M18 Motorway at Bessacarr with 6D75, the 08:45 Scunthorpe - Doncaster Decoy loaded rails.

Intermodal : The morning intermodal from Selby to Felixstowe is routed via Lincoln. On 11th February 2013, GBRf Class 66/7 No.66730 'Whitemoor' (right) approaches the junction with 4Z79, the 12:00 Selby - Felixstowe.

A solitary Class 153 'Sprinter' unit heads for Doncaster with 2K36, the 11:54hrs from Lincoln Central.

Variety 'Under the Wires'
ECML (North)
Arksey

Limestone : Sporting the old EWS Maroon & Gold livery, 'Shed' No.66126 (top left) passes Arksey on 19th January 2015 heading south with 6M96, the 13:21 Milford - Tunstead empty bogie limestone hoppers.

Arksey is two miles north of Doncaster station on the ECML.

Flyash : Occasional flows of flyash run from Drax ps to Earles, for use in the manufacture of cement.

Here, on 13th May 2014, FHH 'Powerhaul' Class 70 No.70005 (middle) heads north at Arksey with a rake of empty 'PCA' wagons, forming 6E45, Earles - Drax. The loaded train runs as 6M45, when required.

Departmental : The departmental 'trip' from Doncaster Decoy to Tyne Yard is 'booked' for a 'shed' but, in early 2016, pairs of DBS Class 90s started to appear - a rare sight indeed!

On 19th January 2016, DBS-liveried No.90036 'Driver jack Mills' + No.90018 'The Pride of Belshill' (below) pass Arksey with 6N70, the 13:30 Doncaster Decoy - Tyne Yard.

ECML (South)
Rossington

Ebange Steel : Class 92s are not an everyday sight on the ECML, once regular performers on the Ebange steel service between Doncaster and Dollands Moor (4O28 / 4E26).

On 22nd August 2013, No.92041 'Vaughan Williams' passes Rossington with 4E26, the 08:13 Dollands Moor - Scunthorpe steel empties.

Today, the train is 'booked' for a DBS Class 66/0 loco.

Intermodal : Class 66/0 No.66001 (middle) passes Rossington with a fully laden 4L45, the 09:36 Wakefield Europort - Felixstowe intermodal.

The Deutsche Bahn Cherry Red livery certainly enhances the appearance of the ubiquitous 'shed'.

Concrete Blocks : One of the EuroPorte Class 66/0s, No.66249 (right), heads 6H96, the late running 21:39 Heck - Peterborough loaded PLASMOR blocks at Rossington.

This train normally runs to Bow (FX) and Biggleswade (FO).

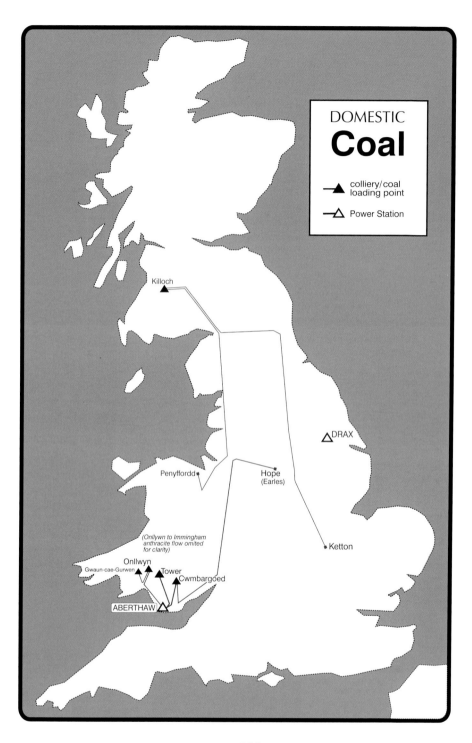

DOMESTIC
Coal

▲ colliery/coal
loading point

△ Power Station

Killoch

DRAX

Penyffordd

Hope
(Earles)

Ketton

*(Onllwyn to Immingham
anthracite flow omited
for clarity)*

Onllwyn

Gwaun-cae-Gurwen

Tower

Cwmbargoed

ABERTHAW

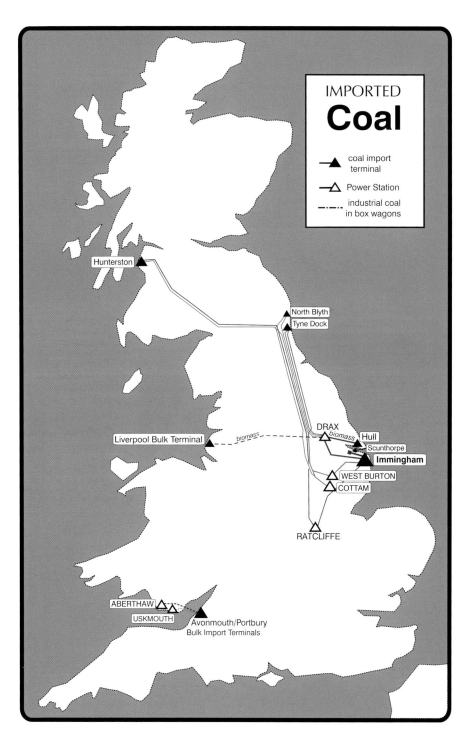

IMPORTED

Coal

▲ coal import terminal

△ Power Station

·–··– industrial coal in box wagons

Hunterston

North Blyth
Tyne Dock

Liverpool Bulk Terminal

biomass

DRAX *biomass*

Hull

Scunthorpe

Immingham

WEST BURTON

COTTAM

RATCLIFFE

ABERTHAW

USKMOUTH

Avonmouth/Portbury
Bulk Import Terminals

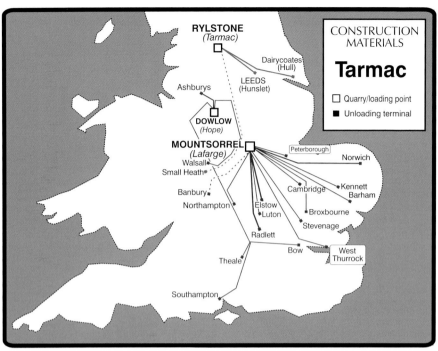

CONSTRUCTION MATERIALS

Tarmac

□ Quarry/loading point
■ Unloading terminal

RYLSTONE
(Tarmac)

Dairycoates
(Hull)

LEEDS
(Hunslet)

Ashburys

DOWLOW
(Hope)

MOUNTSORREL
(Lafarge)

Walsall
Small Heath

Peterborough

Norwich

Banbury

Northampton

Cambridge

Kennett
Barham

Elstow
Luton

Broxbourne

Stevenage

Radlett

Bow

West
Thurrock

Theale

Southampton

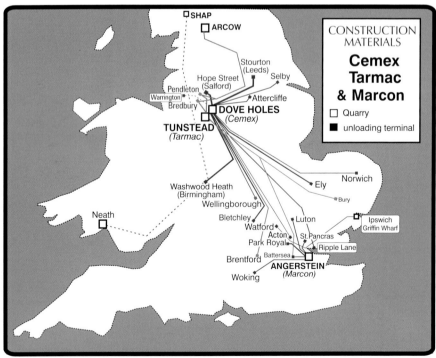

CONSTRUCTION MATERIALS

Cemex
Tarmac
& Marcon

□ Quarry
■ unloading terminal

□ SHAP

□ ARCOW

Stourton
(Leeds)

Selby

Hope Street
(Salford)

Pendleton

Warrington

Bredbury

Attercliffe

DOVE HOLES
(Cemex)

TUNSTEAD
(Tarmac)

Washwood Heath
(Birmingham)

Ely

Norwich

Neath

Bury

Wellingborough

Bletchley

Luton

Watford

Ipswich
Griffin Wharf

Acton

St.Pancras

Park Royal

Battersea

Ripple Lane

Brentford

ANGERSTEIN
(Marcon)

Woking

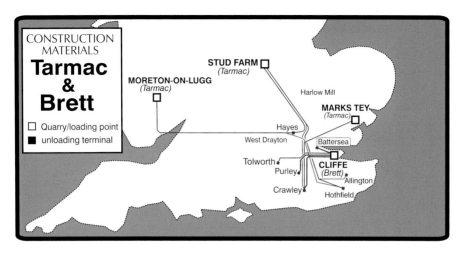

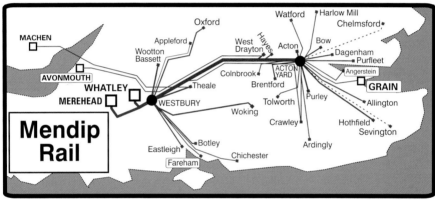

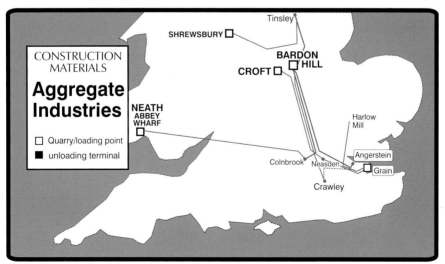

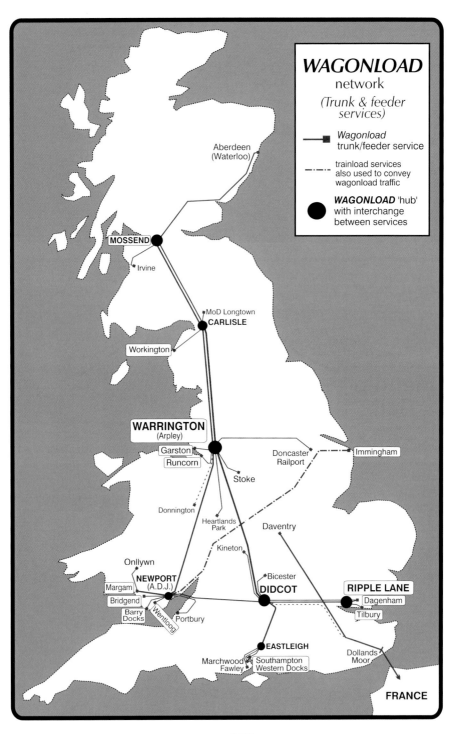

133

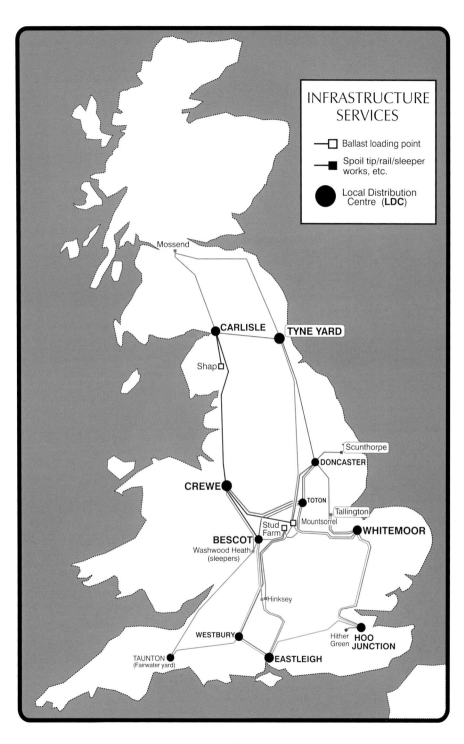

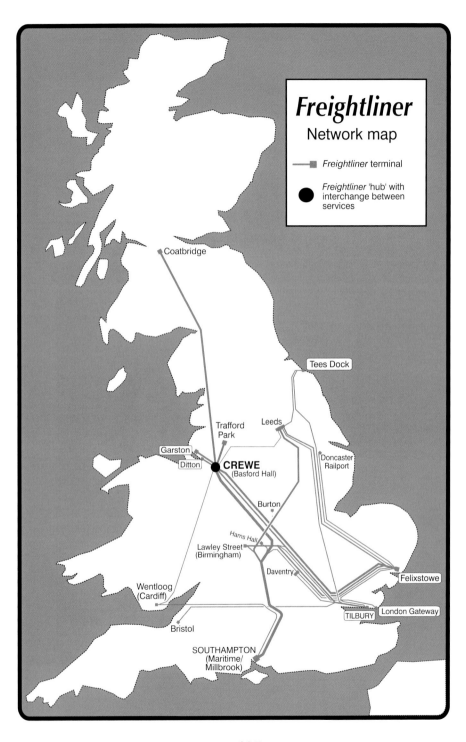

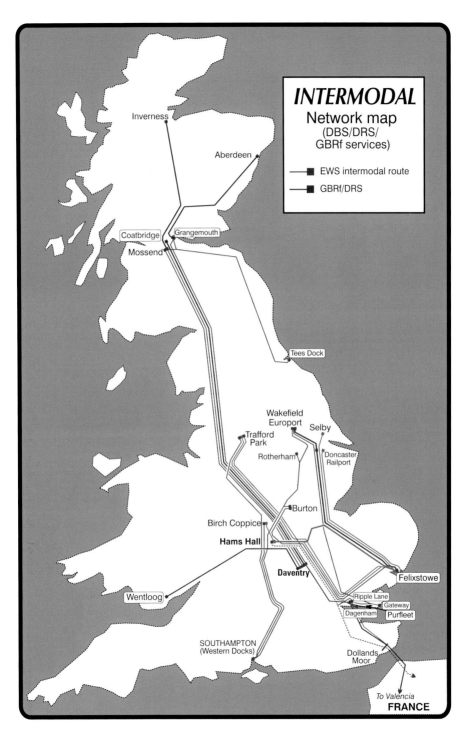

INTERMODAL
Network map
(DBS/DRS/
GBRf services)

■■ EWS intermodal route
■ GBRf/DRS

Inverness

Aberdeen

Coatbridge Grangemouth
Mossend

Tees Dock

Wakefield
Europort   Selby
Trafford
Park
Rotherham   Doncaster
Railport

Burton
Birch Coppice
Hams Hall

Daventry   Felixstowe

Wentloog
Ripple Lane
Gateway
Dagenham   Purfleet

SOUTHAMPTON
(Western Docks)
Dollands
Moor

To Valencia
FRANCE

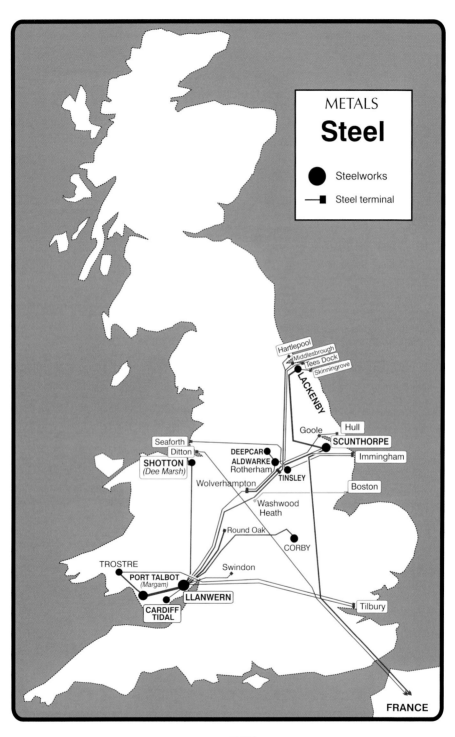

METALS
Steel

● Steelworks

━■ Steel terminal

Hartlepool
Middlesbrough
Tees Dock
Skinningrove
LACKENBY

Goole
Hull
SCUNTHORPE
Immingham

Seaforth
Ditton
DEEPCAR
ALDWARKE
Rotherham
SHOTTON
(Dee Marsh)
TINSLEY

Wolverhampton
Boston

Washwood
Heath

Round Oak
CORBY

TROSTRE
Swindon
PORT TALBOT
(Margam)
LLANWERN
Tilbury
CARDIFF
TIDAL

FRANCE

137

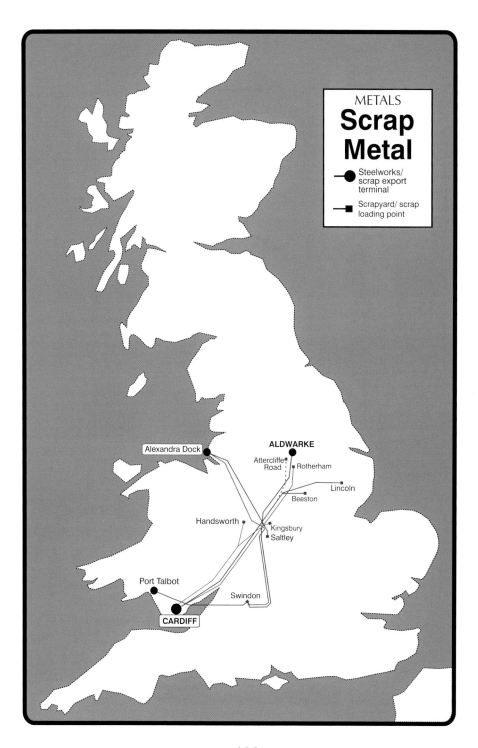

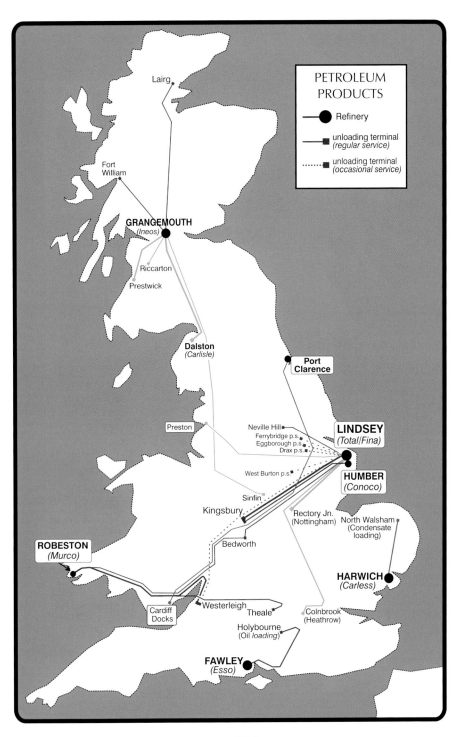

PETROLEUM
PRODUCTS

● Refinery

■ unloading terminal
(regular service)

■ unloading terminal
(occasional service)

Lairg

Fort
William

GRANGEMOUTH
(Ineos)

Riccarton

Prestwick

Dalston
(Carlisle)

Port
Clarence

Preston

Neville Hill
Ferrybridge p.s.
Eggborough p.s.
Drax p.s.

LINDSEY
(Total/Fina)

West Burton p.s.

HUMBER
(Conoco)

Sinfin

Kingsbury

Rectory Jn.
(Nottingham)

North Walsham
(Condensate
loading)

ROBESTON
(Murco)

Bedworth

HARWICH
(Carless)

Cardiff
Docks

Westerleigh

Theale

Colnbrook
(Heathrow)

Holybourne
(Oil loading)

FAWLEY
(Esso)

139

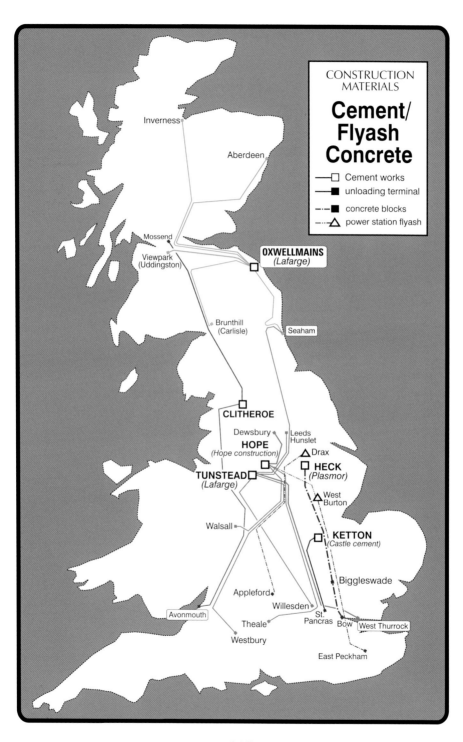

CONSTRUCTION
MATERIALS

Cement/
Flyash
Concrete

☐ Cement works
■ unloading terminal
■ concrete blocks
△ power station flyash

Inverness

Aberdeen

Mossend

Viewpark
(Uddingston)

OXWELLMAINS
(Lafarge)

Brunthill
(Carlisle)

Seaham

CLITHEROE

Dewsbury

Leeds
Hunslet

HOPE
(Hope construction)

Drax

TUNSTEAD
(Lafarge)

HECK
(Plasmor)

West
Burton

Walsall

KETTON
(Castle cement)

Biggleswade

Appleford

Willesden

Avonmouth

St.
Pancras

Bow

West Thurrock

Theale

Westbury

East Peckham

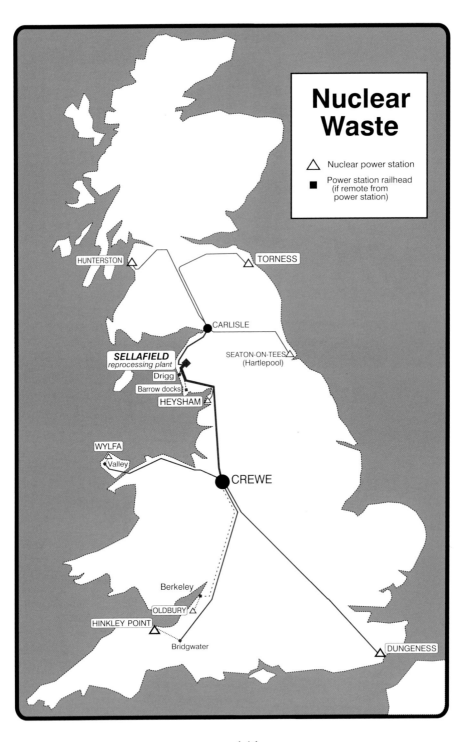

Nuclear Waste

△ Nuclear power station

■ Power station railhead
(if remote from power station)

HUNTERSTON △

TORNESS △

CARLISLE

SELLAFIELD
reprocessing plant

SEATON-ON-TEES △
(Hartlepool)

Drigg

Barrow docks

HEYSHAM △

WYLFA △
Valley

CREWE

Berkeley

OLDBURY △

HINKLEY POINT △

Bridgwater

DUNGENESS △

141

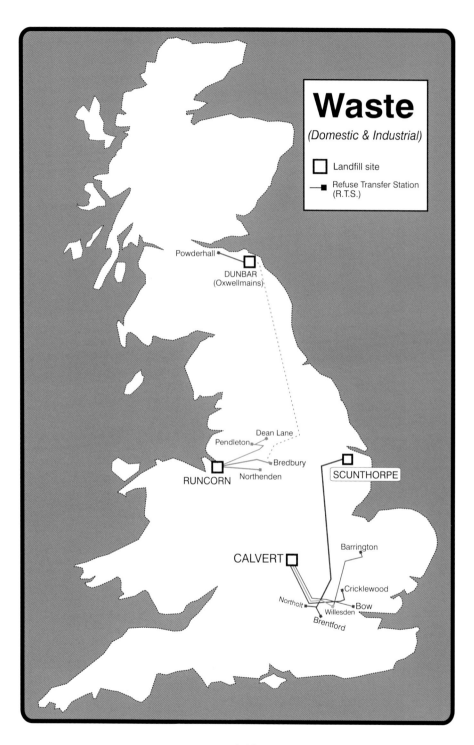

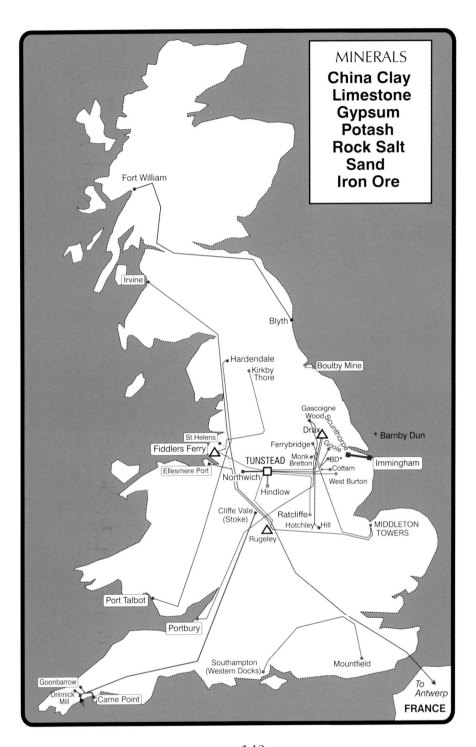

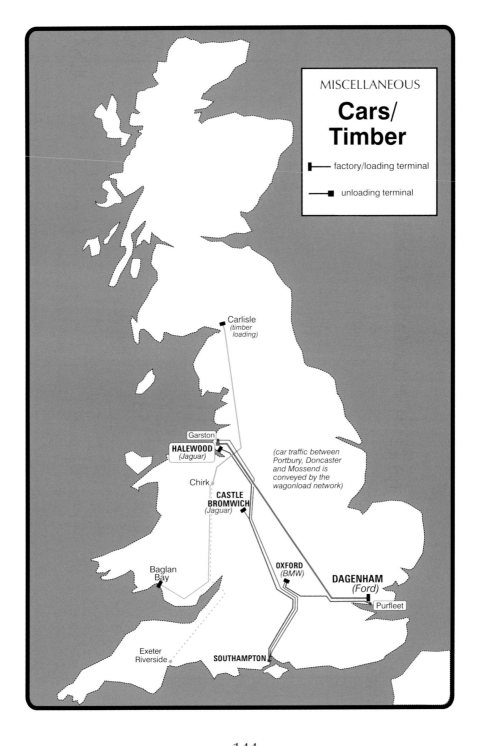

MISCELLANEOUS

Cars/ Timber

⊢■ factory/loading terminal

■— unloading terminal

Carlisle
(timber loading)

Garston

HALEWOOD
(Jaguar)

Chirk

CASTLE BROMWICH
(Jaguar)

(car traffic between Portbury, Doncaster and Mossend is conveyed by the wagonload network)

Baglan Bay

OXFORD
(BMW)

DAGENHAM
(Ford)

Purfleet

Exeter Riverside

SOUTHAMPTON

INDEX OF 'HOTSPOTS'

Acton Bridge	86-87
Acton Mainline.........................	36-37
Ashford....................................	31
Banbury...................................	20-21
Barnetby..................................	122-25
Basingstoke..............................	26-27
Bath..	9
Bedwyn...................................	25
Bristol.....................................	8-9
Cardiff.....................................	10-11
Cargo Fleet..............................	107
Carlisle....................................	94-96
Camden Road...........................	46-47
Cheltenham Spa.......................	15
Chester....................................	85
Chesterfield..............................	58-59
Church Fenton.........................	110-11
Clapham Junction.....................	32-33
Coatbridge Central...................	100
Colton Junction(York)..............	110-11
Cossington...............................	62-63
Dalwhinnie...............................	99
Dartford...................................	30
Dawlish....................................	7
Didcot......................................	22-24
Doncaster.................................	114-16
Eastleigh..................................	28-29
Eaglescliffe..............................	108-09
Ely...	53
Fareham...................................	27
Gravesend................................	30
Gloucester................................	15
Gospel Oak..............................	46-47
Grangetown..............................	107
Harrow.....................................	44-45
Hellifield..................................	93
Helsby.....................................	91
Holytown..................................	98-99
Ipswich....................................	50-51

Kensington Olympia................	32-33
Leamington Spa.......................	76-77
Leyland....................................	92
Loughborough..........................	62-63
Manchester Piccadilly..............	83
Mirfield...................................	117
Motherwell...............................	98-99
Newark....................................	57
Newcastle.................................	106-7
Newport...................................	12-14
Nuneaton.................................	64-66
Par..	7
Peak Forest..............................	84-85
Pelaw......................................	106-7
Peterborough...........................	54-55
Preston....................................	92
Prestonpans.............................	103
Rannoch...................................	101
Rugby......................................	67-69
Severn Tunnel Junction...........	16-17
Shrewsbury...............................	75
Slateford..................................	102
Stafford...................................	78-81
Stainforth.................................	120-21
Stirling....................................	104
Stratford..................................	48-49
Swinton....................................	118-19
Tamworth.................................	73-75
Thornaby..................................	108-09
Toton yard...............................	60-61
Upper Holloway (GOBLIN)........	46-47
Wakefield.................................	113
Wandsworth Road....................	32-33
Warrington...............................	88-90
Water Orton.............................	70-72
Wellingborough........................	56
Westbury..................................	18
West Ealing..............................	34-35
West Ruislip.............................	43
Whifflet...................................	100
Willesden Junction...................	38-42

In addition to the above, additional timetables are available by subscribing to the online version of Freightmaster - these currently include: Reading, Barking, Trimley, Bletchley, Walsall, Worcester, Leicester, Northampton, Derby, Lincoln, Spalding and many others!!

(For further details, please see page 126)